AF334701

Best Friends

CONTINUUM · NEW YORK

Best Friends

A PICTORIAL CELEBRATION

By The Winners Of
The Parade-Kodak
National
Photo Contest

Introduction By
Walter Anderson

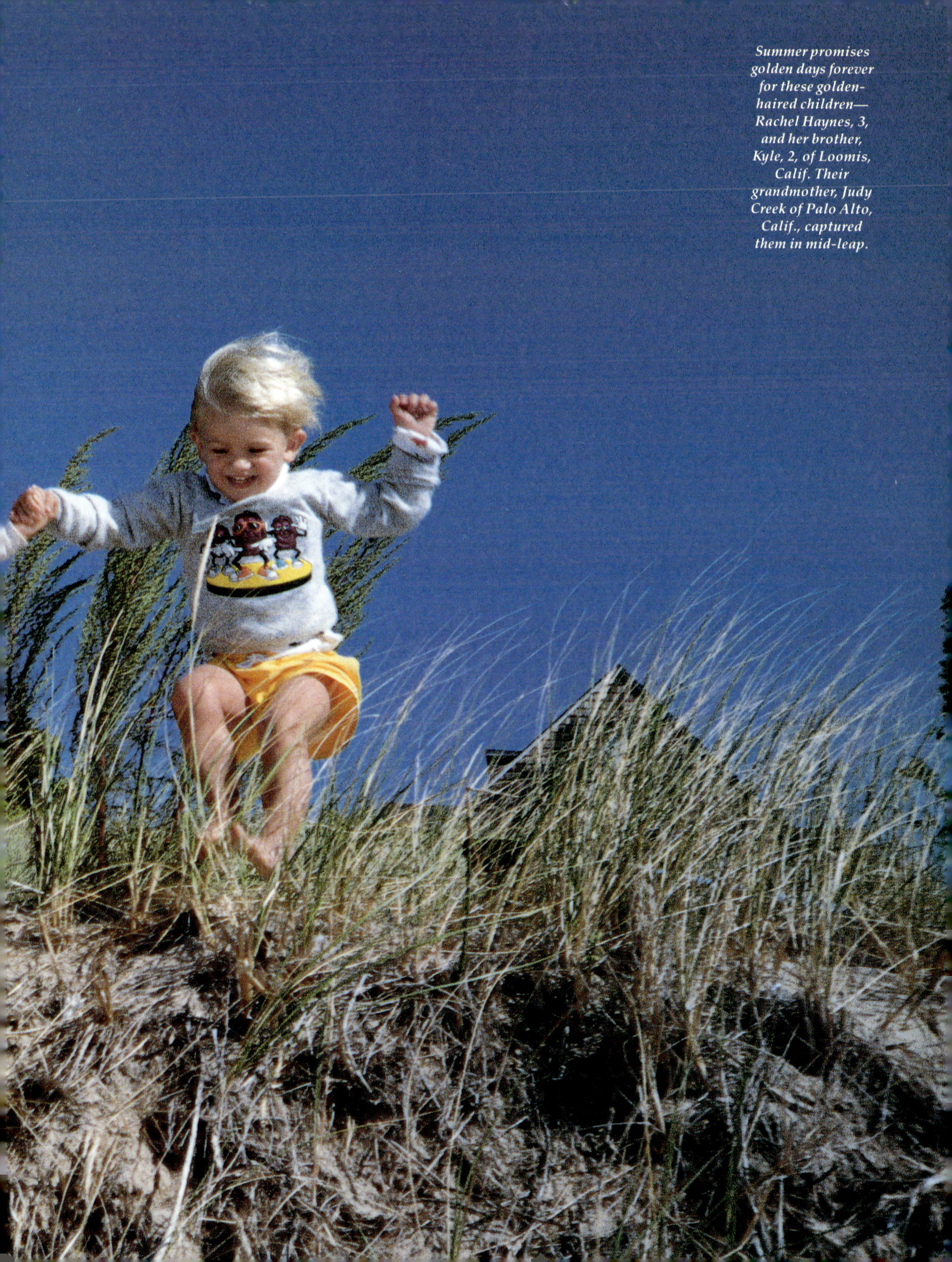

Summer promises
golden days forever
for these golden-
haired children—
Rachel Haynes, 3,
and her brother,
Kyle, 2, of Loomis,
Calif. Their
grandmother, Judy
Creek of Palo Alto,
Calif., captured
them in mid-leap.

1991

The Continuum Publishing Company
370 Lexington Avenue, New York, NY 10017

Copyright © 1991 by Parade Publications, Inc.

Design by Ira Yoffe

Printed in Hong Kong

Library of Congress Cataloging-in-Publication Data
Best friends : a pictorial celebration
/ by the winners of the Parade-Kodak National Photo Contest
: introduction by Walter Anderson.
p.   cm.
ISBN 0-8264-0534-7
1. Photography—Portraits.
2. Friendship—Pictorial works.
I. Eastman Kodak Company.
II. Parade (New York, N.Y.)
TR680.B465 1991

779' .2' 0973—dc20   *91-3096 CIP*

"For You, Mom":
Kevin Perazzelli, 3,
presents a bouquet
to his mother,
Margaret Perazzelli
of Delmar, N.Y.,
who took this
photo.

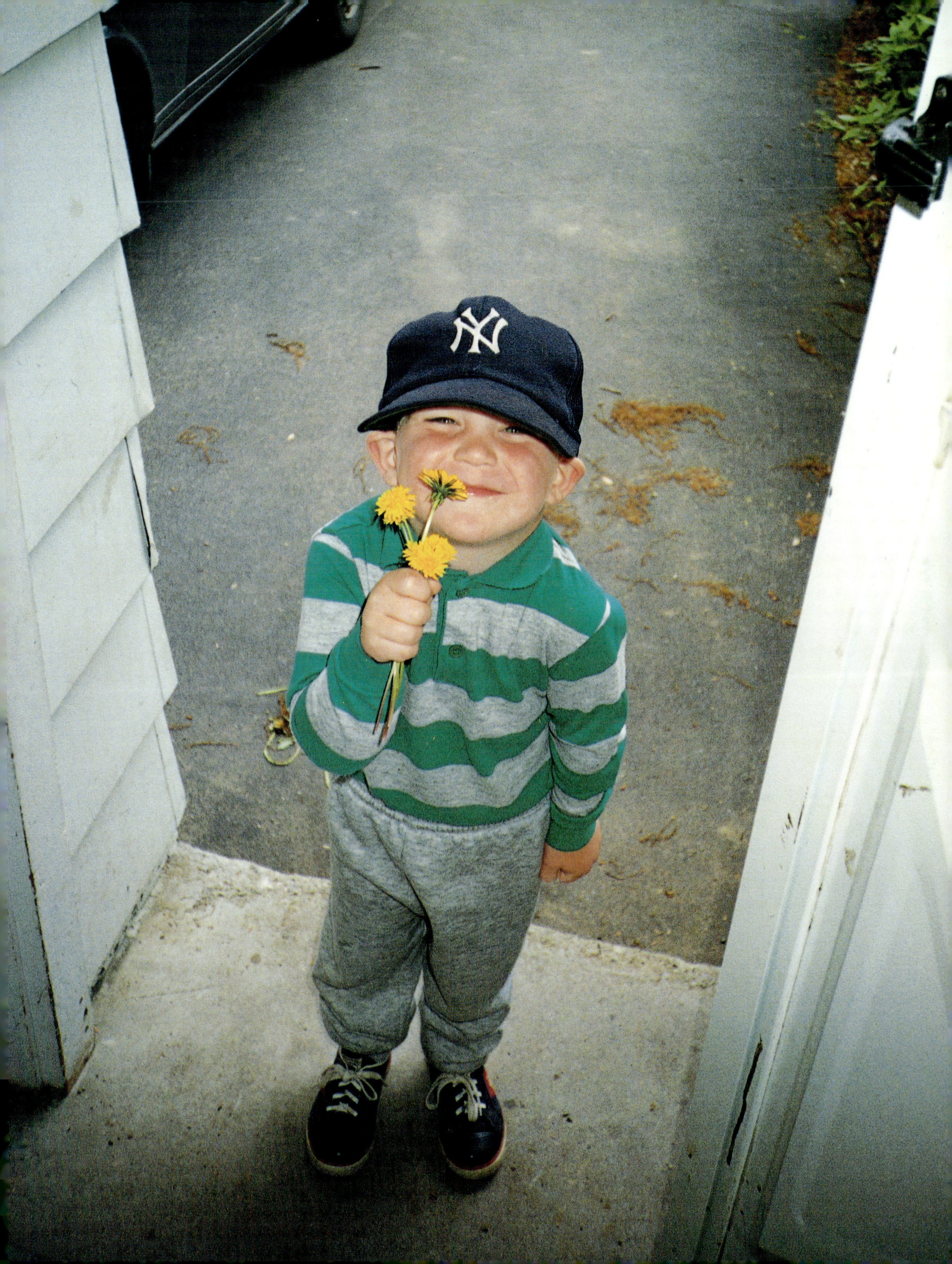

Walter Anderson

Mud Men: Brothers
Robin (left), 5, and
Christopher, 6, on a
rainy afternoon in
Houston. Photo by
their father, F.
Donald Barbaree.

Best friends are everywhere, and they come in all sizes, shapes, colors and ages. I think you'll find that truism borne out in the beautiful, touching and heart-warming photographs that make up this book. These pictures were the winners in the fourth annual National Photo Contest, co-sponsored by *Parade* Magazine and Eastman Kodak Company. The competition drew more than 200,000 entries from all over the country, a record total.

This outpouring of pictures reflects to a degree, the pulling power of *Parade*, which is carried every Sunday in most of the nation's leading newspapers and which has a circulation of 35 million, the largest in the world. But it also is a tribute to the energy, artistry and skill of the American picture-taking public, whose numbers are unmeasurable. The *Parade-Kodak* competition is open to amateurs as well as professionals; in fact, the overwhelming majority of these pictures were taken by ordinary folks who like to carry a camera with them on their vacations or travels, or just to use it for family shots or neighborhood scenes.

The announced theme of the competition, "Best Friends," obviously struck a responsive chord in these enterprising amateurs. As you'll see as you look through the pages that follow, there are friends indeed all over, and in the darndest of places. One Californian found one snorkeling off Grand Cayman Island—a golden-colored fish. A four-month-old North Carolina infant found hers in a doll just as hairless as she is. And a young lad from New York recorded his friendship by having his picture taken in the act of handing some wildflowers to his mother—who snapped the photo herself.

Most of these "best friends," though, are just that—couples together, parents with their children, youngsters playing with their friends, their pets, their toys. This is the stuff of everyday life, and it makes a fine picture album of the people and nation we are.

Our judges in the competition were the Pulitzer Prize-winning photographer Eddie Adams, the psychologist Dr. Joyce Brothers, the author Alex Haley, the comedienne Carol Burnett and Michael Eisner, chairman and chief executive officer of the Walt Disney Company. All have told me of the difficulty they had in selecting 100 winners from the huge outpouring of top-quality submissions.

They were especially impressed, as I was, by the large number of pictures devoted to family activities. Parents take pictures of children—that has always been so. But nowadays, children are also taking pictures of their parents, and of the other members of their family. That shows, if anything, that photography increasingly is a pastime that appeals to the young. Cameras have become far more accessible, sensitive and easy to operate than ever before. And if the photographer is blessed with just a bit of imagination, ingenuity and creativity—not to mention patience—he or she can produce a picture that often verges on the realm of art.

I believe that many of the photos in this book do just that. This is a unique pictorial compilation of the warmth, humanity and friendliness of Americans today, and I salute the men, women—yes, and children—
who have helped put it together.

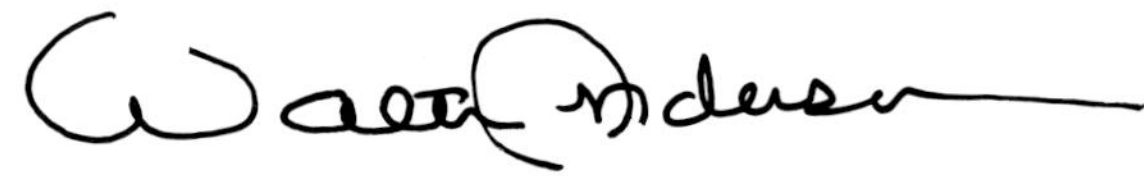

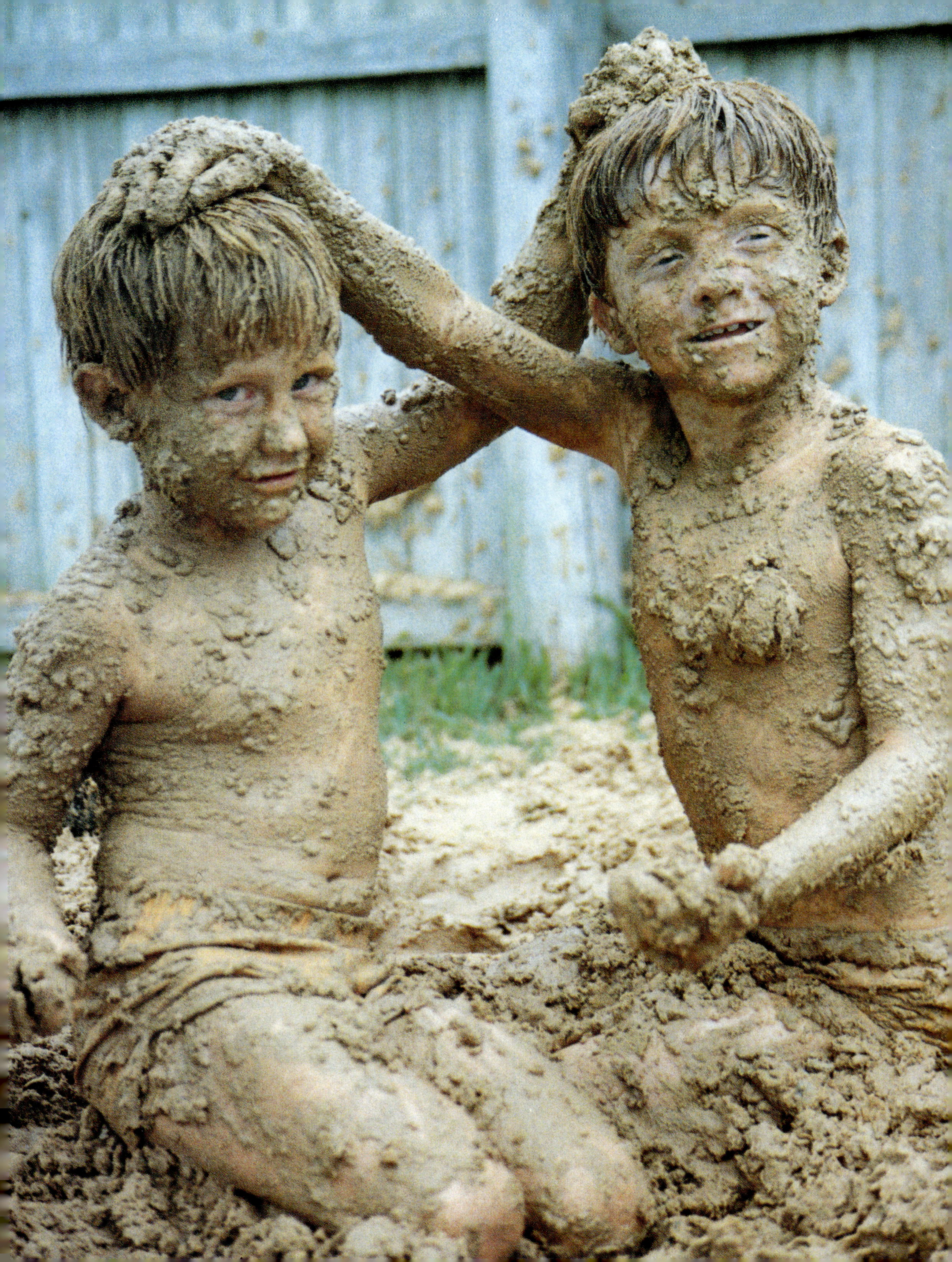

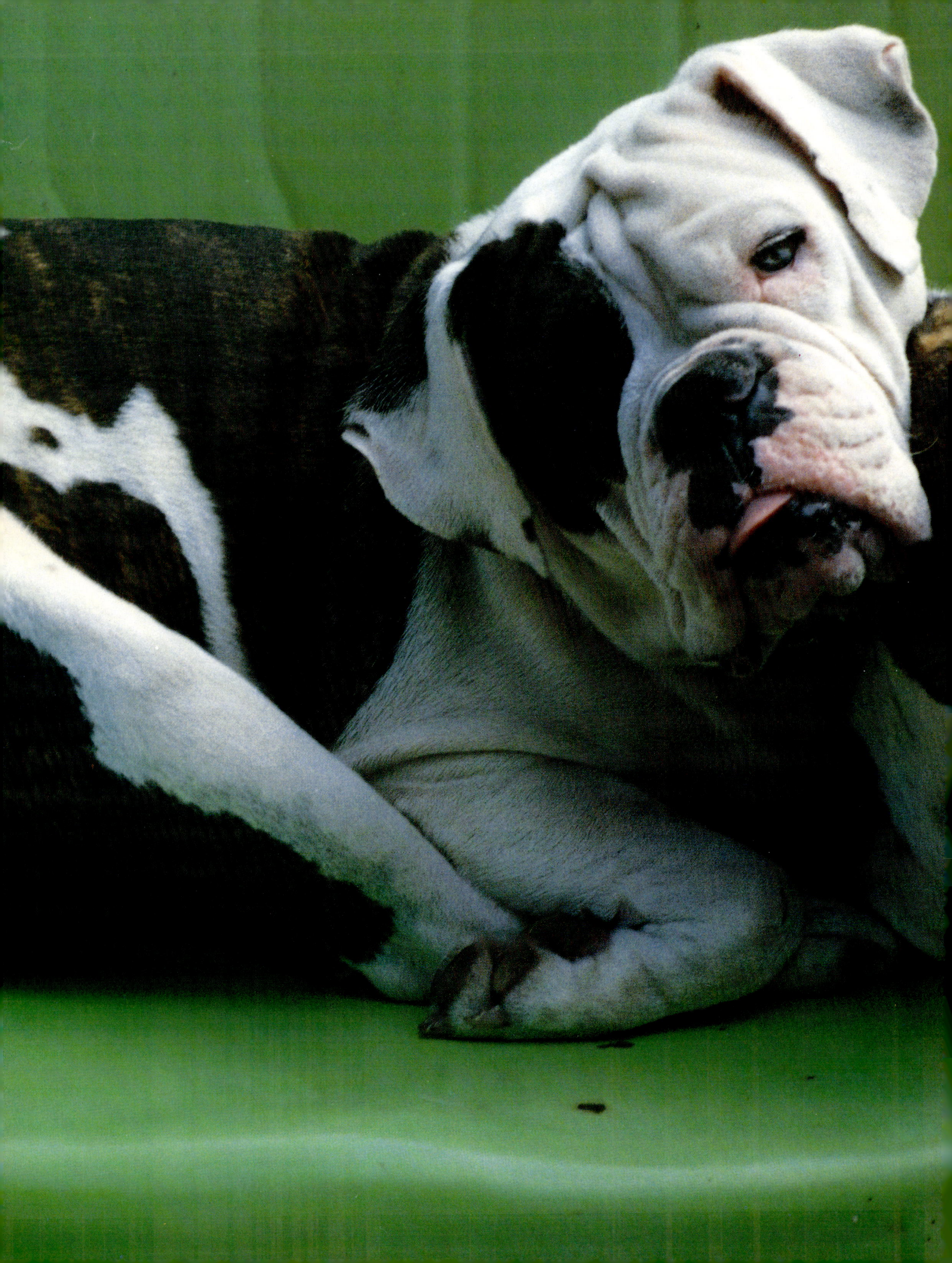

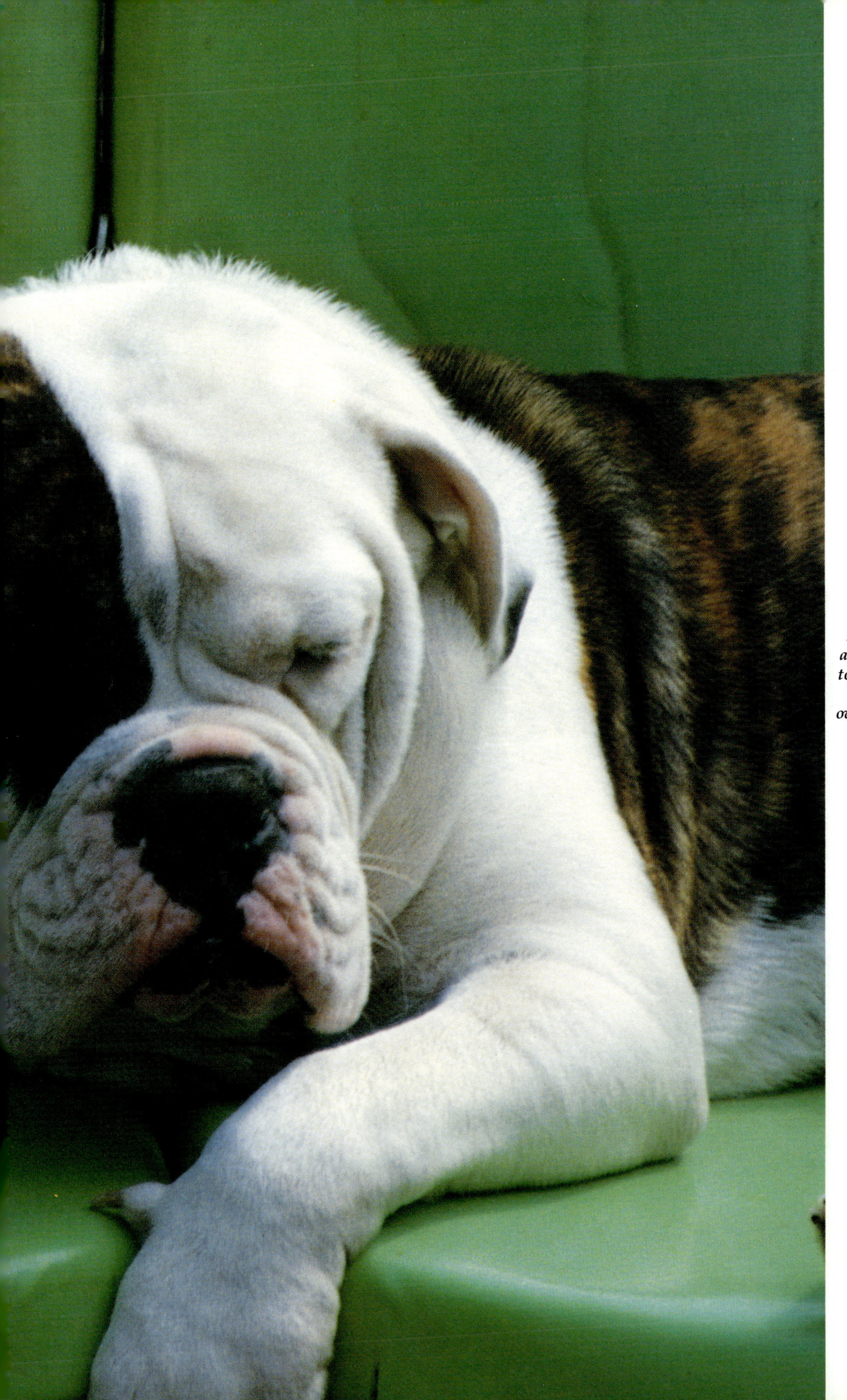

Dog Tired: Justin and Justine cozy up to catch some zzzzs. Photo by their owner, Tom Byrne of Eufaula, Ala.

"It's Just You and Me, Kid": Baby sitter Ronda Rippstein, 21, with Stephen Champion, 3, on a clear spring evening. Photo by Katherine Michele Shupe of Provo, Utah.

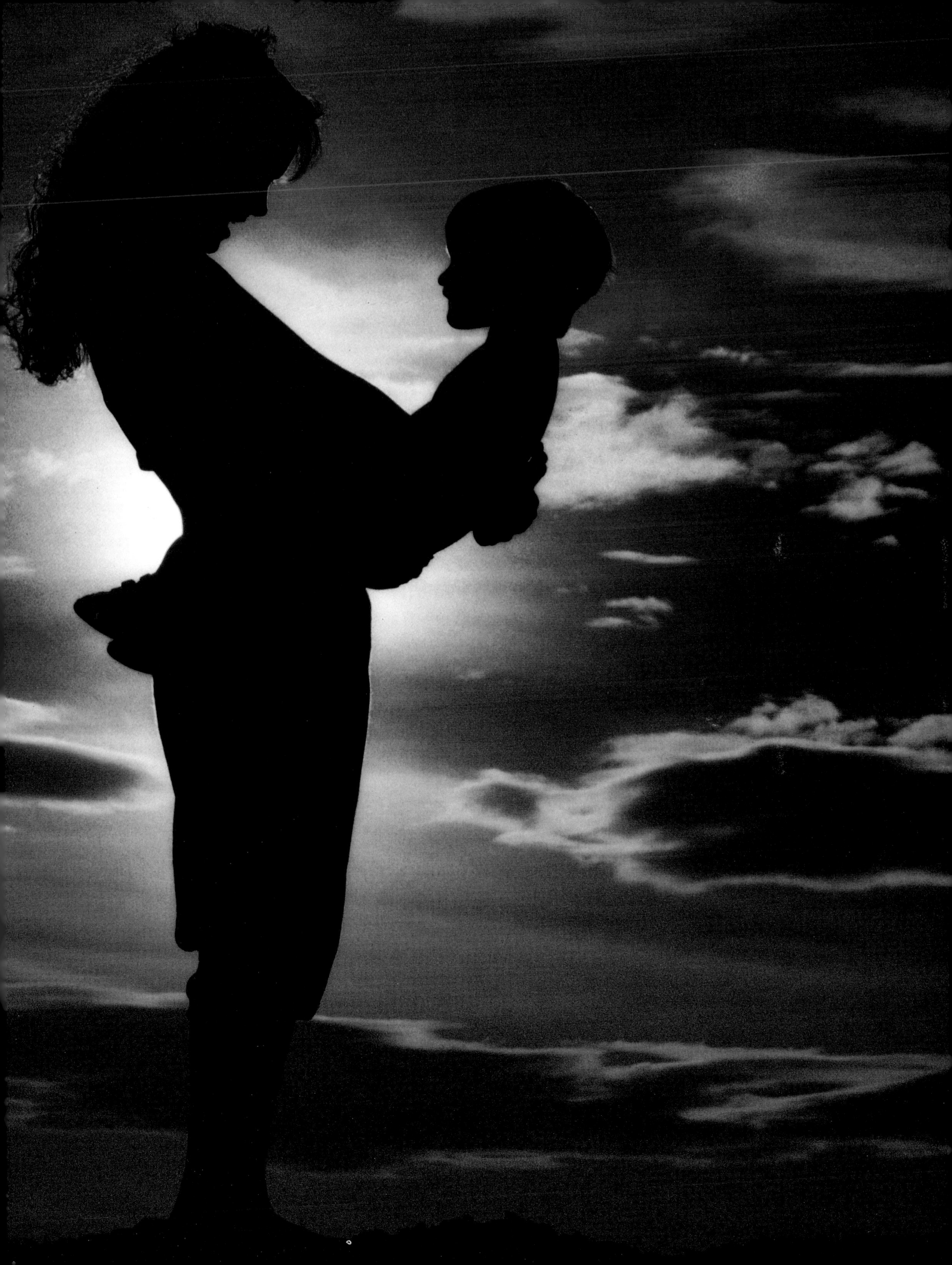

"True is the sentence we are sometimes told:
A friend is worth far more than bags of gold."
—Leonora Christina

"Forsake not an old friend; for the new is not comparable
to him: a new friend is as new wine; when it is old, thou
shalt drink it with pleasure."
—Ecclesiastes 9:10

"The truth is friendship is to me every bit as sacred and
eternal as marriage."
—Katherine Mansfield

"For there is no friend like a sister
In calm or stormy weather;
To cheer one on the tedious way,
To fetch one if one goes astray,
To lift one if one totters down,
To strengthen whilst one stands."
—Christina Rossetti

"A friend may well be reckoned the masterpiece of Nature."
—Ralph Waldo Emerson

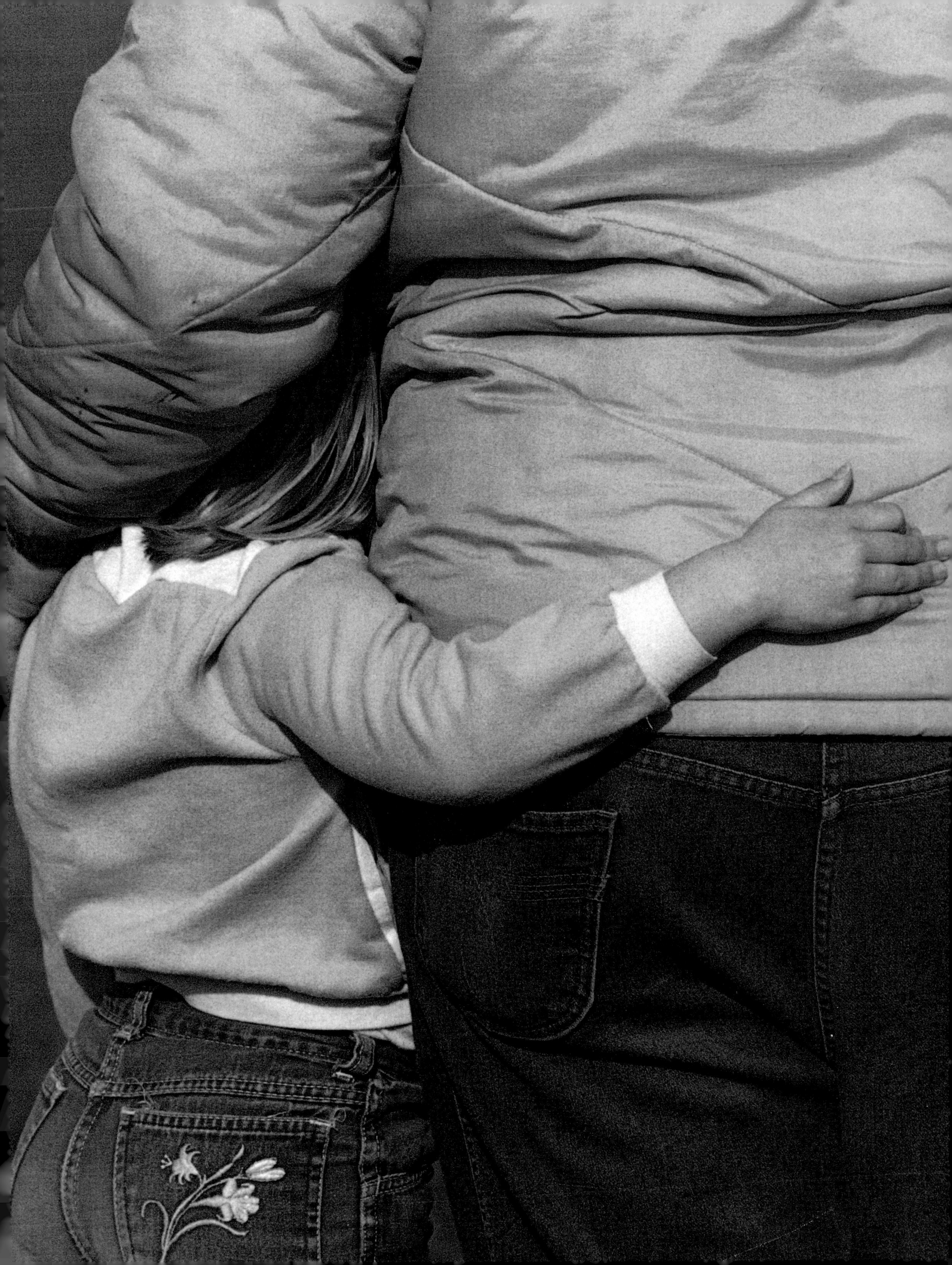

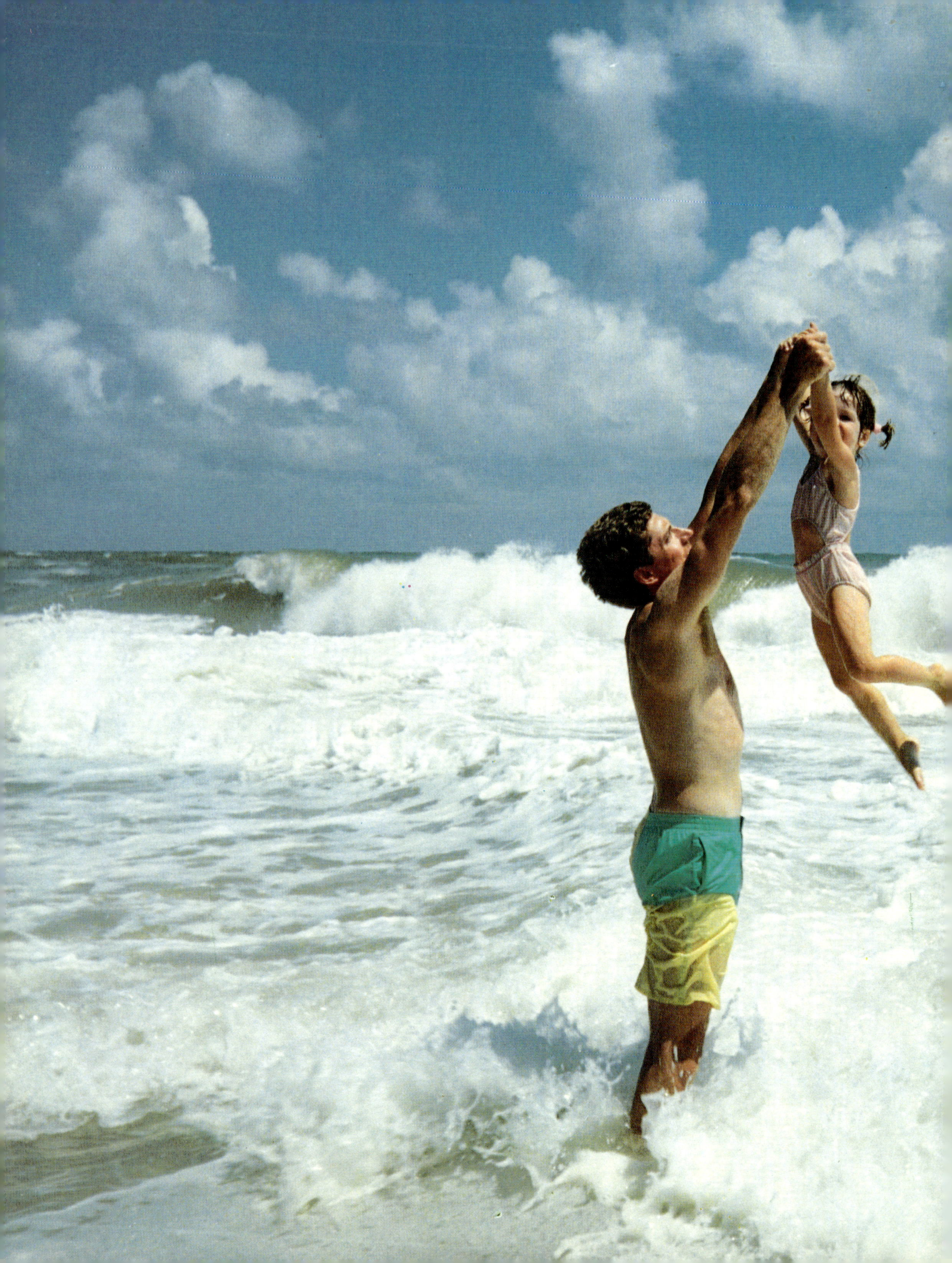

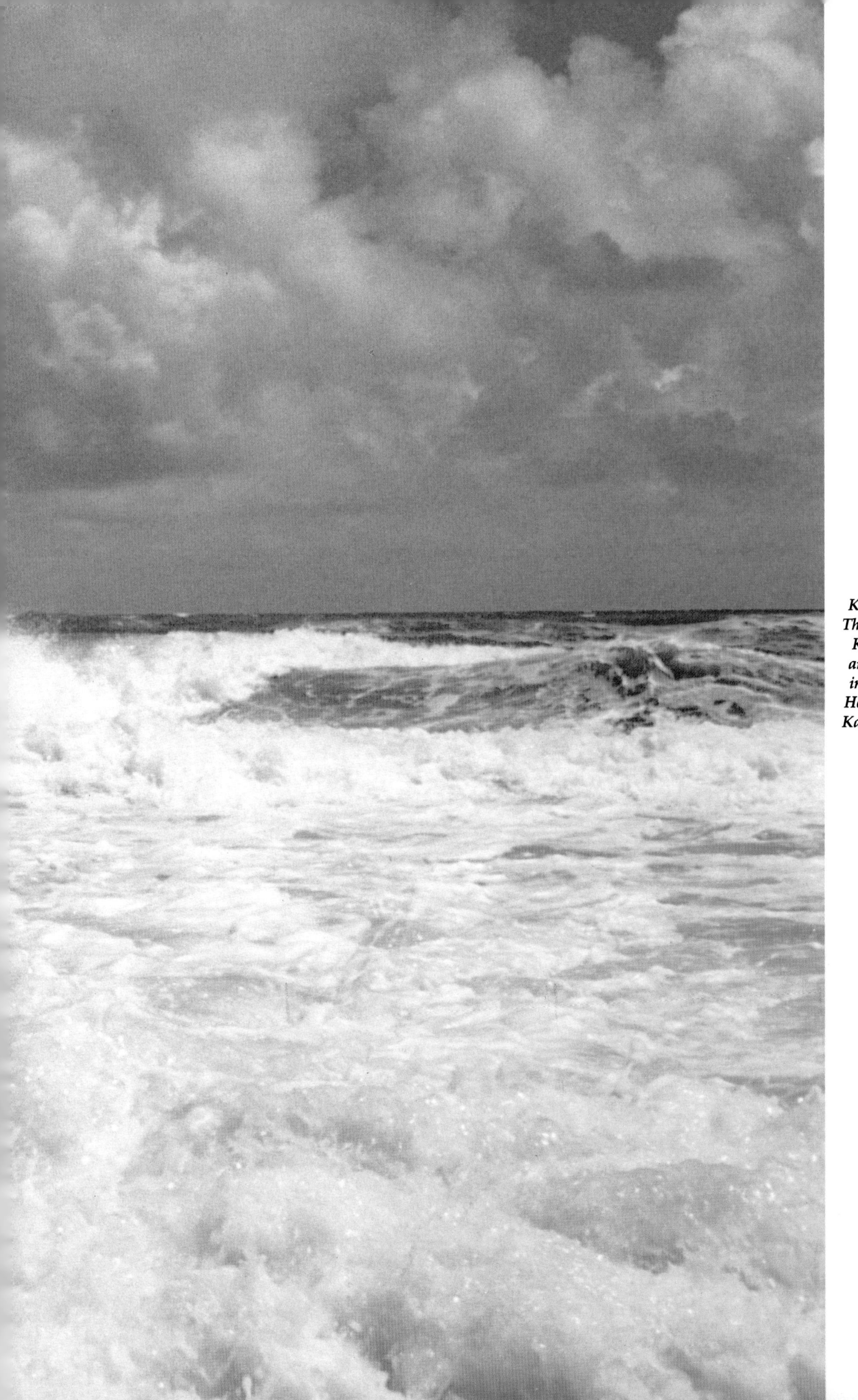

Katie at the Beach: Three-year-old Mary Kathleen Renehan and her father, Ray, in the surf off Nags Head, N.C. Photo by Katie's mother, Mary Renehan of Baltimore.

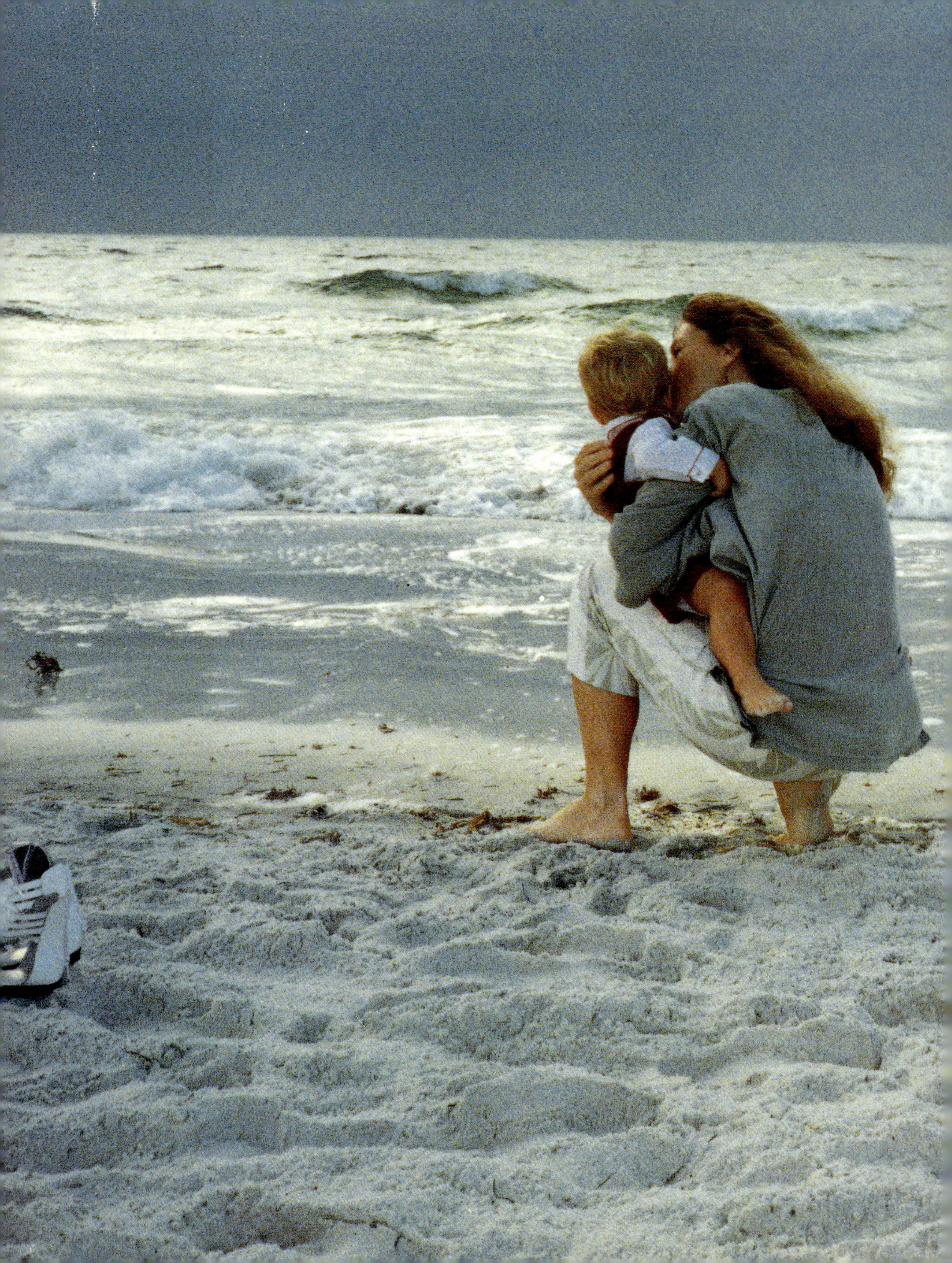

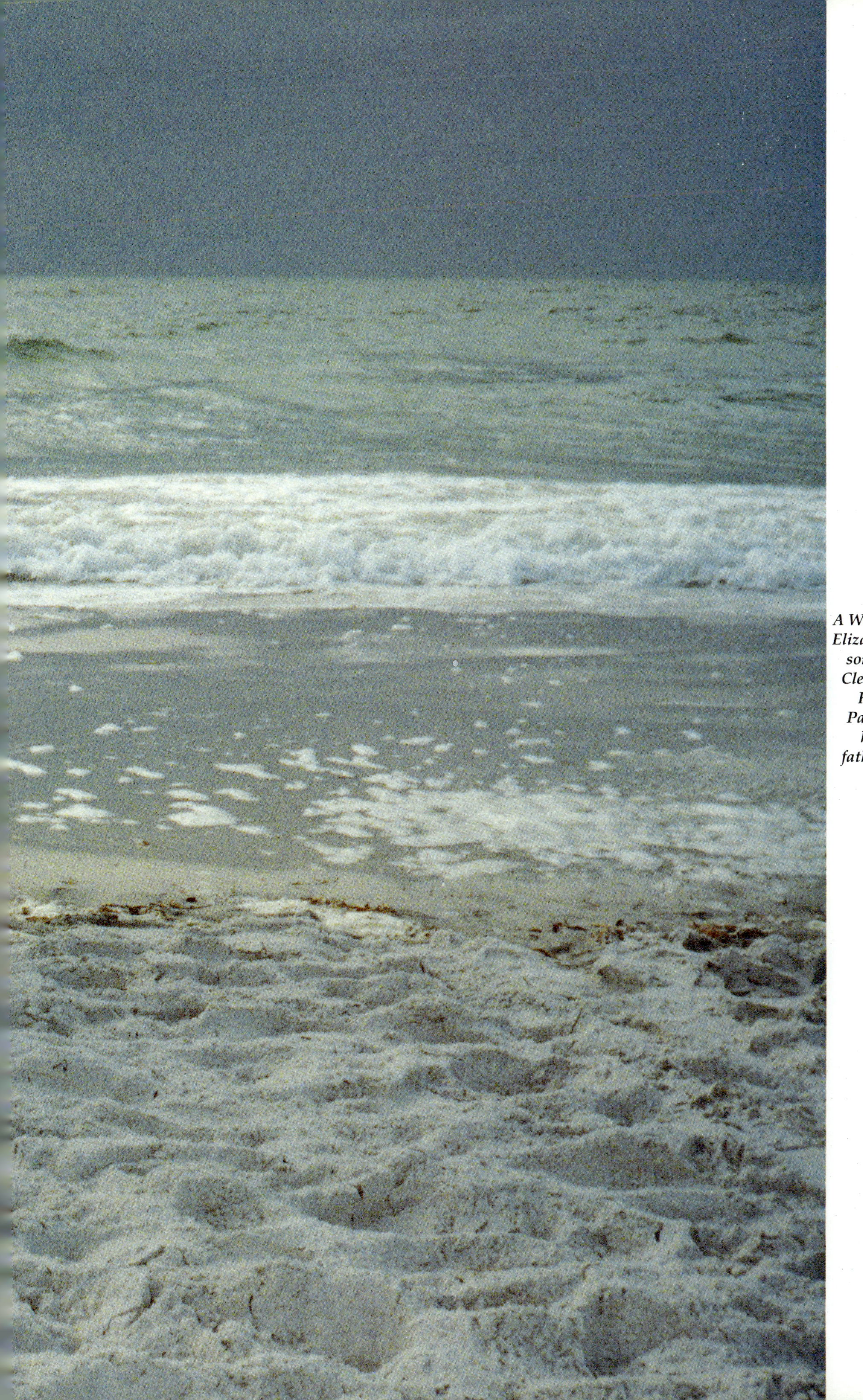

A Winter Afternoon: Elizabeth Doone and son, Matthew, at Clearwater Beach, Fla. Photo by Patrick Doone—husband and father—of Tampa.

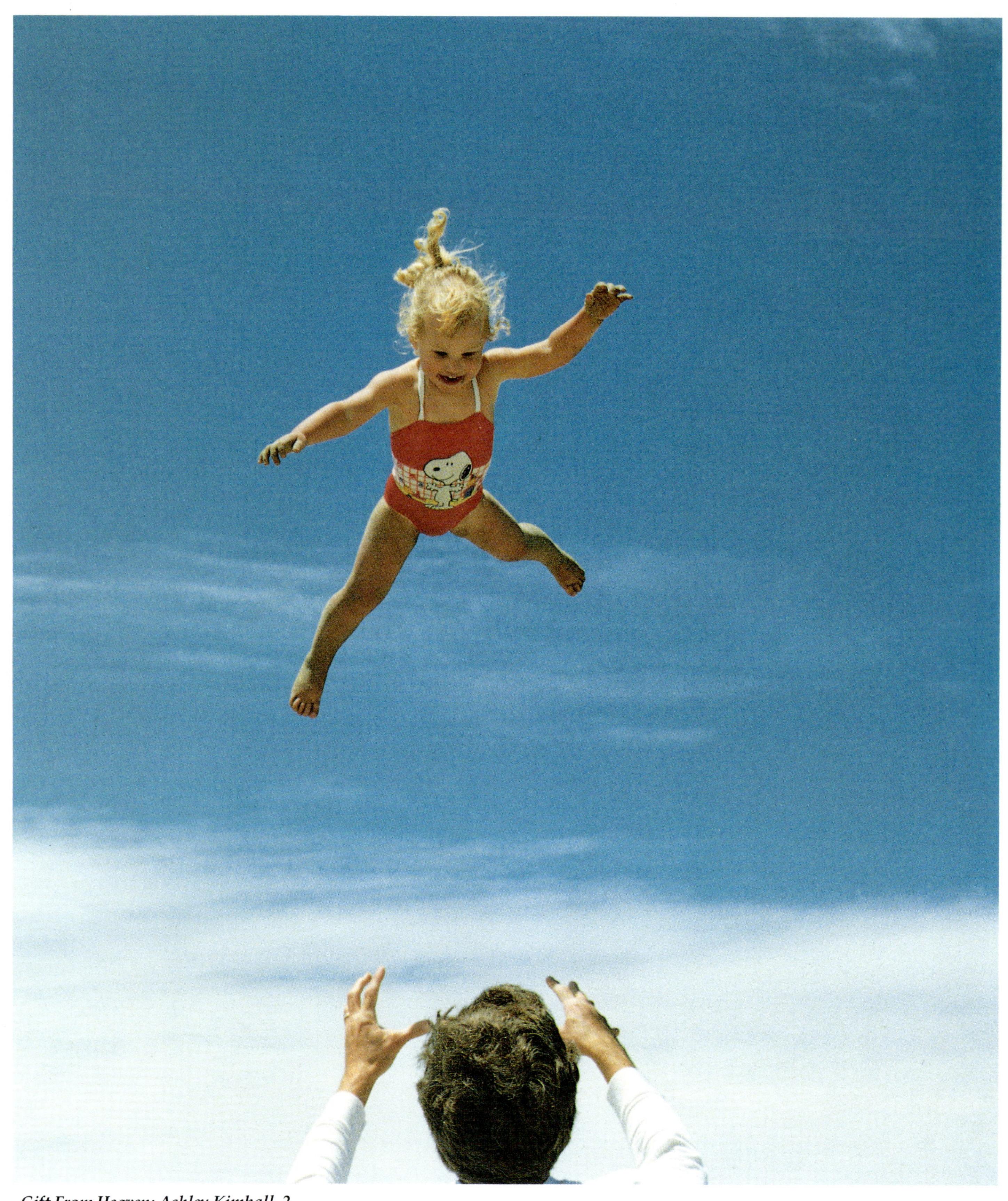

Gift From Heaven: Ashley Kimball, 2, drops into the arms of her father, Bob. Photo by Ashley's mom, Nancy Kimball of Cupertino, Calif. (taken lying on her back on the beach).

Robert Dantzler, 3, makes quite a splash at the family reunion as he jumps into the waiting arms of his dad, David. Photo by Cynthia S. Emerson of Memphis, Tenn.

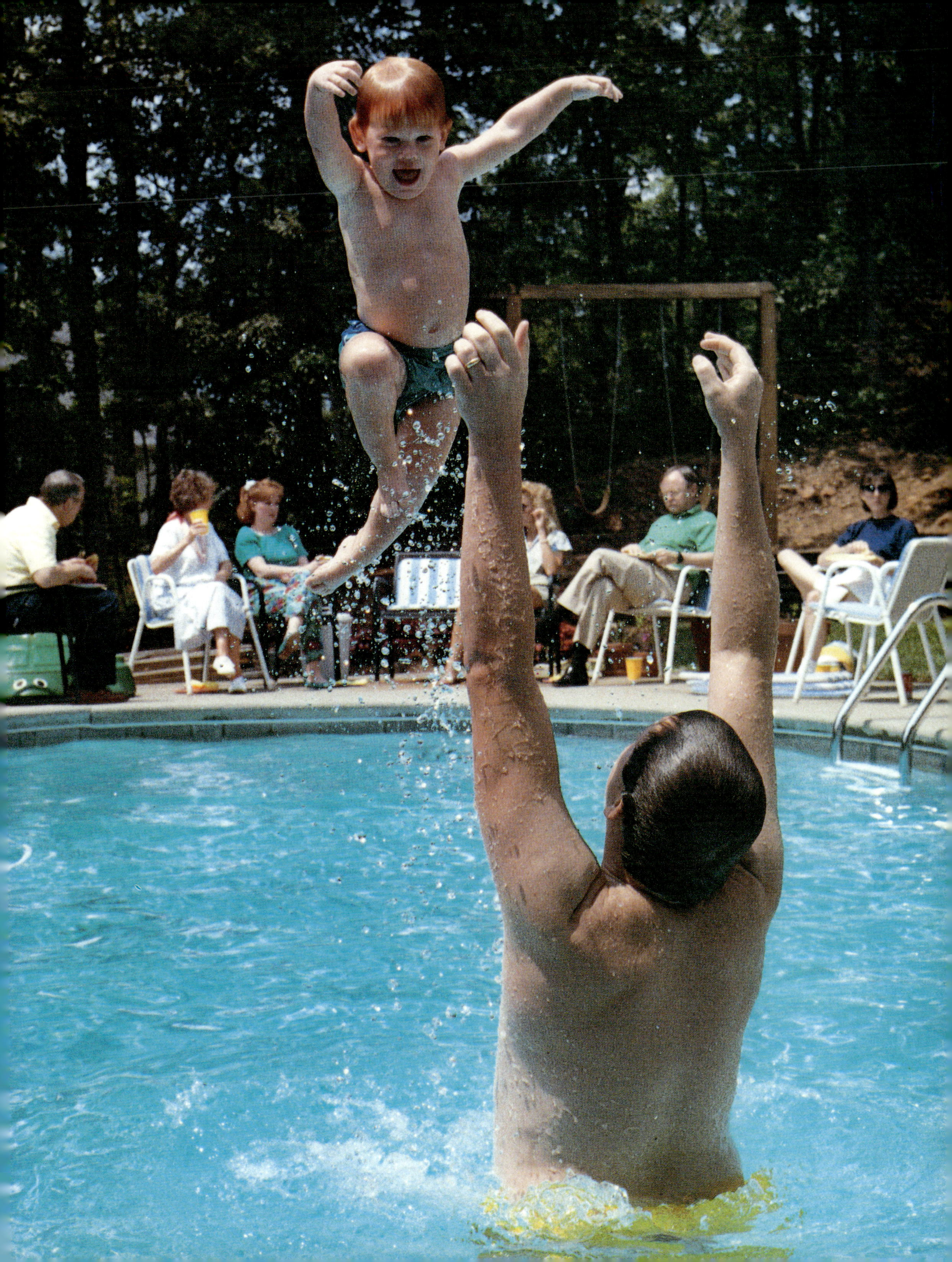

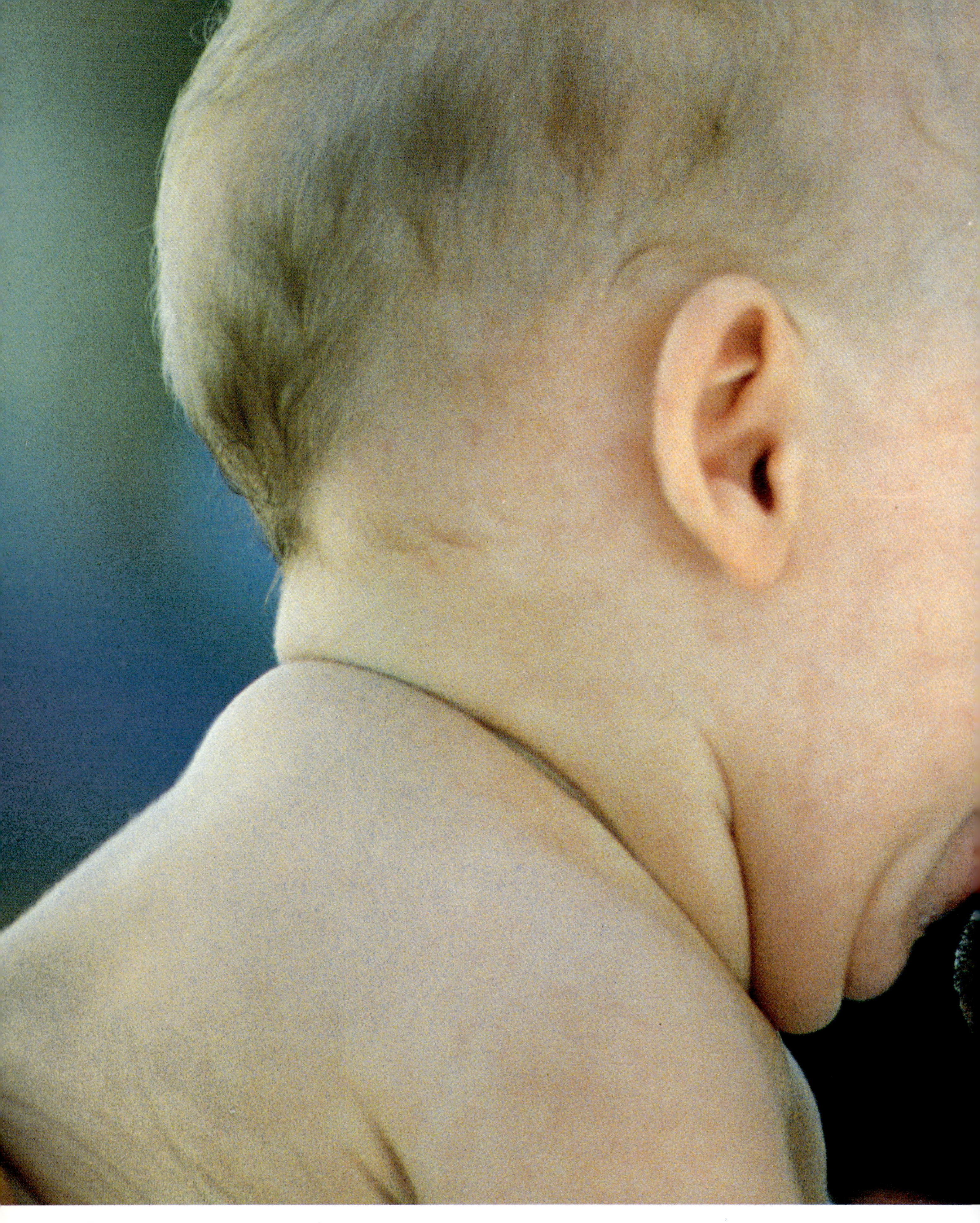

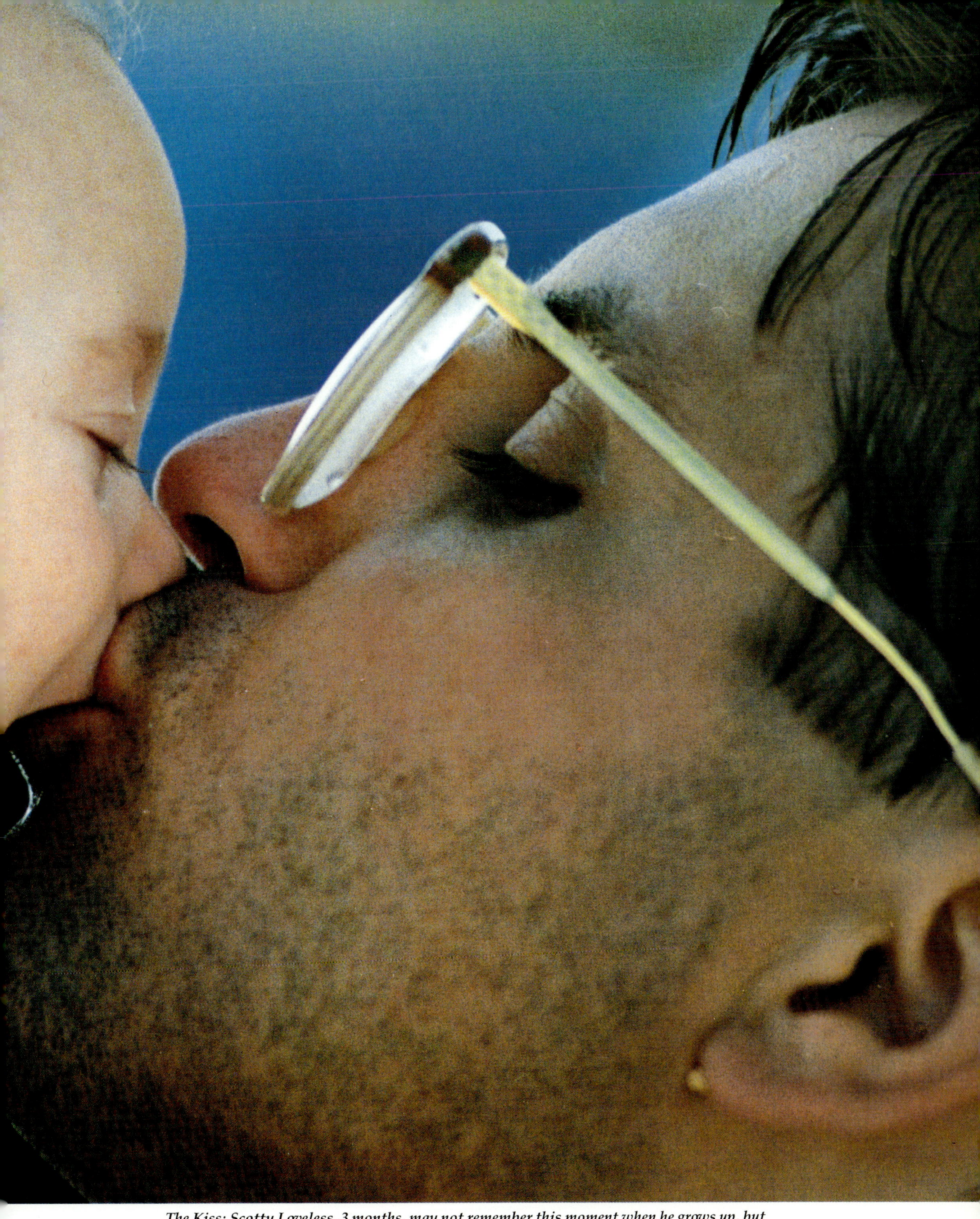

The Kiss: Scotty Loveless, 3 months, may not remember this moment when he grows up, but he'll know his dad, Scott, loves him. Photo by Minette Loveless, Scotty's mom.

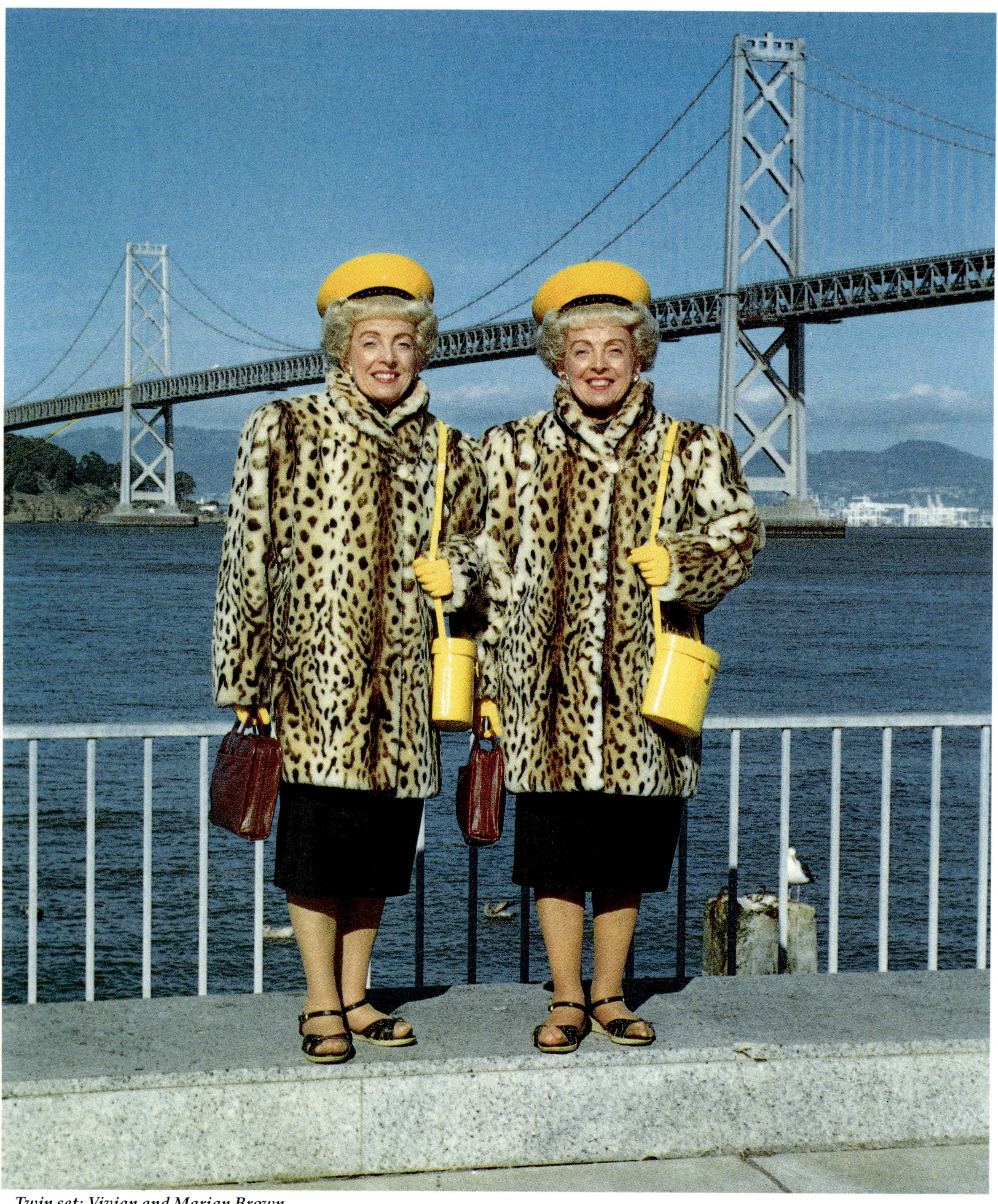

Twin set: Vivian and Marian Brown by the Oakland Bay Bridge in San Francisco. Photo by Lana Christensen of Portland, Ore.

Double Vision? Miss Elsa and Miss Edith Johnson of Gresham, Ore., told Kay Caldwell of Gresham—who took the twins' picture—that yes, indeed, they're best friends.

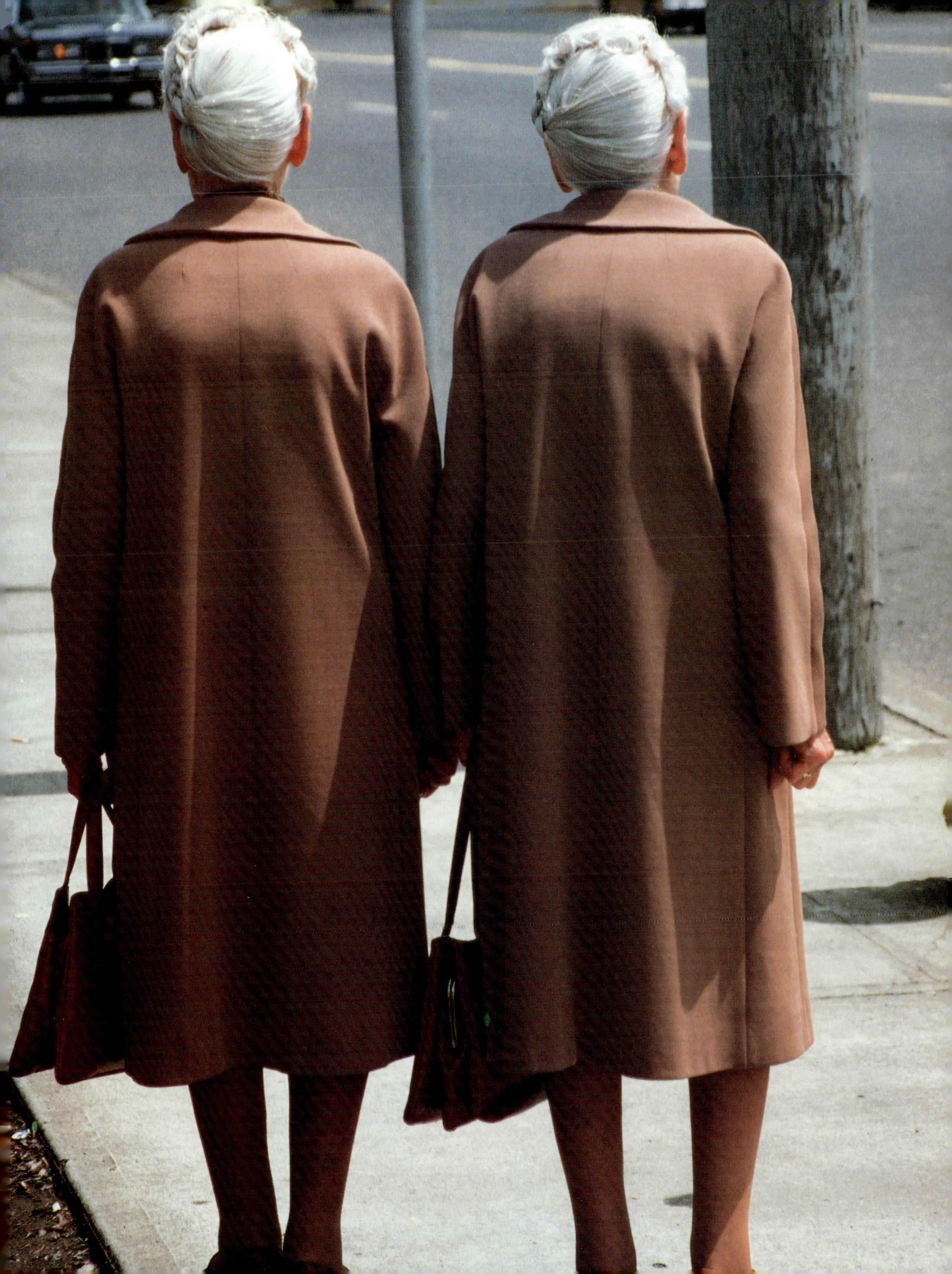

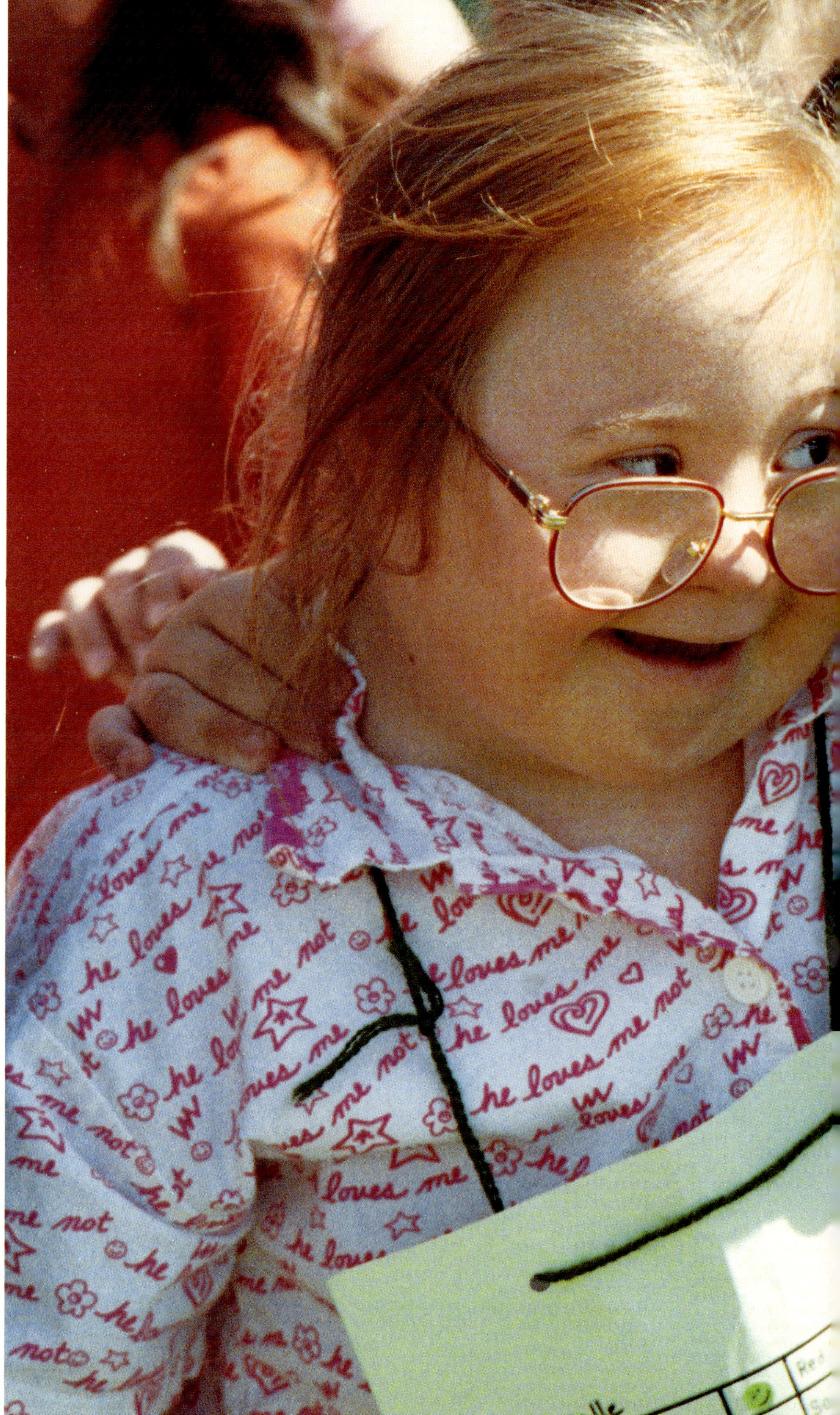

"We Won!" Danielle Spears and her friend, Kristopher Richmond, both 7, share a victory during their school's field day. Photo by Danielle's mother, Carolyn Spears of Arlington, Tex.

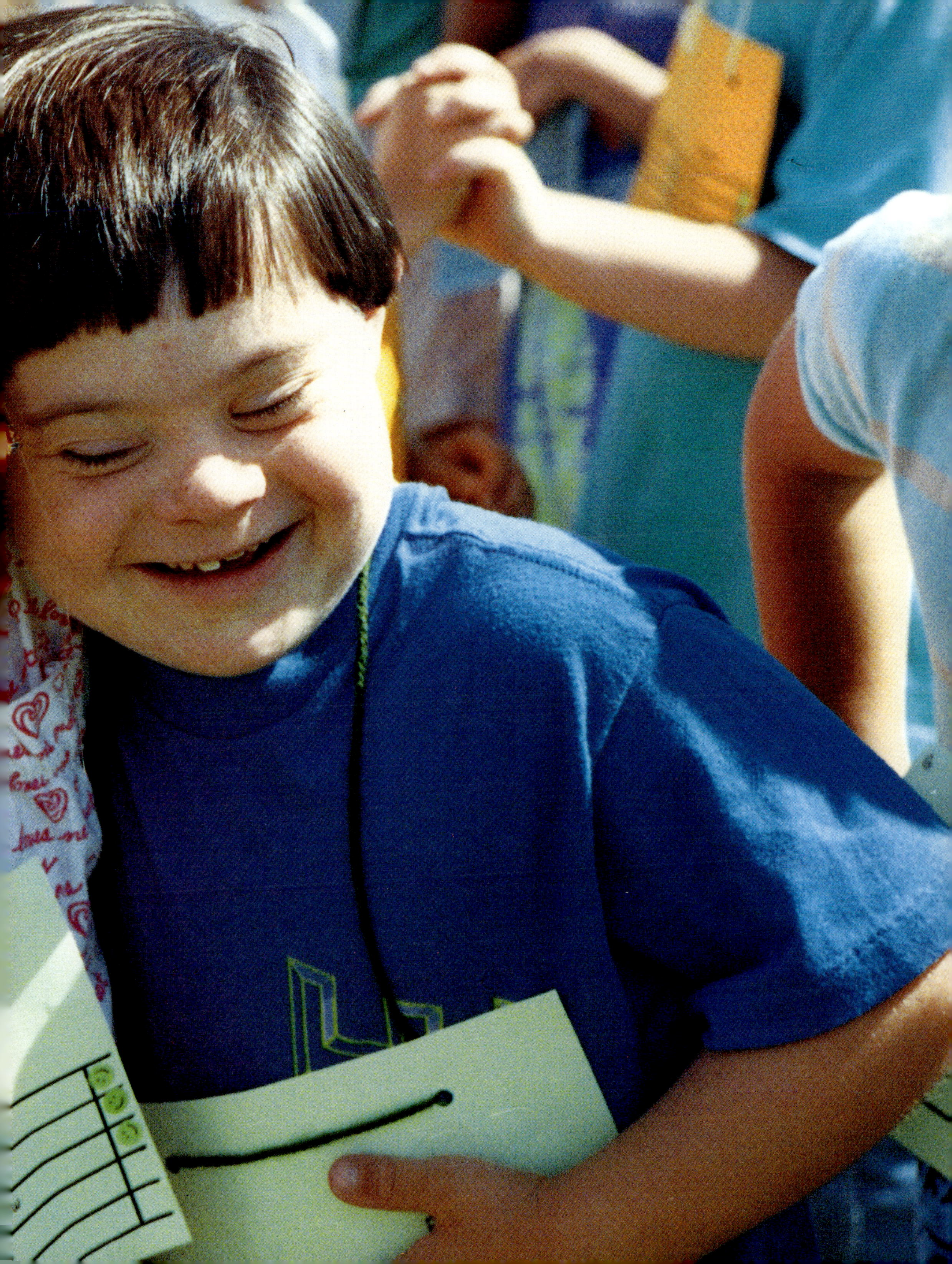

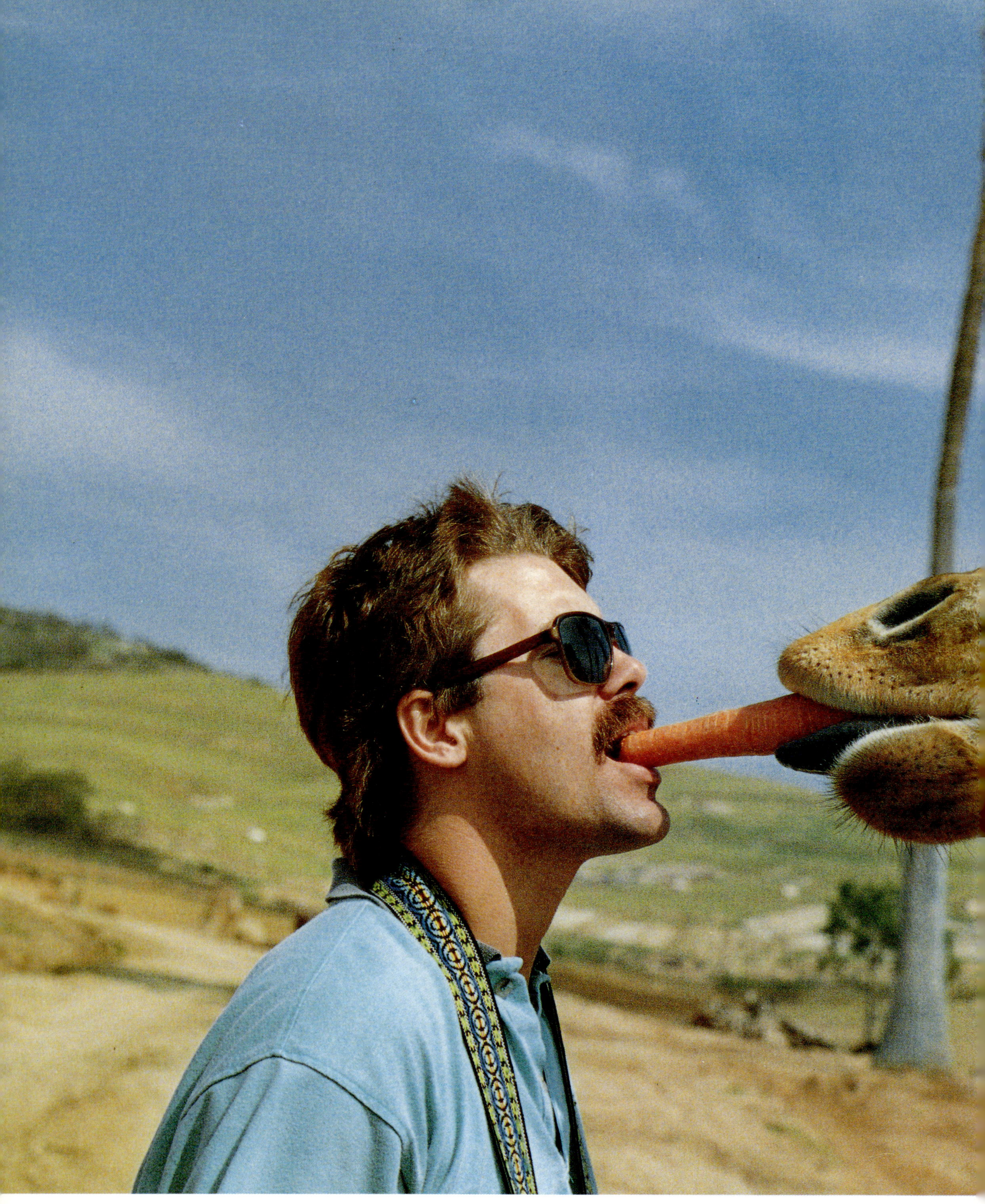

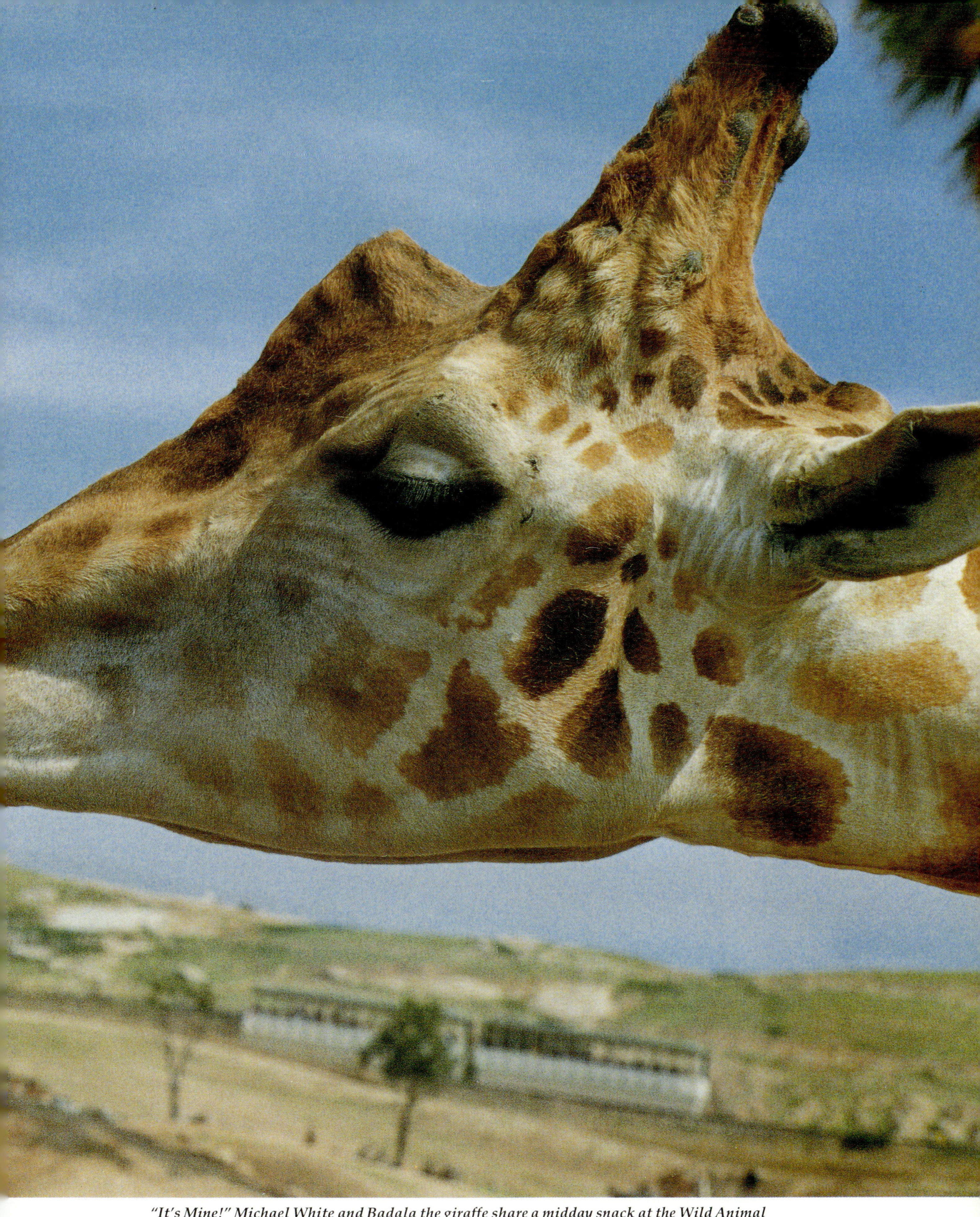

"It's Mine!" Michael White and Badala the giraffe share a midday snack at the Wild Animal Park in Escondido, Calif. Photo by Katherine M. Goldmann of Leucadia, Calif.

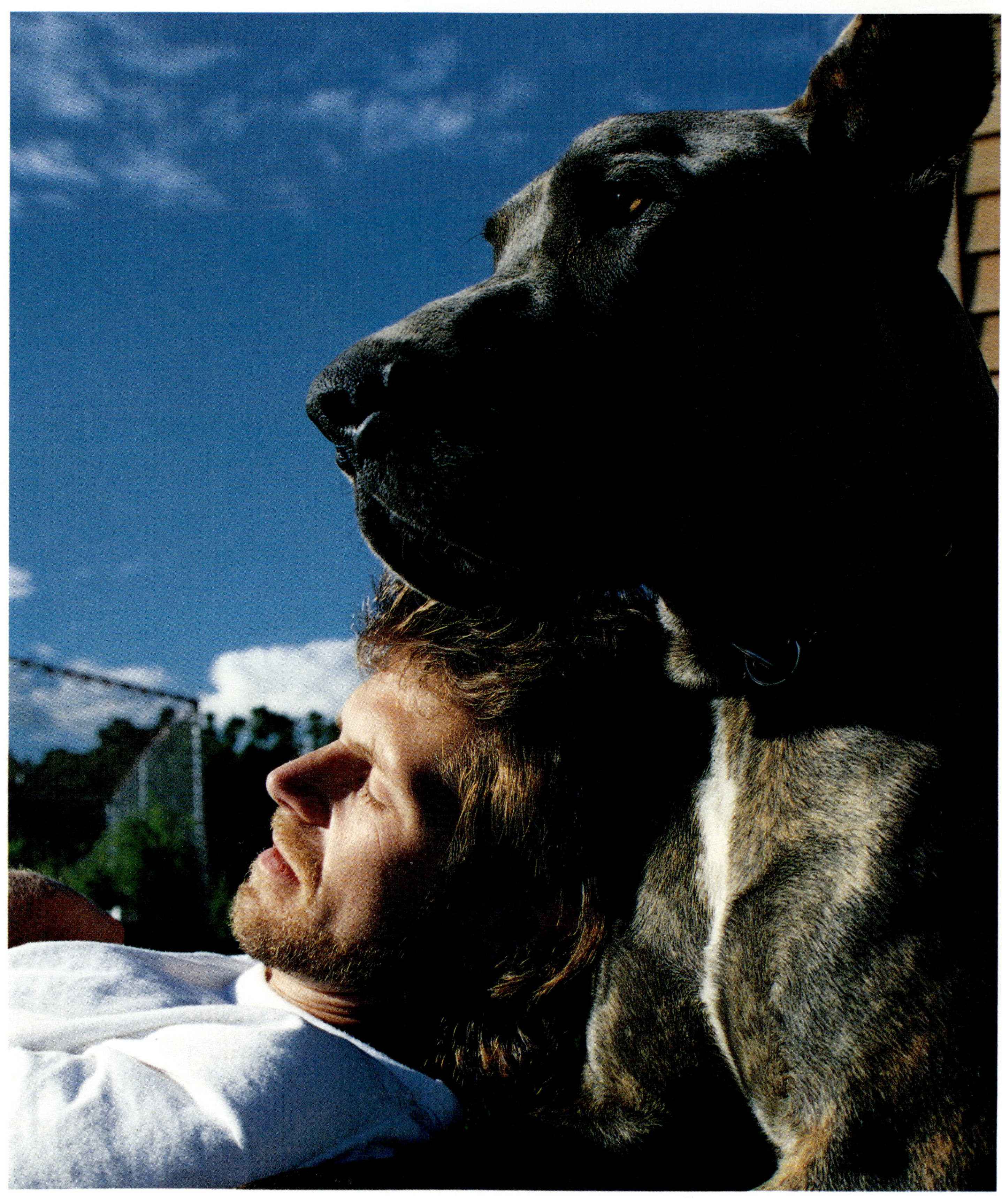

Richard Risch catches a nap on the grass under the watchful eye of the family dog, Mingus. Photo by Richard's wife, Marsha. They live in Hudson, Wis.

Dress-alikes: Emma Elizabeth Herzog 10 months, and canine pal, Sophie Irene, 3 years. Photo by Marshall J. Cohen of Houston, Tex.

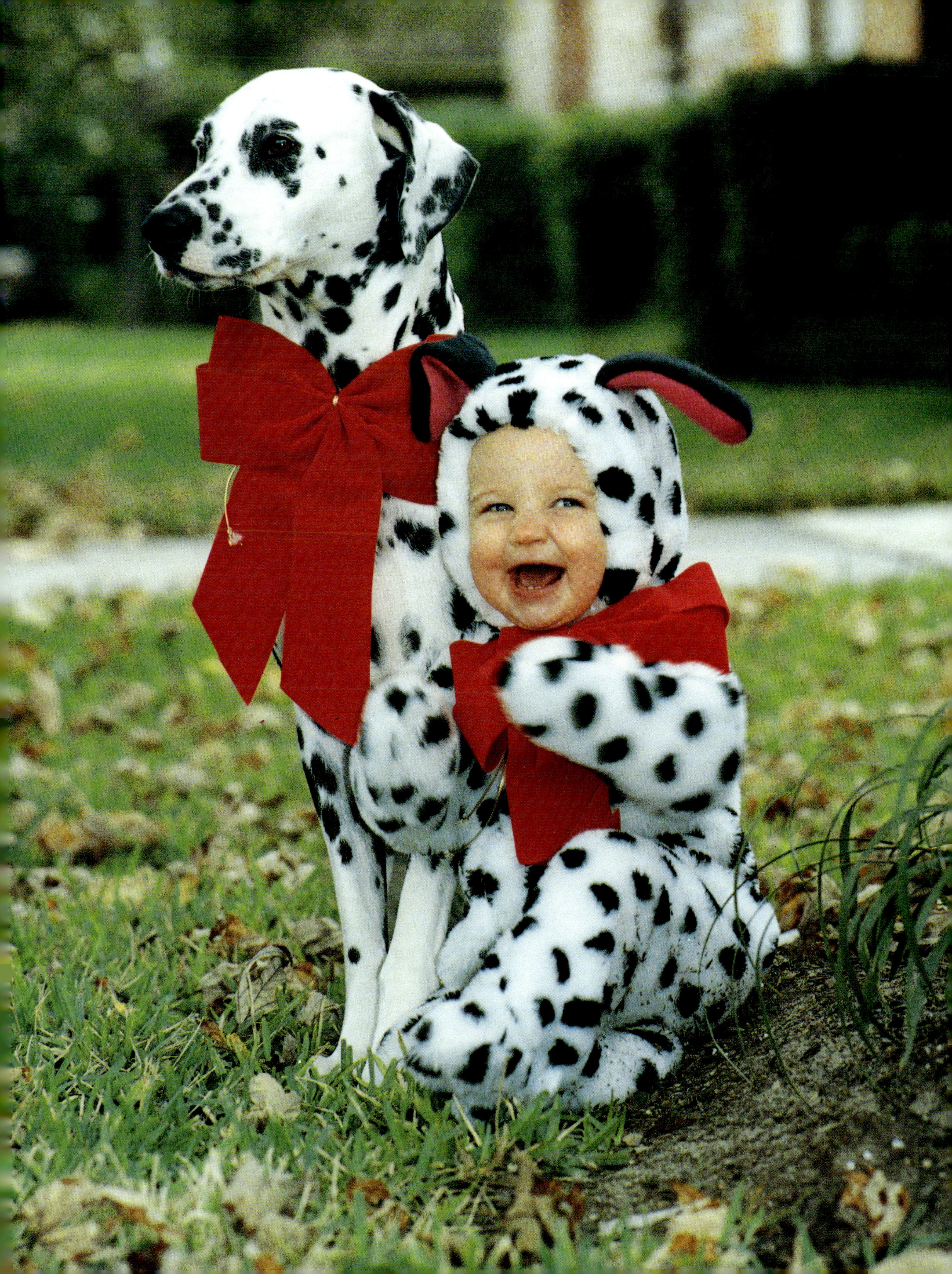

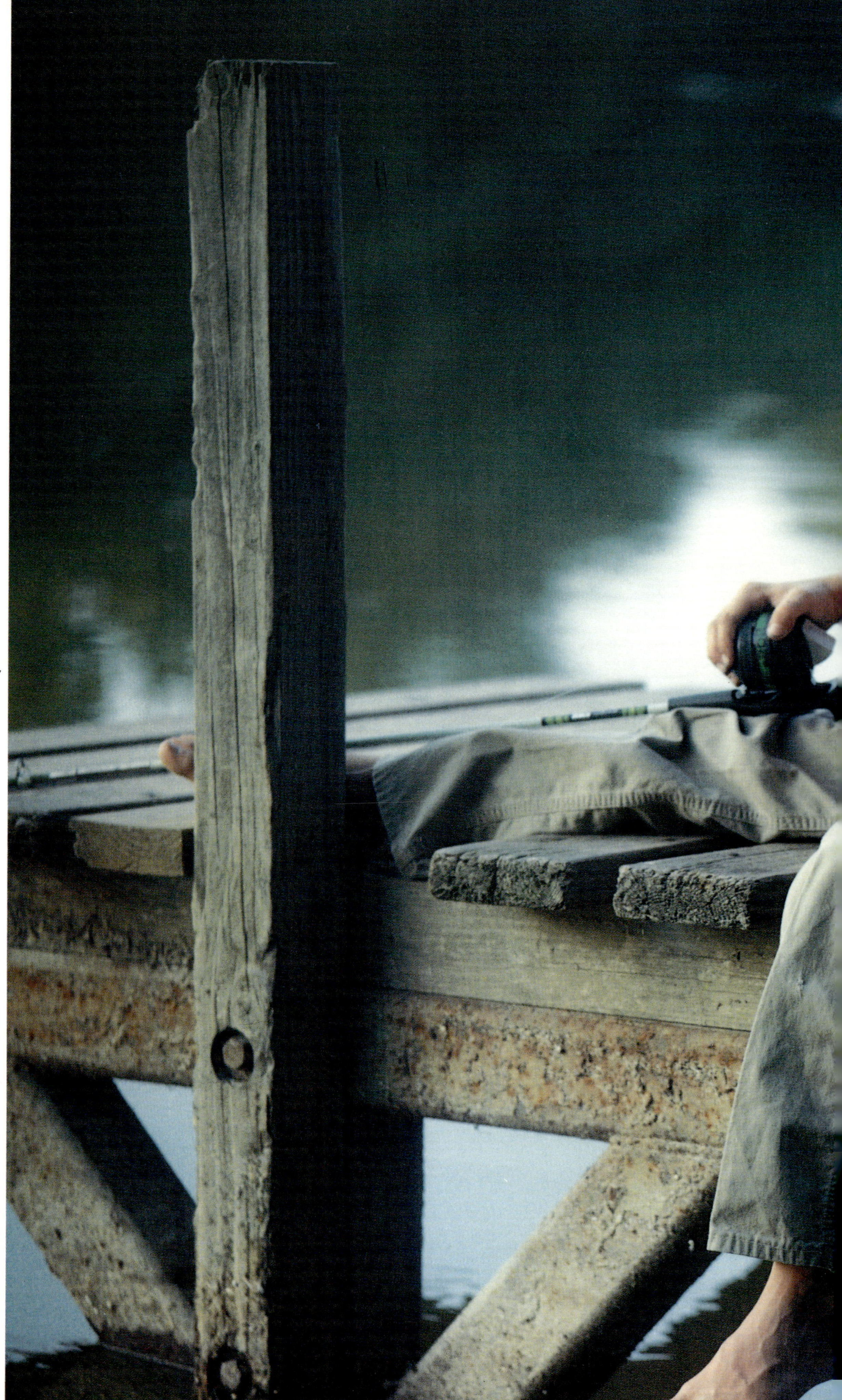

Barefoot Boy With Dog: It could be a painting, but it's a photograph—of Jeremy Southwell, 9, with Melissa. Jeremy's mother, Rebecca J. Klein of Grand Rapids, Mich., took the picture.

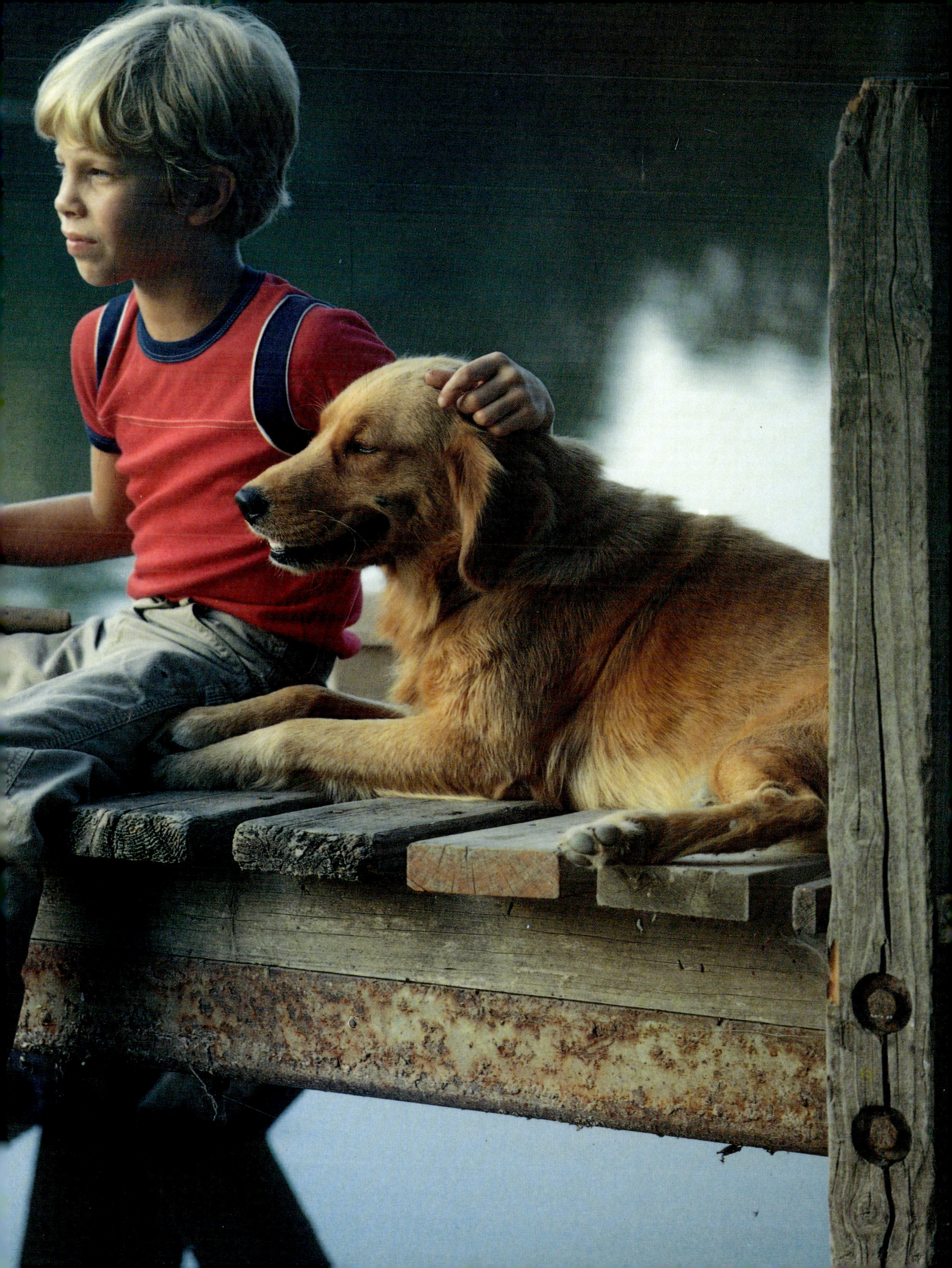

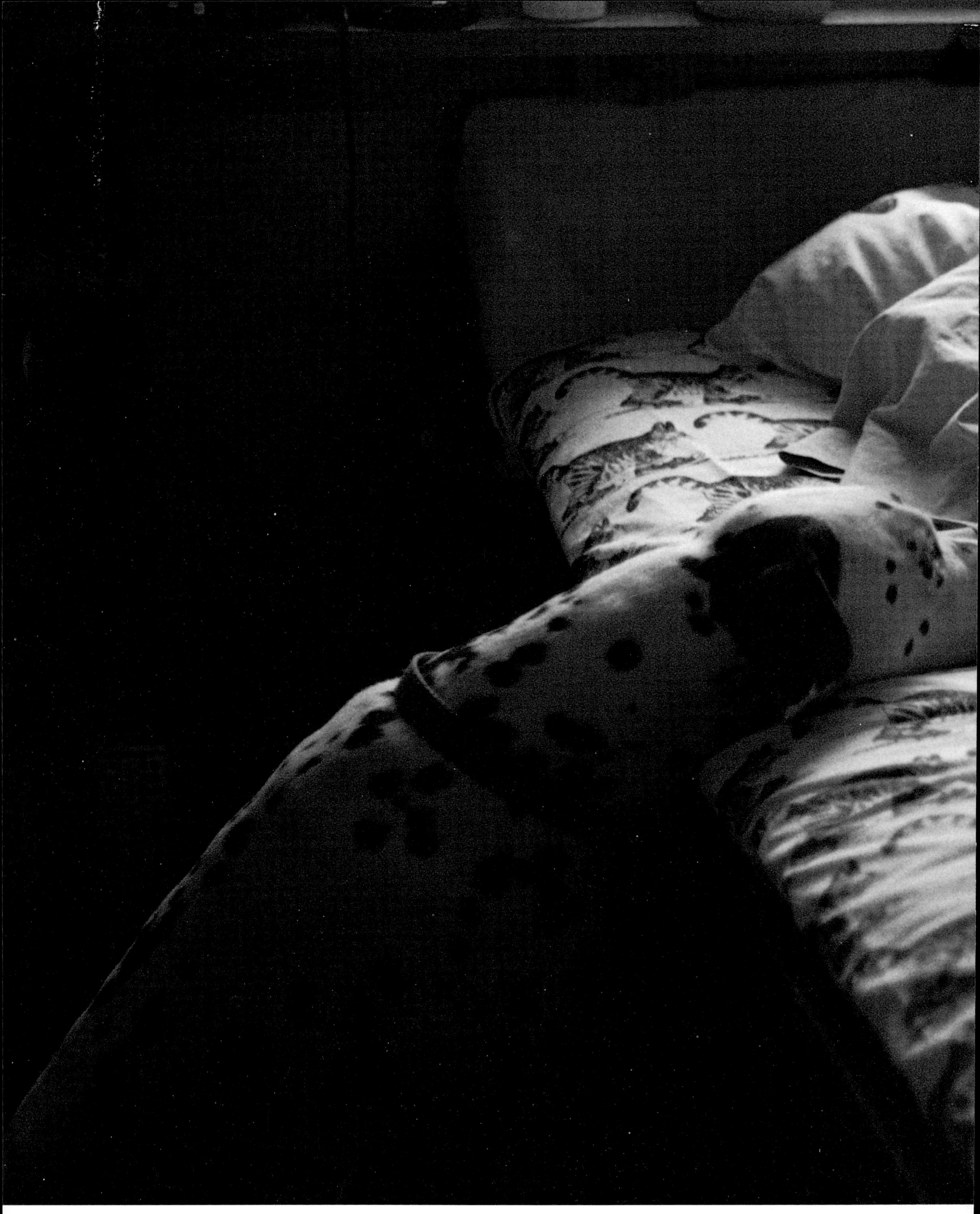

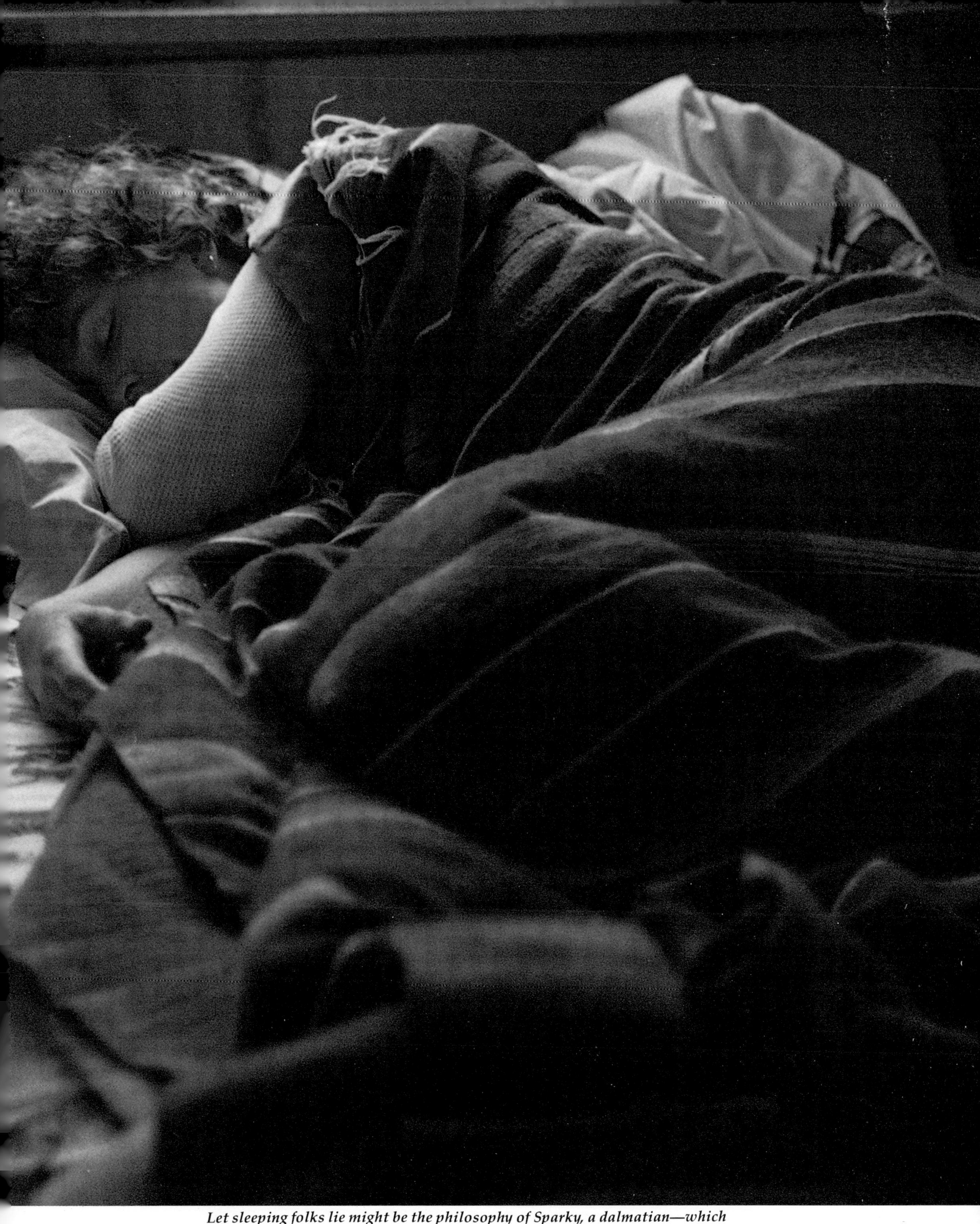

Let sleeping folks lie might be the philosophy of Sparky, a dalmatian—which allows Maryanne Knox to sleep undisturbed. Photo by Chris Bondante of Tucson.

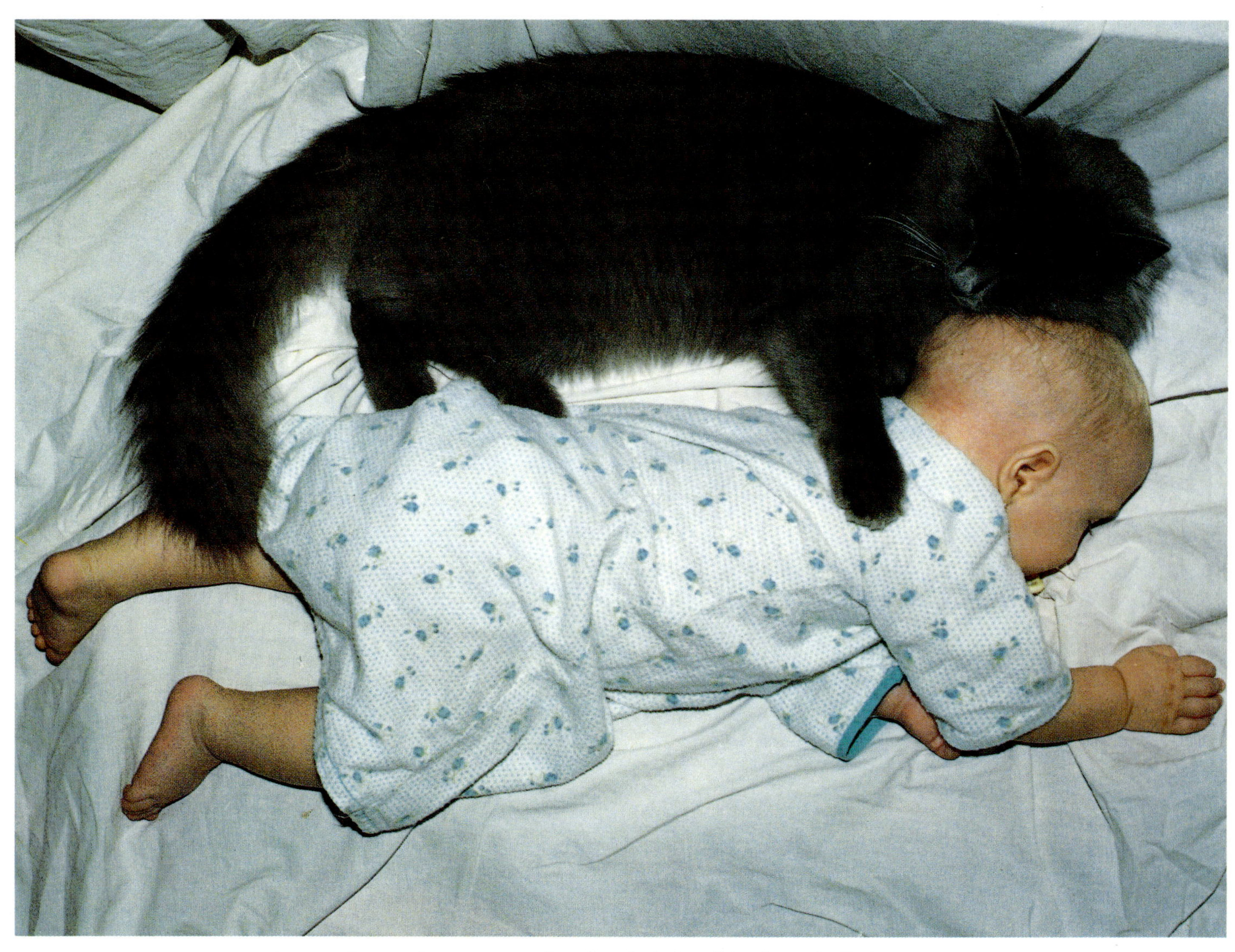

Catnap: Ryan Lehman, 5 months, already is fast friends with Chelsea. Photo by Ryan's father, Scott Lehman of Phoenix.

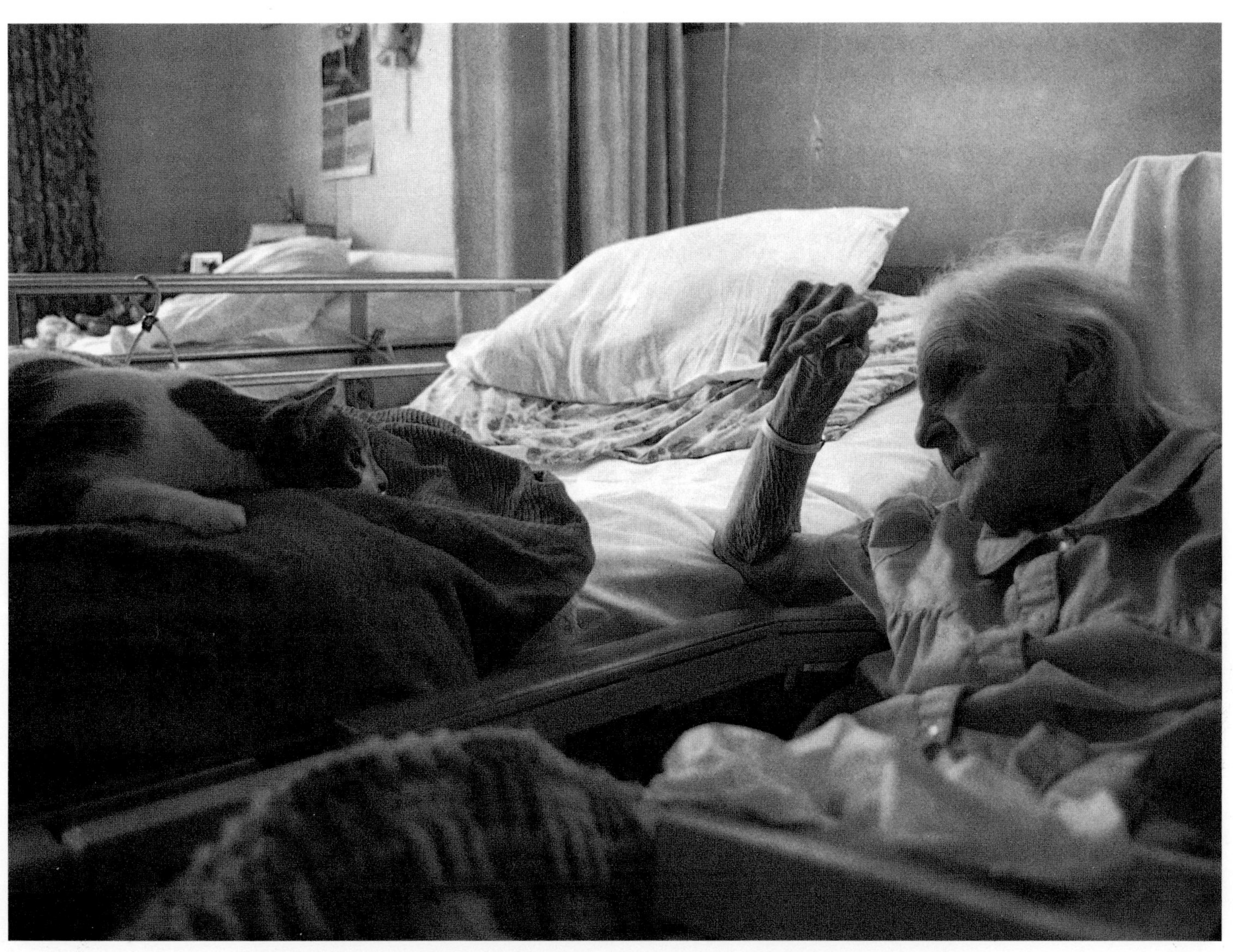

A Very Special Understanding: Marion B. Potter, 97, and Mickey in a Portland, Maine, nursing home. Photo by Paule French of Portland.

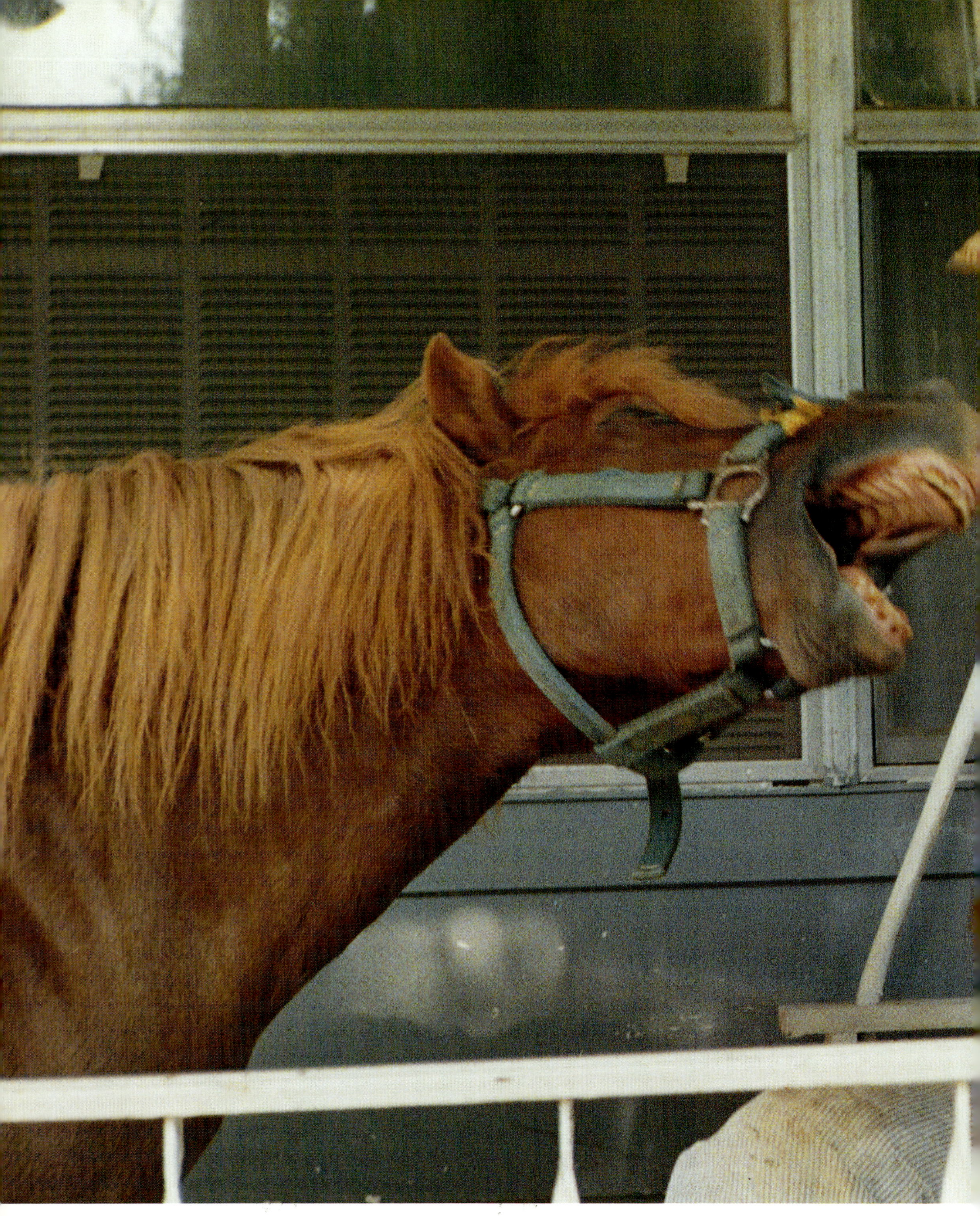

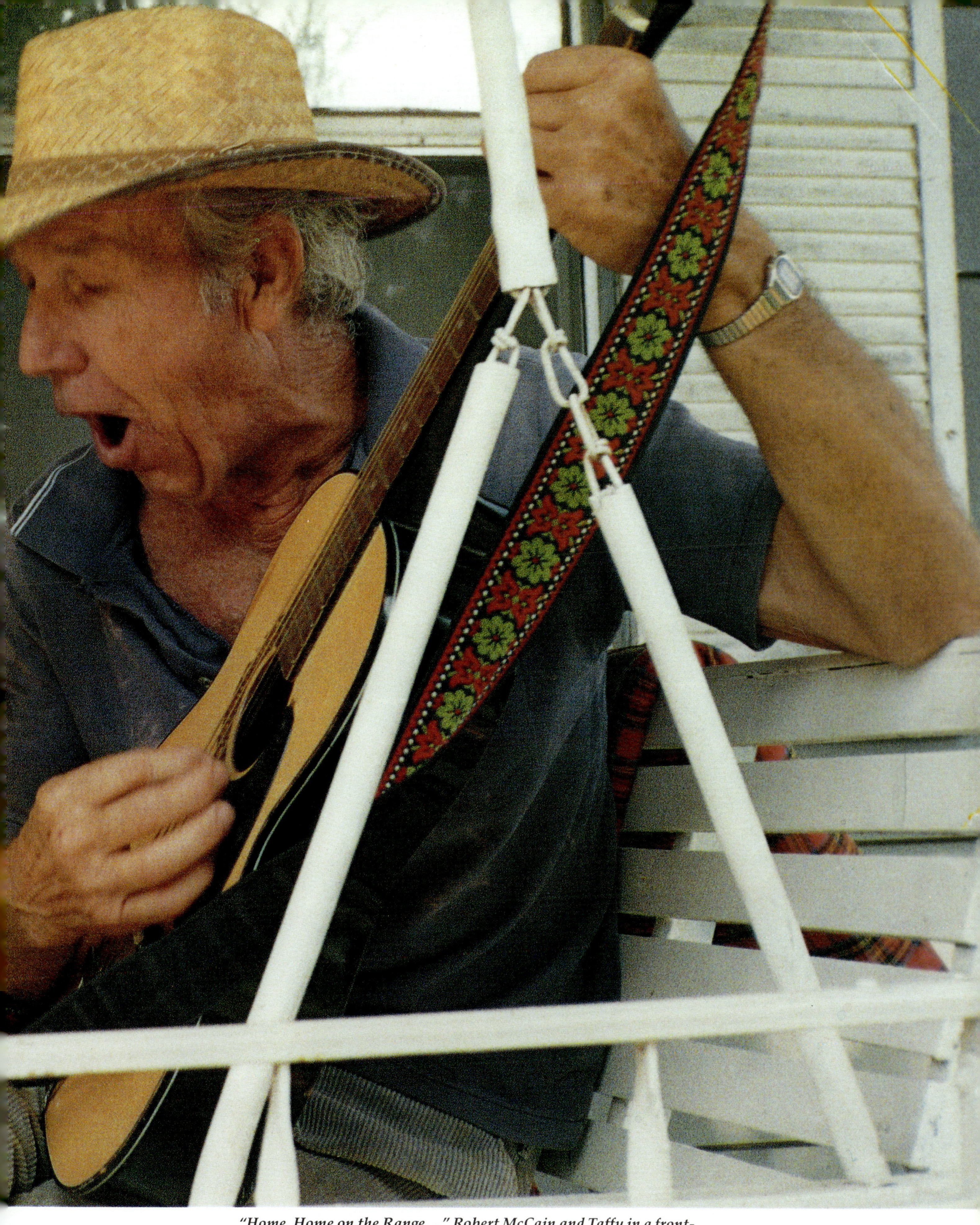

"Home, Home on the Range…" Robert McCain and Taffy in a front-porch duet in Washington County, Fla. Photo by Robert's wife, Audrey.

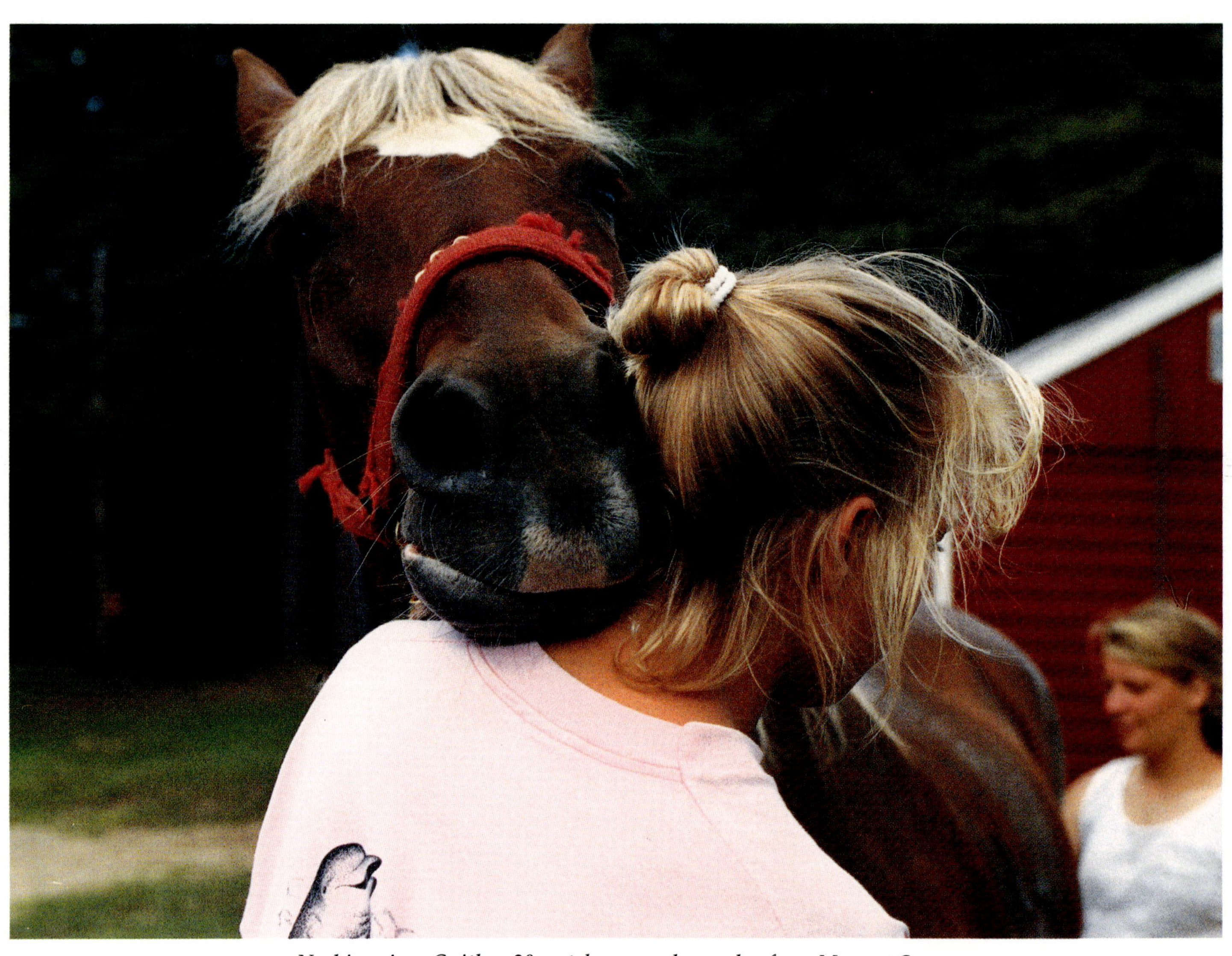

Necking: Amy Gaither, 20, catches some horseplay from Mom at Camp Oceanwood in Ocean Park, Maine. Photo by Amy's friend, Lynn E. Kilroy of Salem, Mass.

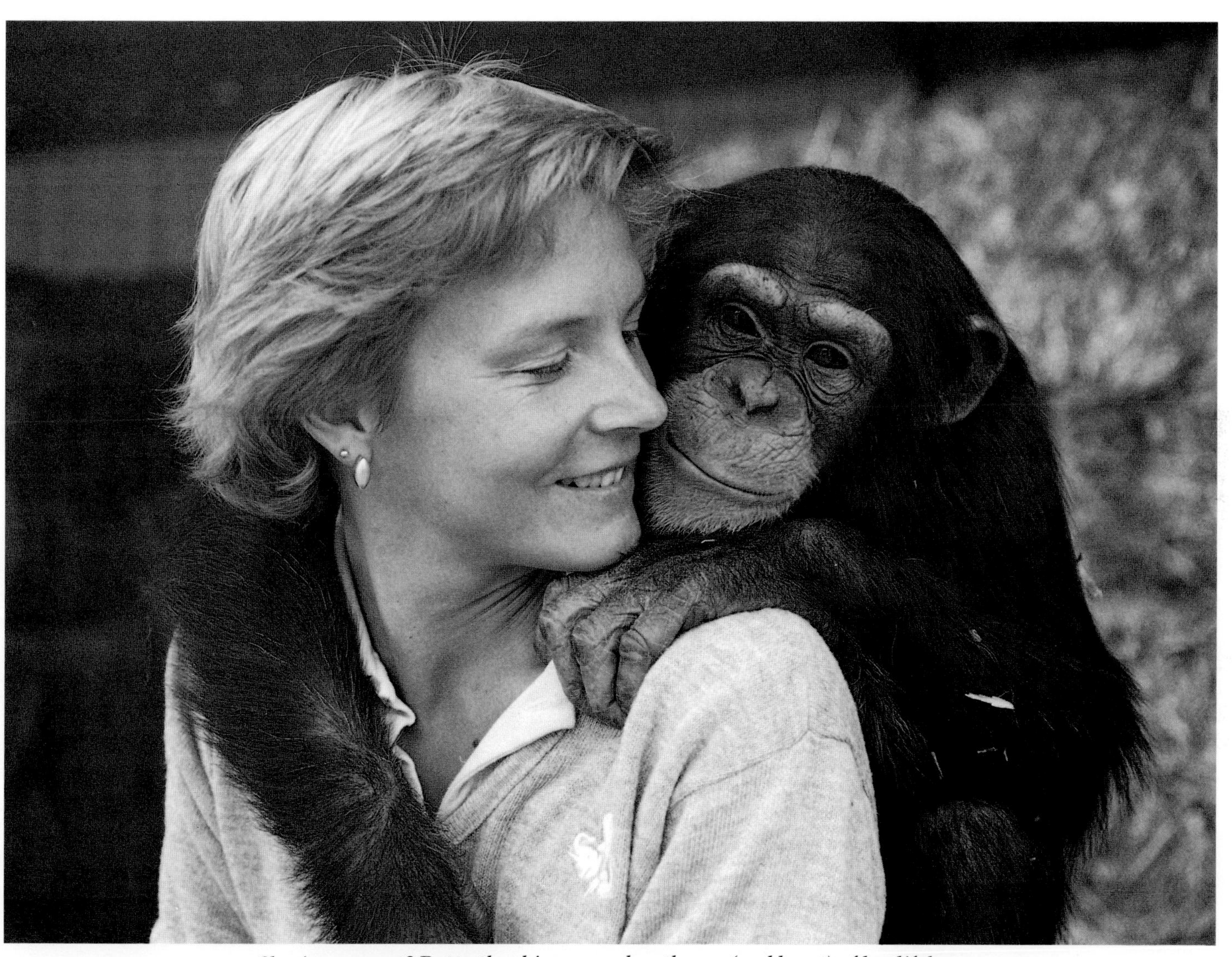

Sharing a secret? Patty the chimpanzee has the ear (and heart) of her lifelong friend, Kim Broadfoot Hussey, an animal trainer at Marine World Africa USA in Vallejo, Calif. Photo by Darryl Bush of San Francisco.

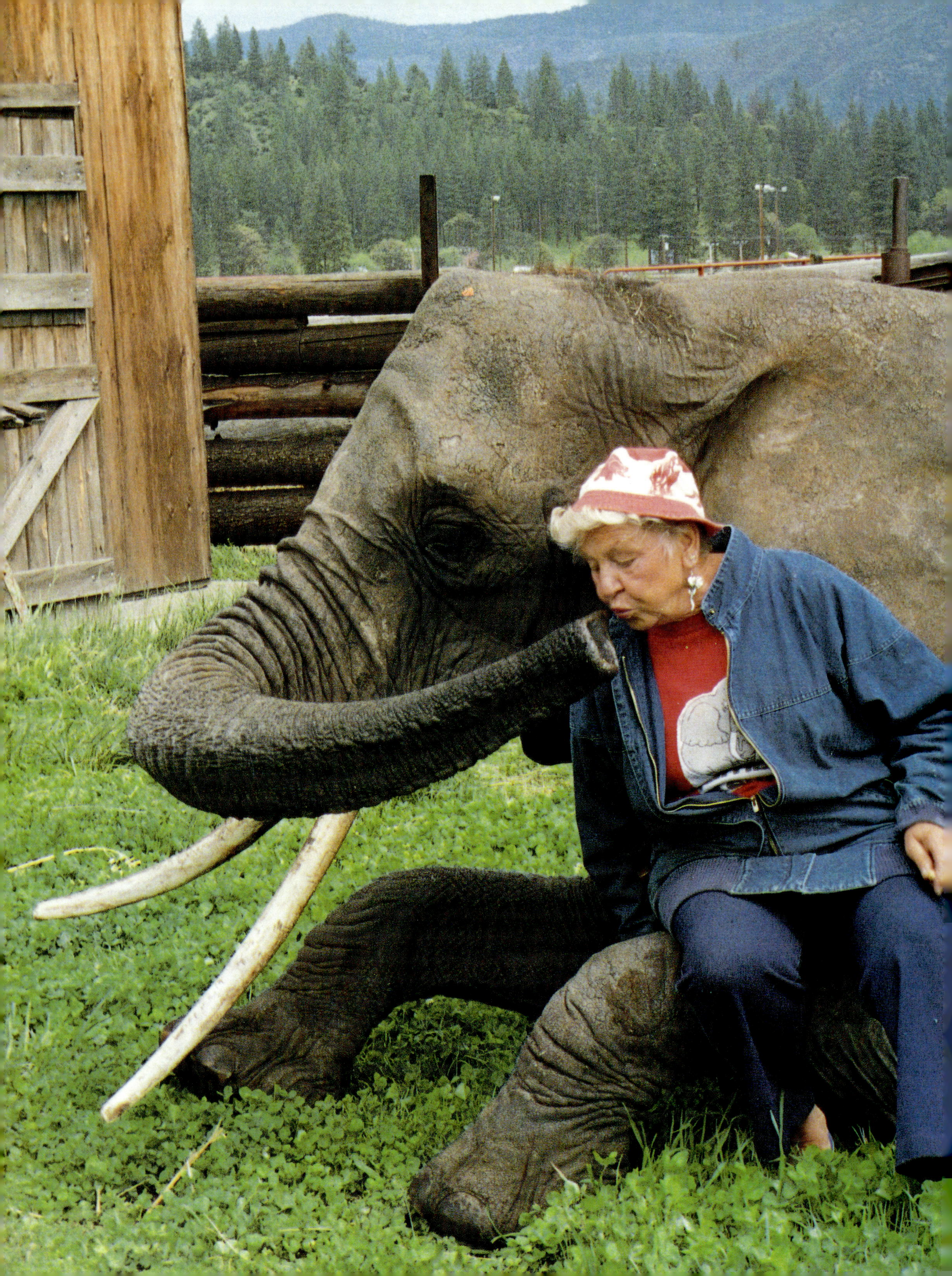

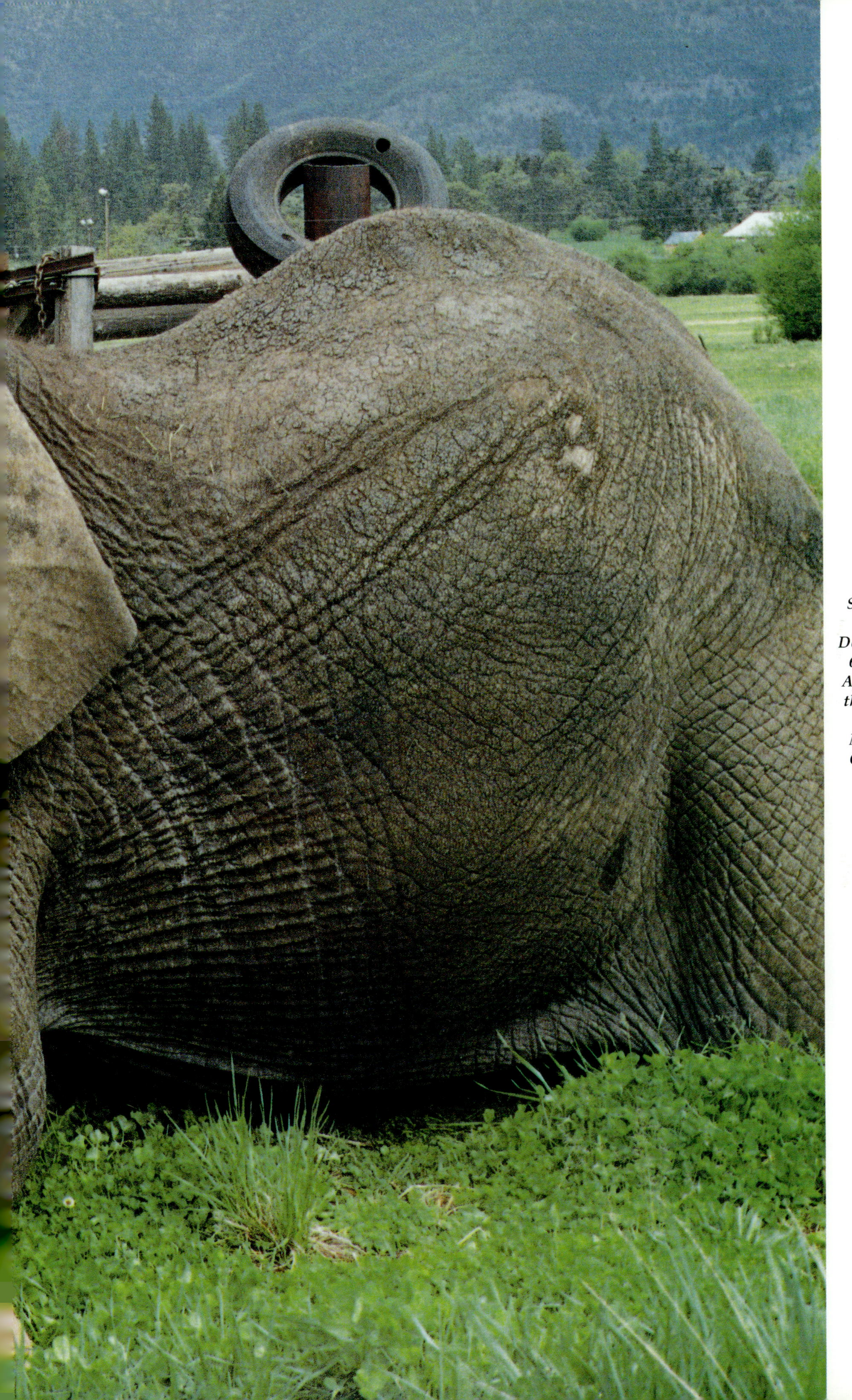

Some Friends Rub Noses…Some Don't: Dotty Olson, 68, with Akili the African elephant at their home in Etna, Calif. Photo by Merlyn Shaffer of Cloverdale, Calif.

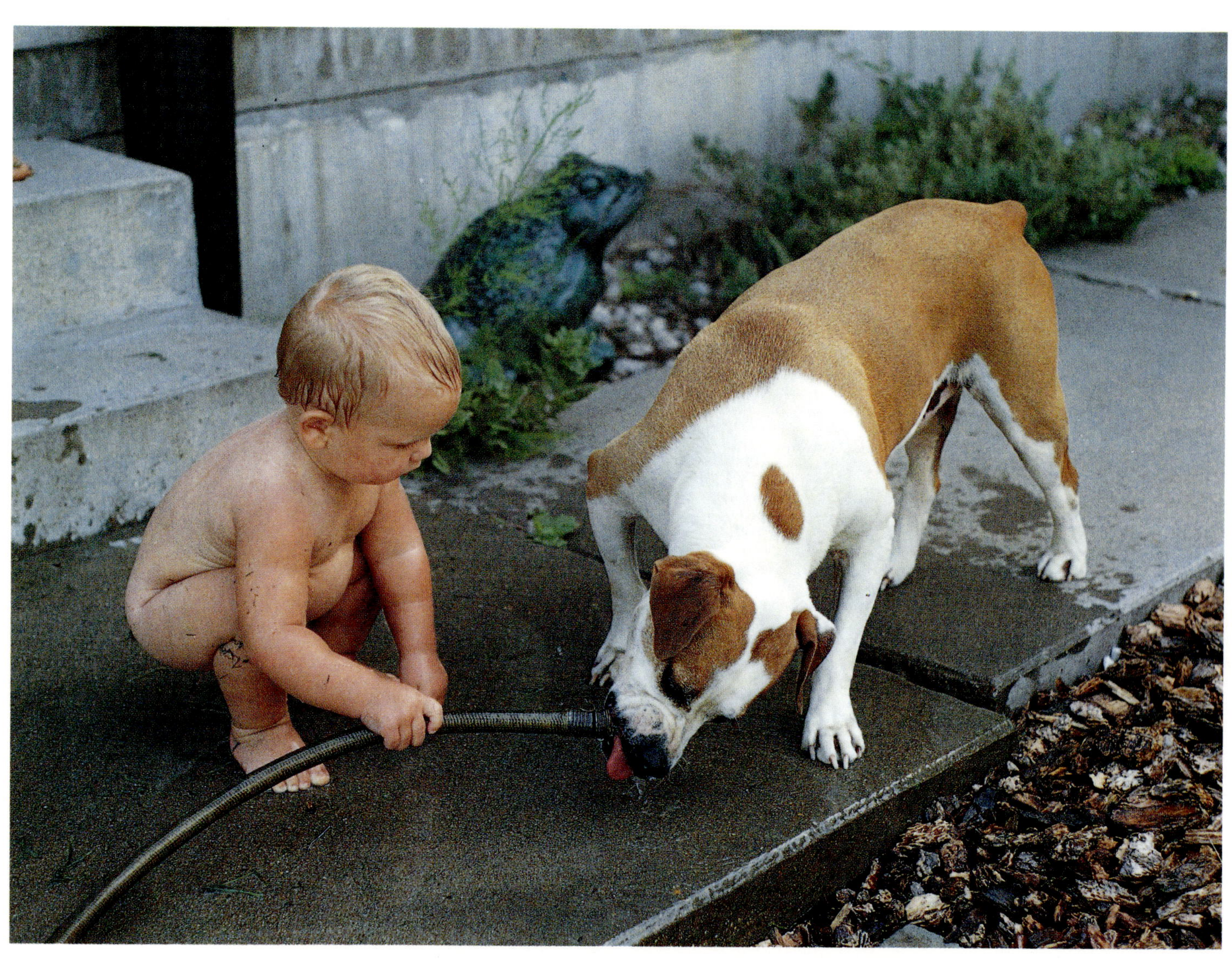

Richard Dean Brandkamp, 14 months old, cools off with Brandy, while Richard's grandmother, Patricia A. Brandkamp of Sedahia, Mo., takes the picture.

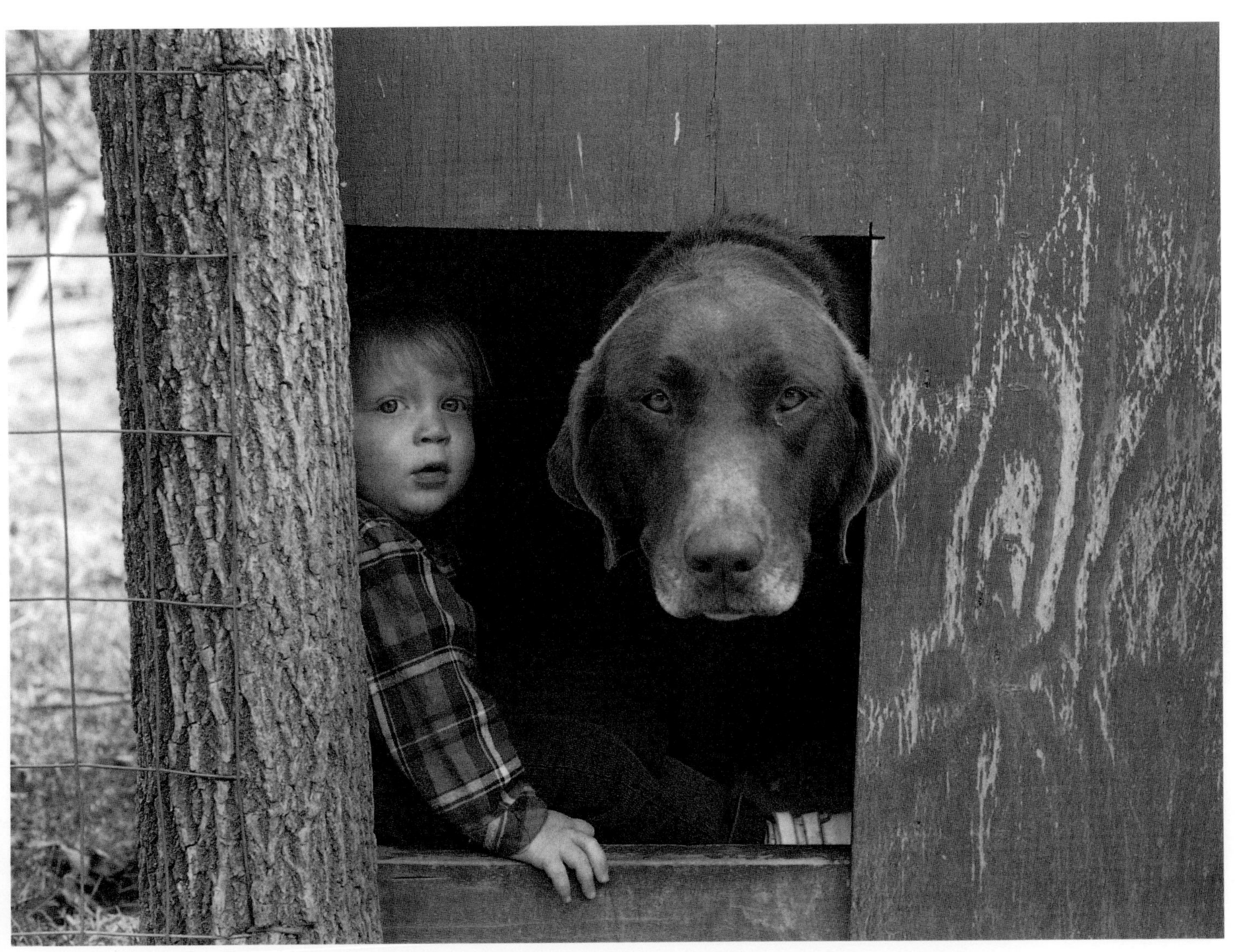

In the Doghouse: Lisa Lyne of Marshall, Va., stepped inside for a moment and discovered her son, Liam, 18 months, and their dog, Jesse, in this pensive pose.

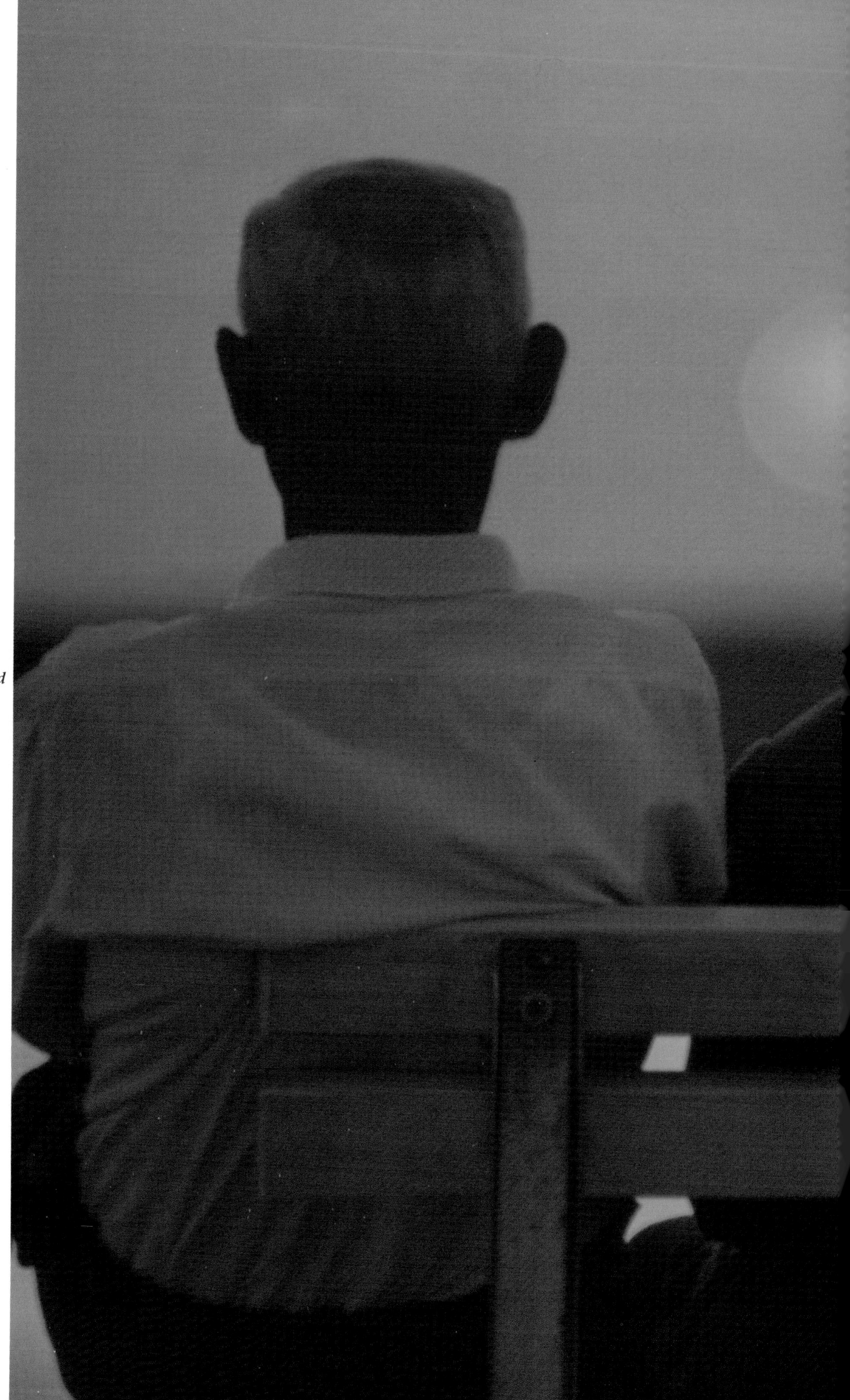

*A Quiet Sharing:
Taken in Patras,
Greece, at day's end
by Bill Petros of
Washington, D.C.*

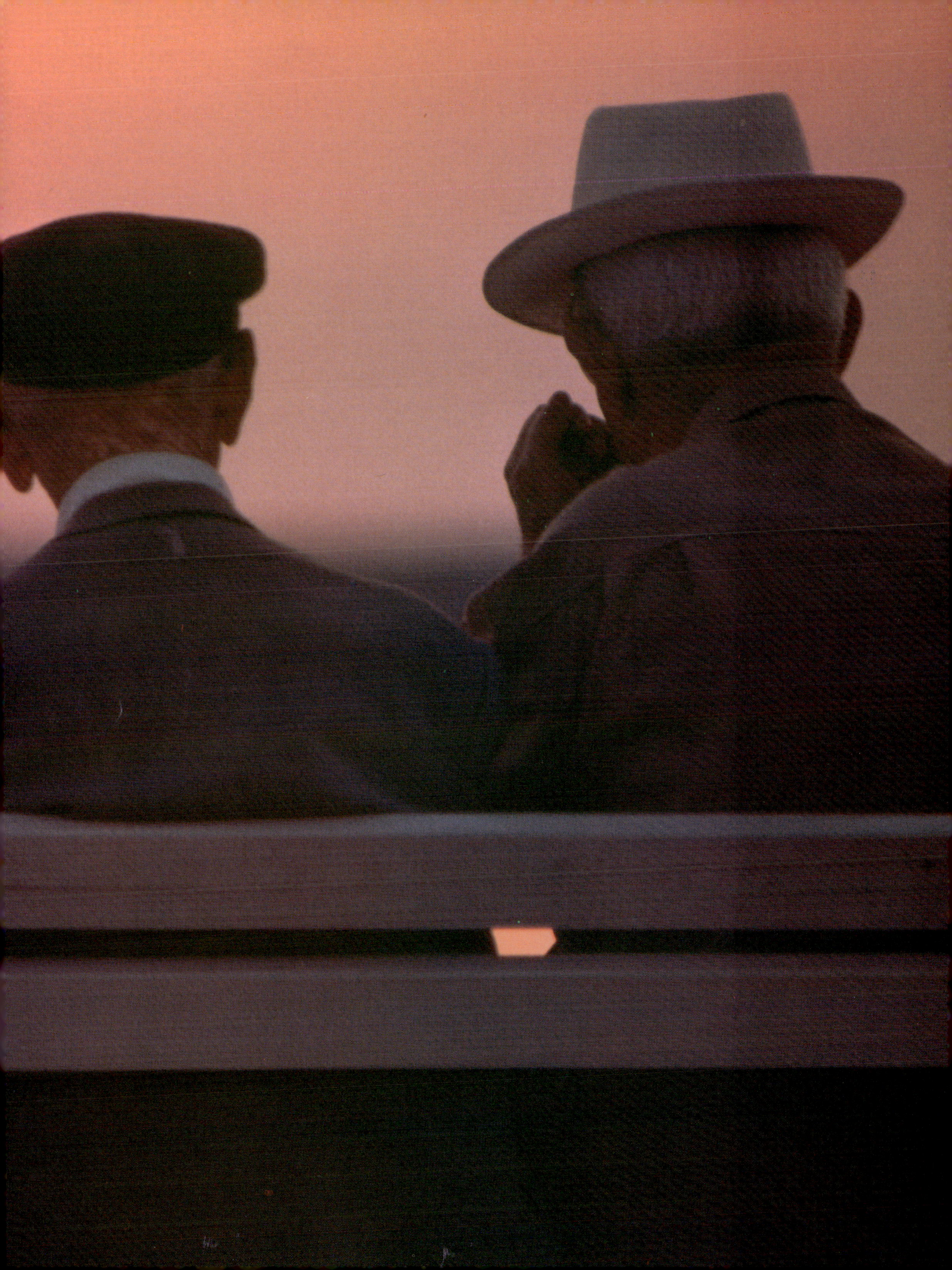

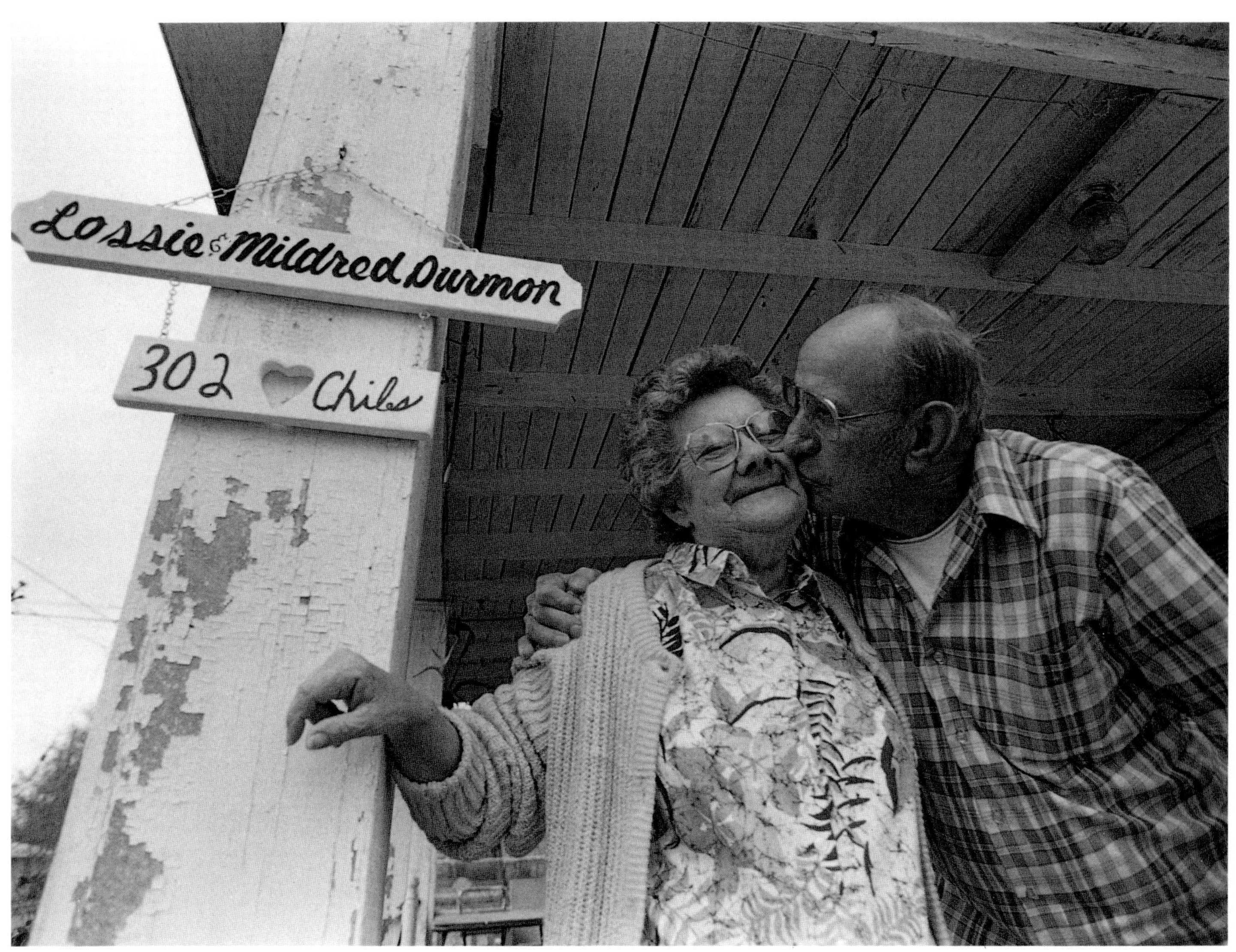

"I Love You Just Because": Lossie Durmon kisses his wife, Mildred, outside their home. Photo by Nancée E. Lewis of Shreveport, La.

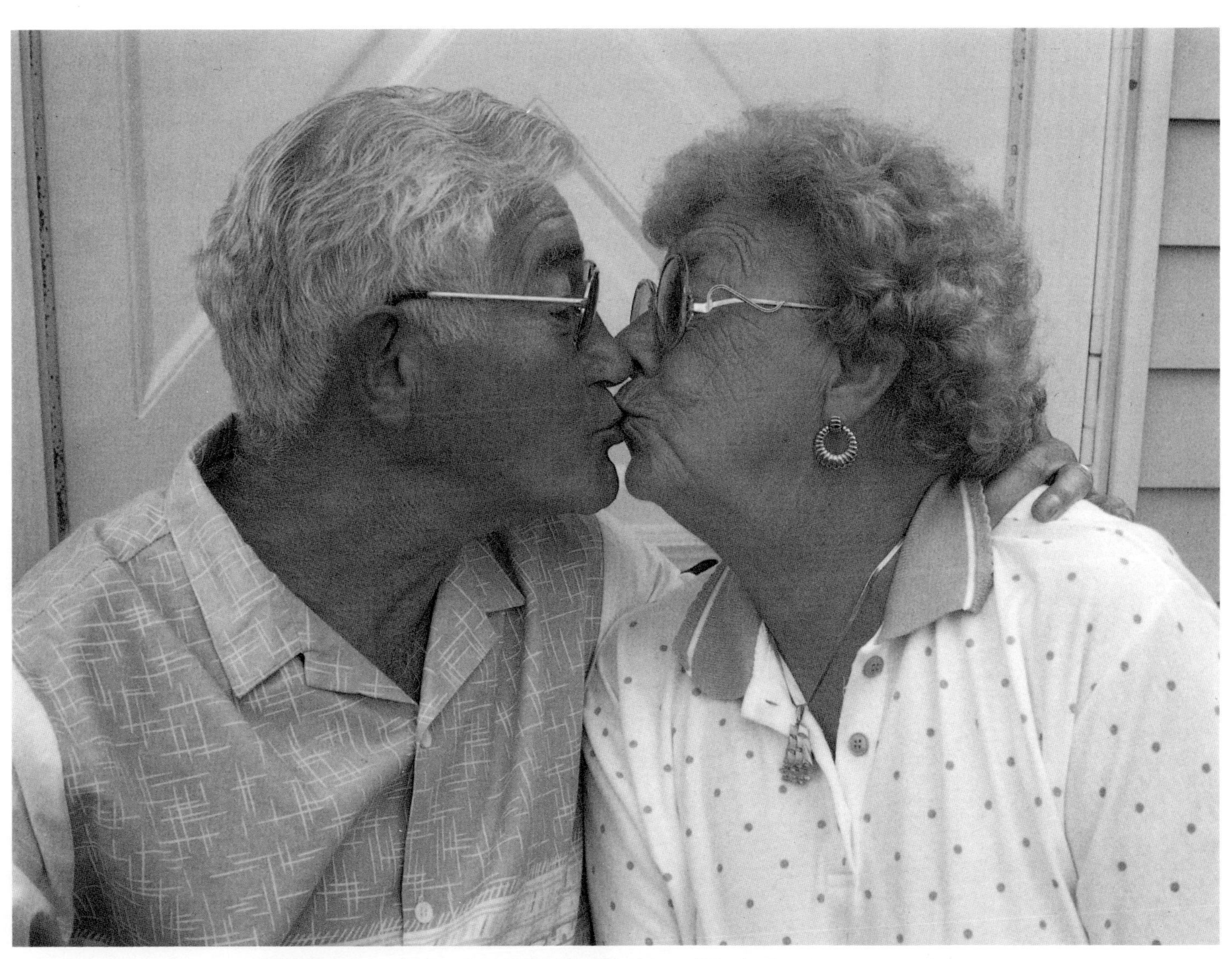

Still Best Friends: Doris and Edwin Hutchins of Peabody, Mass., married since 1947. Photo by their granddaughter, Suzanne Hutchins of Beverly, Mass.

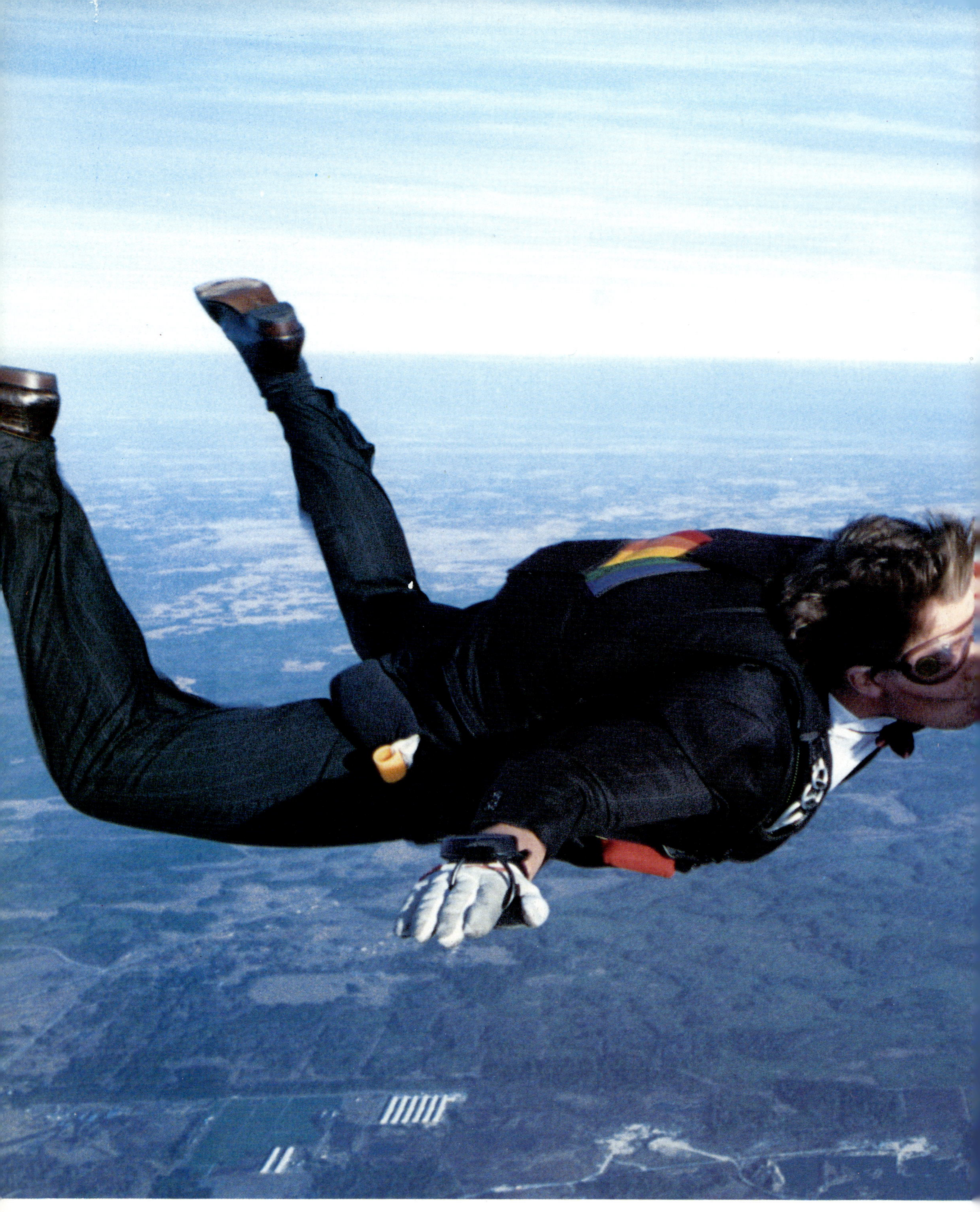

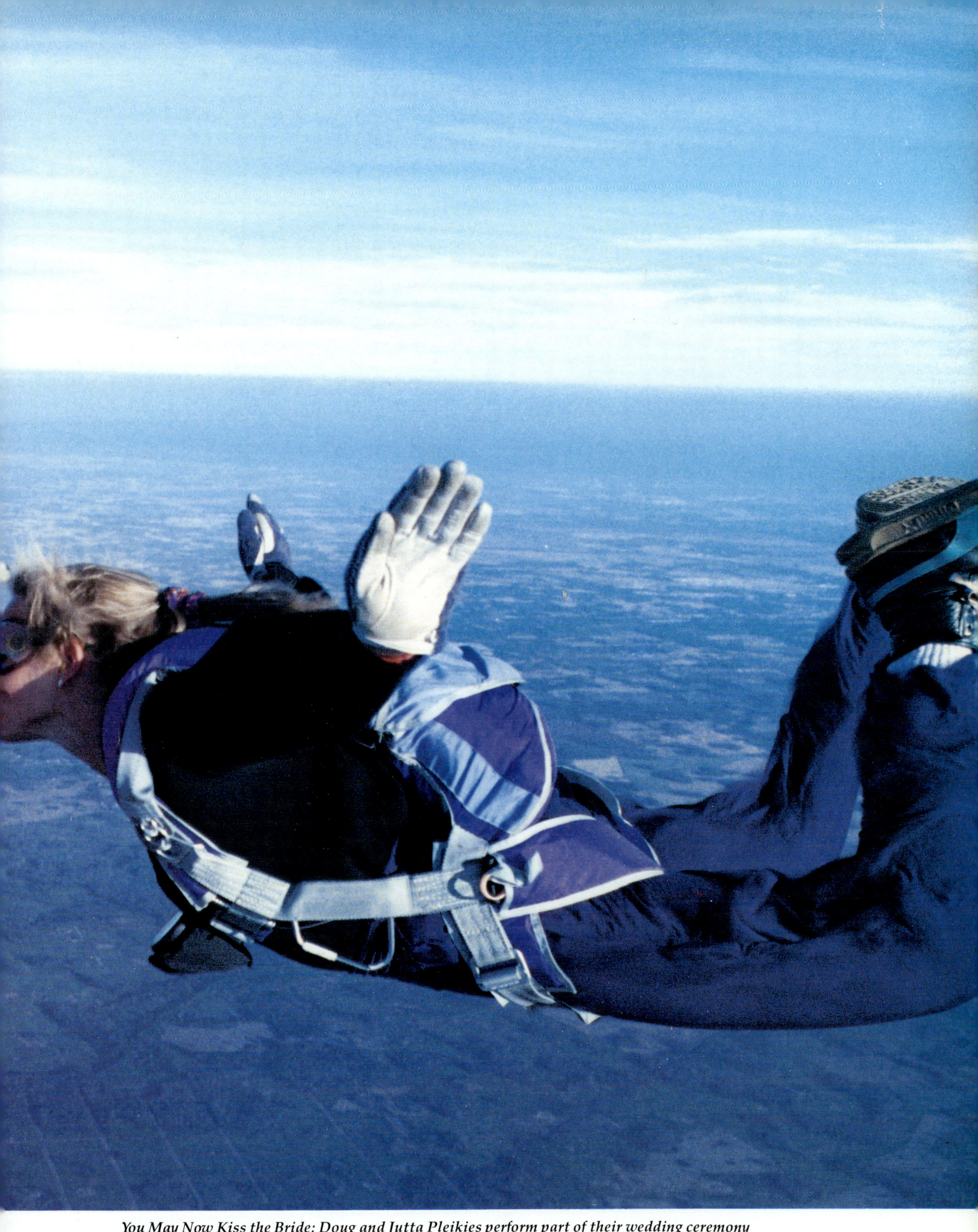

You May Now Kiss the Bride: Doug and Jutta Pleikies perform part of their wedding ceremony with a skydive from Cloud Nine. Dave Floyd of Zephyrhills, Fla., recorded it for the family album.

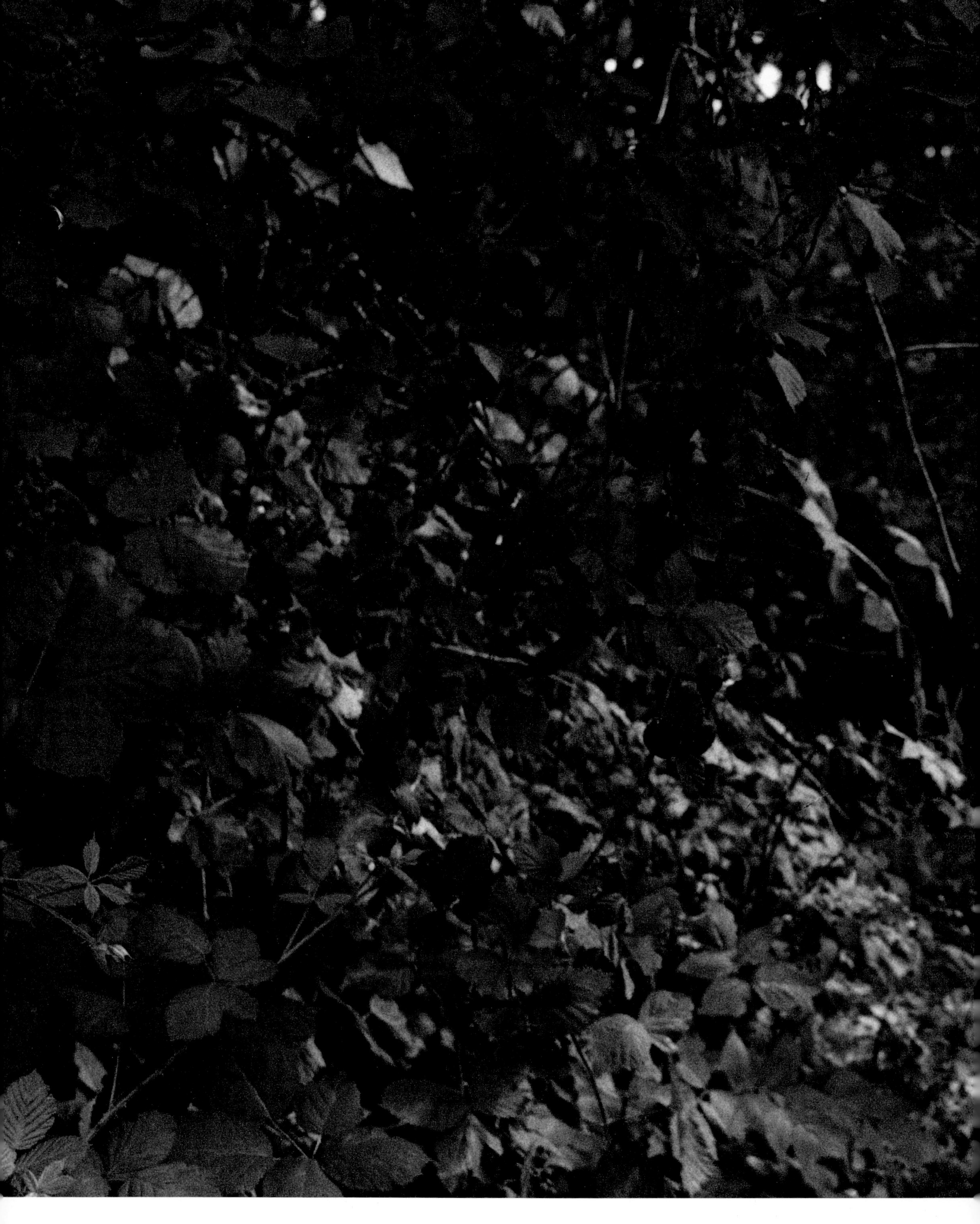

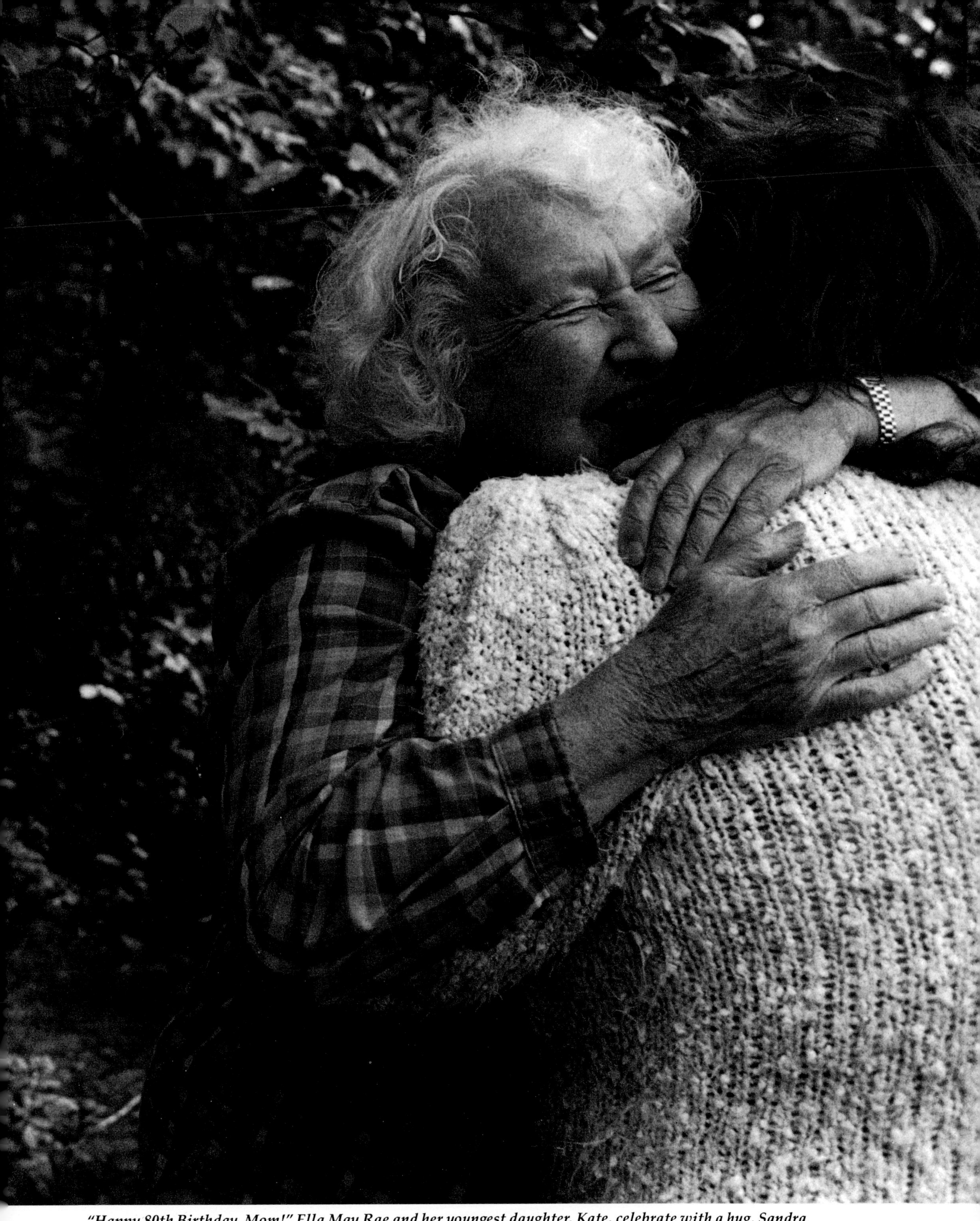

"Happy 80th Birthday, Mom!" Ella May Rae and her youngest daughter, Kate, celebrate with a hug. Sandra L. Hoover—granddaughter and niece—snapped the picture in Kirkland, Wash., their hometown.

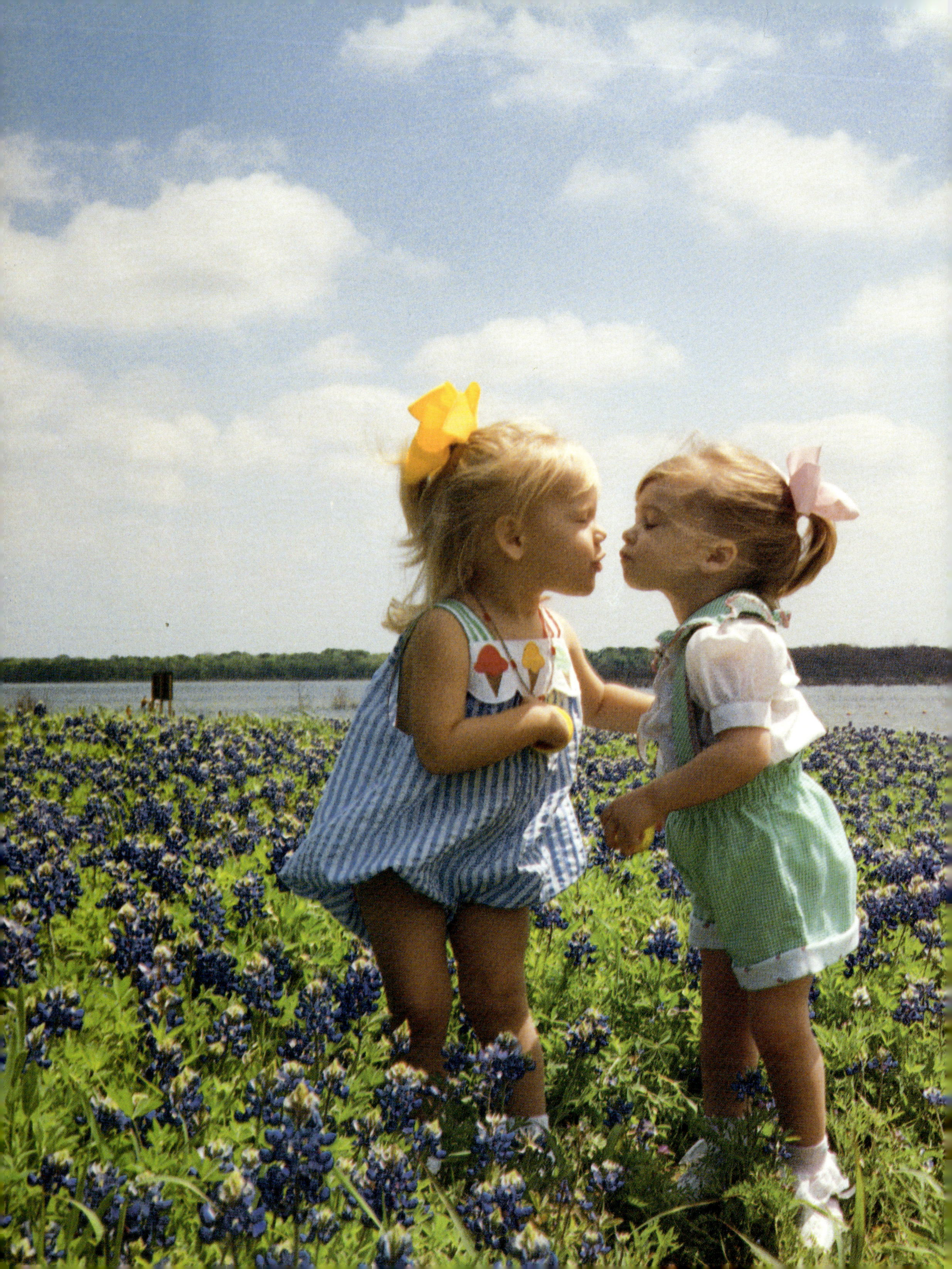

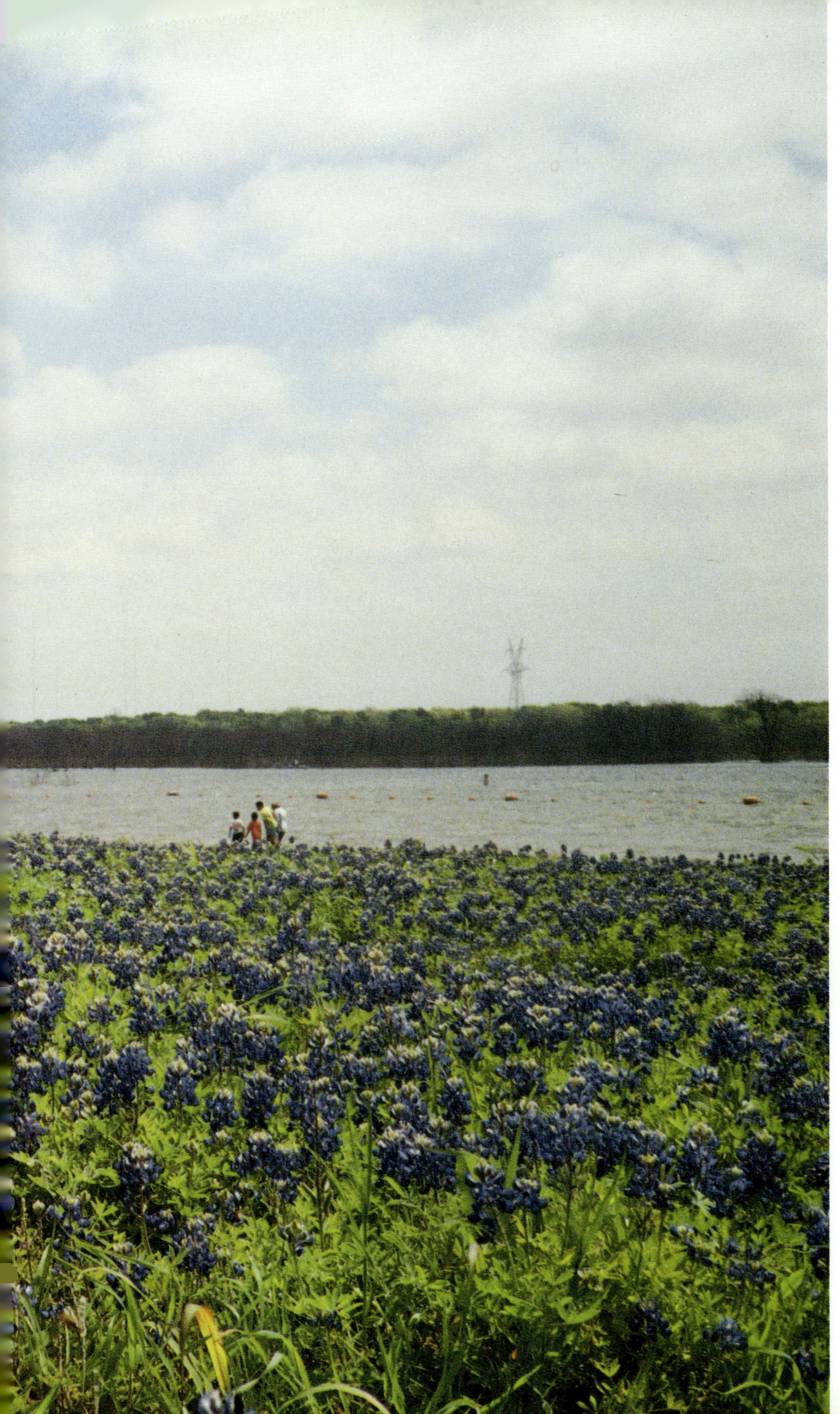

*Flowers of Texas:
Miranda Carrie
Amman and Rachel
Elizabeth Nelson,
both 2, get ready for
a little kiss in a field
of bluebonnets, the
state flower.
Rachel's mother,
Cynthia Amman of
Arlington, Tex., took
the photo.*

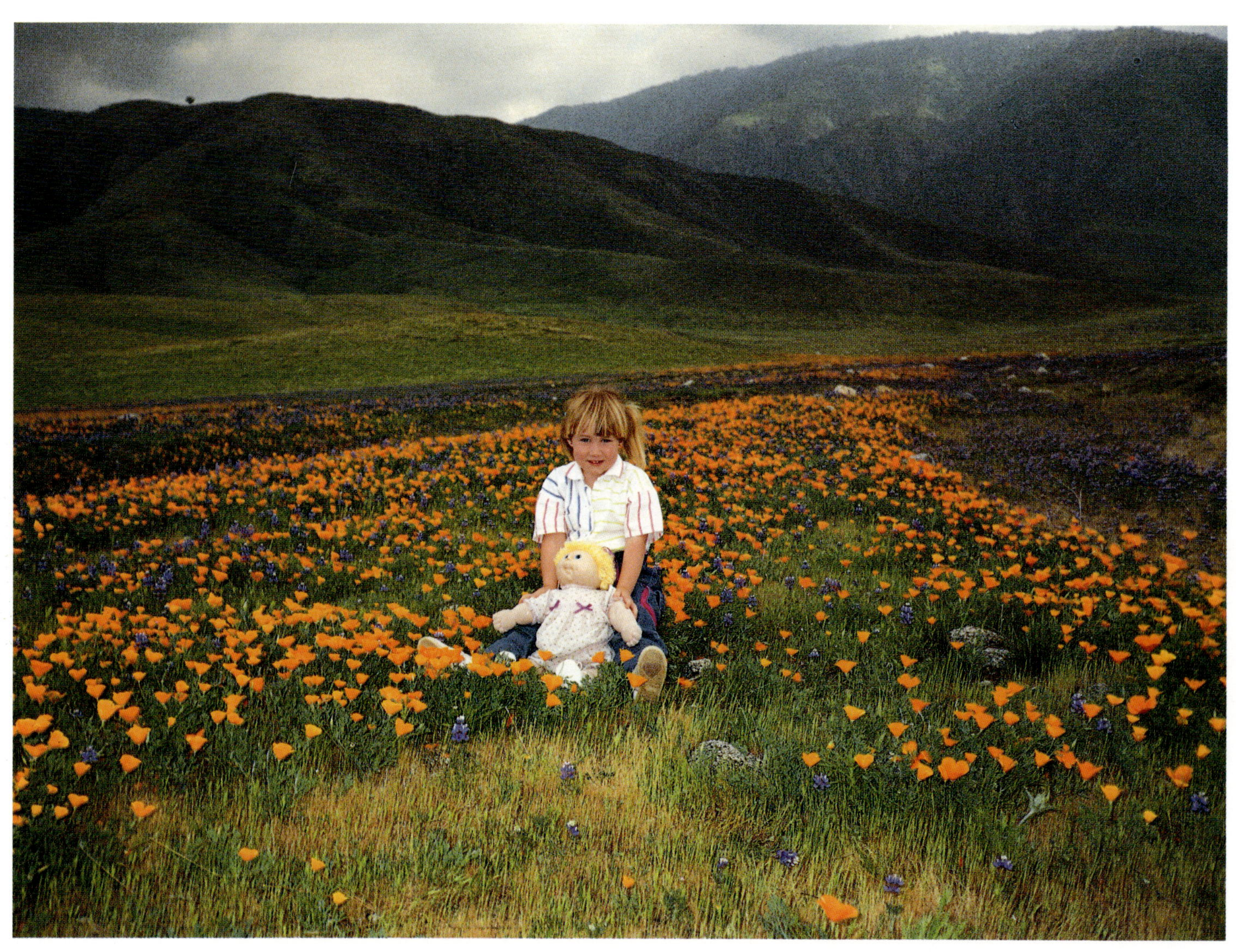

*Springtime Blossoms: Fairest of them all is Cassie Renee Hallum, 4, whose
mother, Susan, photographed her in Arvin, Calif.*

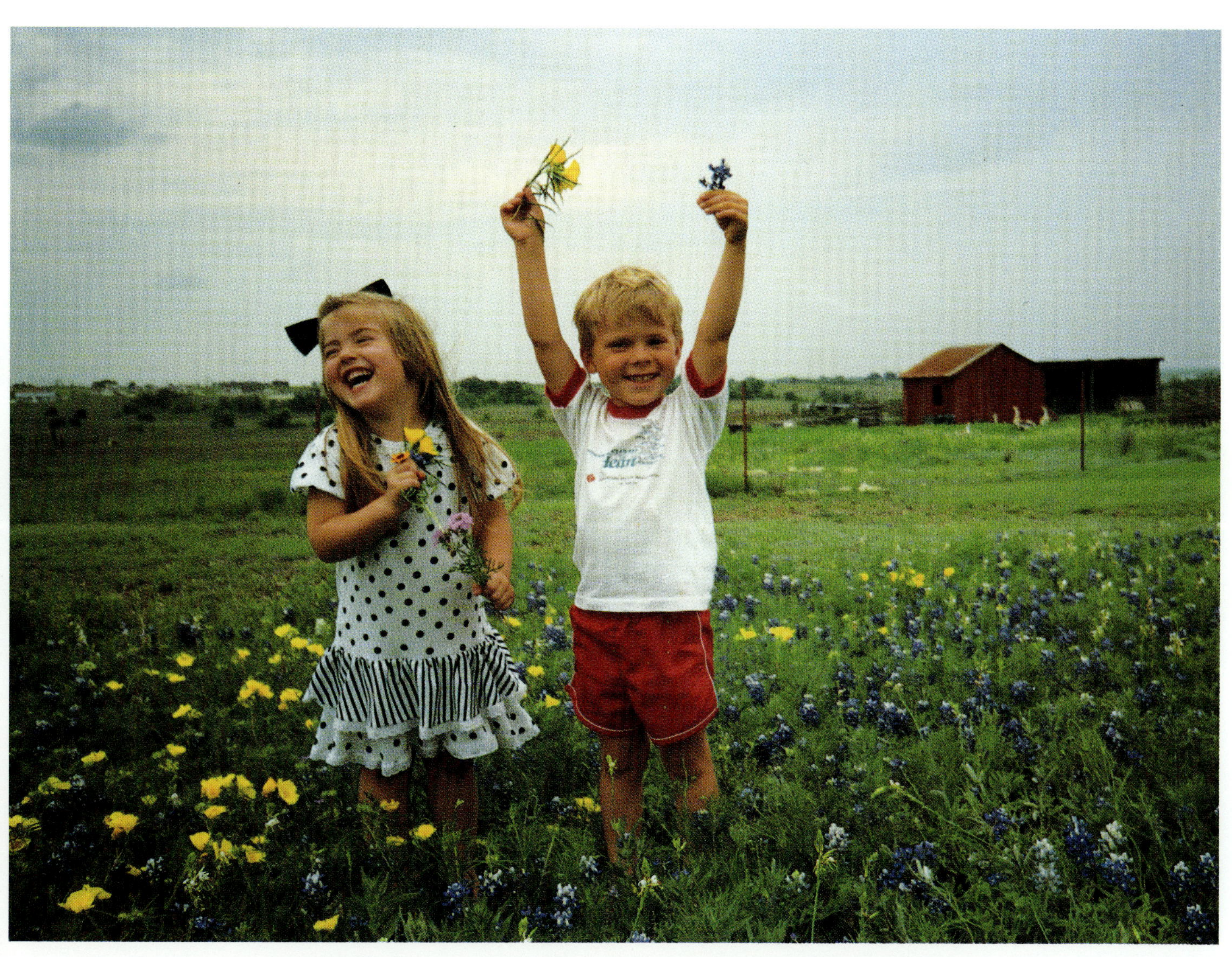

*Sarah Phillips, 3, and Clinton Muery, 4, among buttercups and bluebonnets in
Hutto, Tex. Photo by Sarah's mother, Lisa Phillips of San Antonio.*

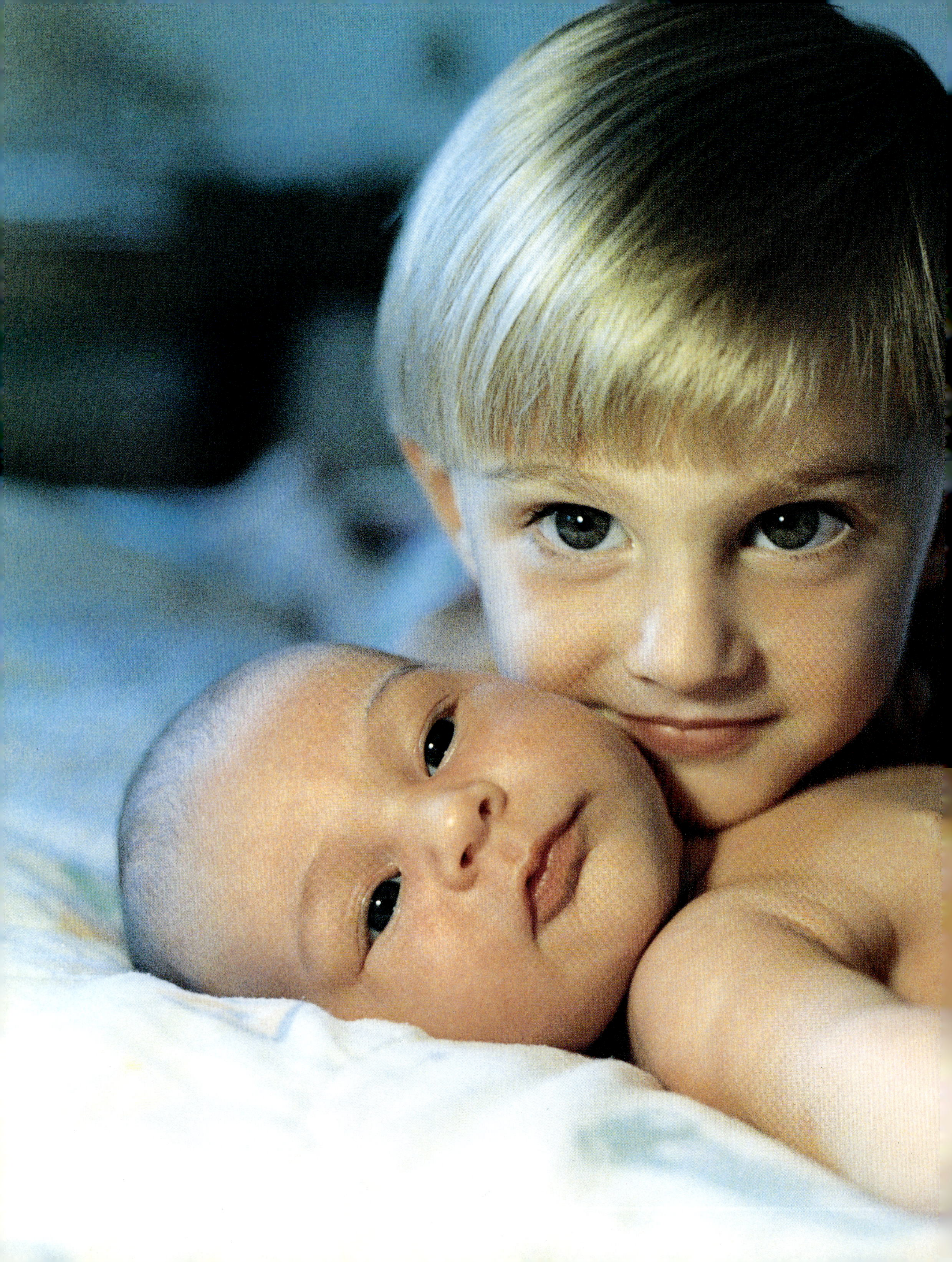

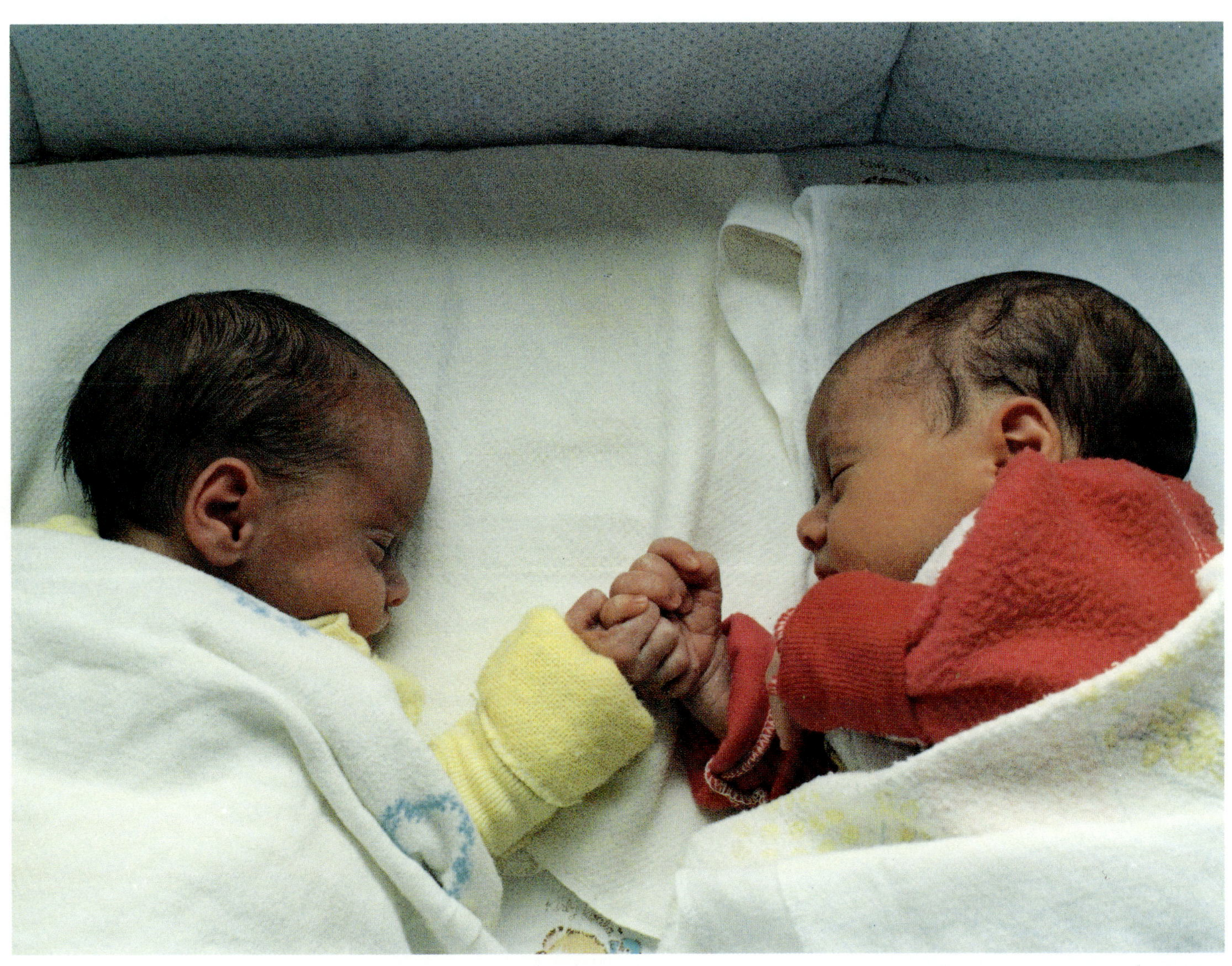

Brothers' Bond: Alexander Luis Musso, 3, and his brother, Timothy Luis, 3 weeks. Alexander has been Timothy's special friend since he witnessed his brother's birth. Photo by their mother, Rebecca Musso of League City, Tex.

Together Again: Newborn Laura E. Hurd (right) is reunited with her twin sister, Janine, who just returned home from a week in the hospital. Photo by their father, Robert John Hurd of Olney, Md.

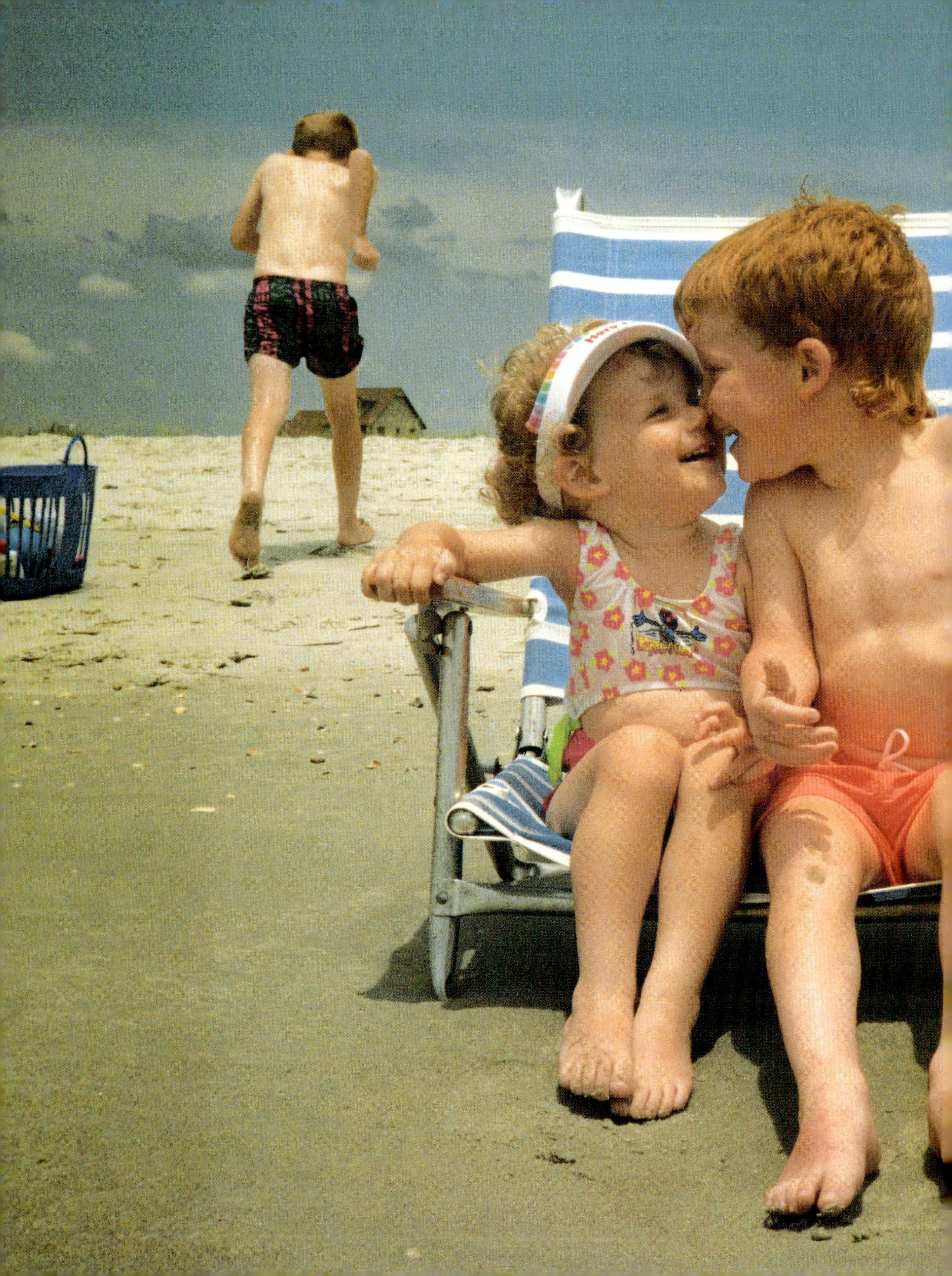

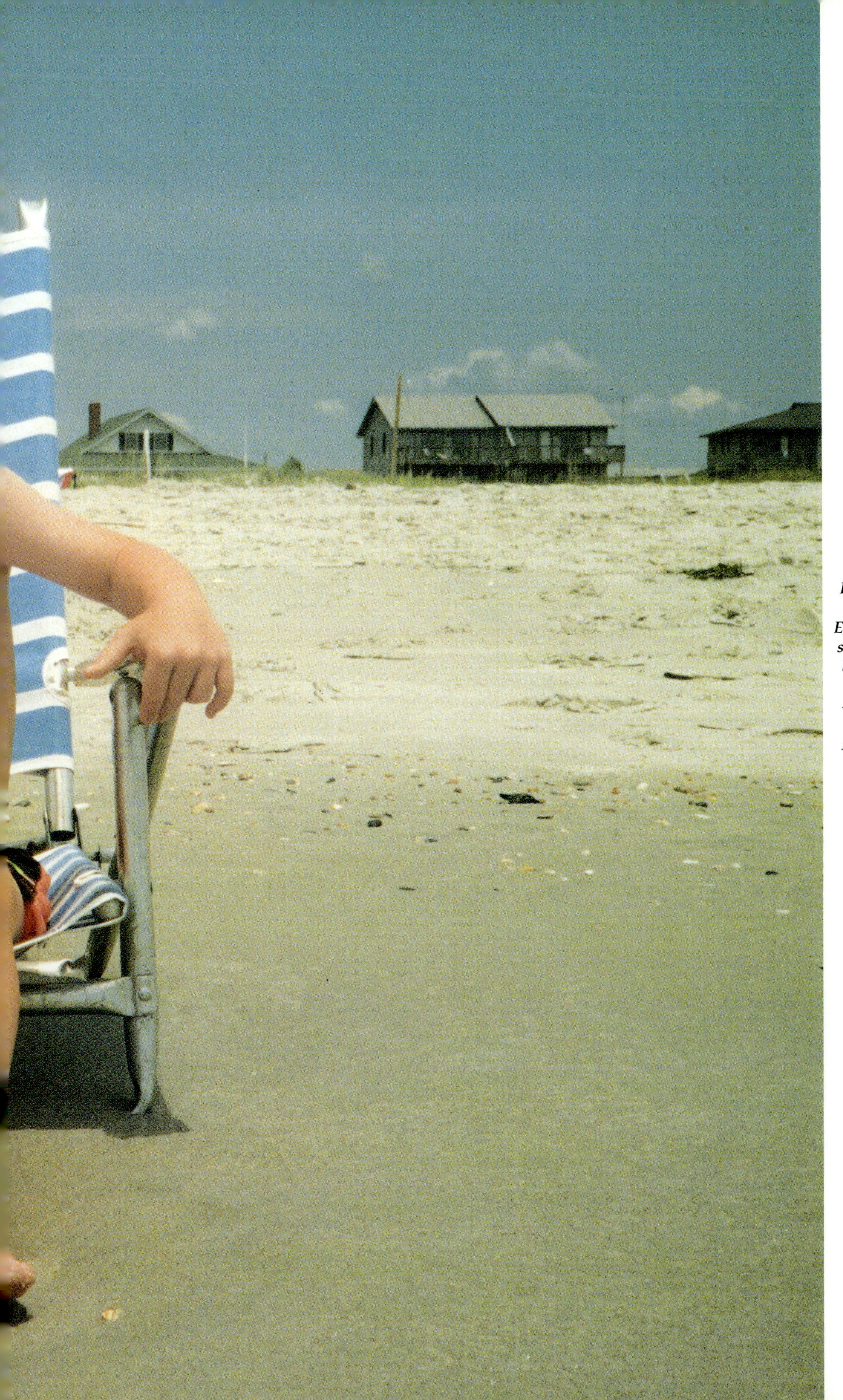

Katherine Ross, 2, and brother Emerson, 4, soak up some sun while big brother, Philip, 8, races away —perhaps to find another chair? Photo by Mary A. Vorberger of Sewickley, Pa.

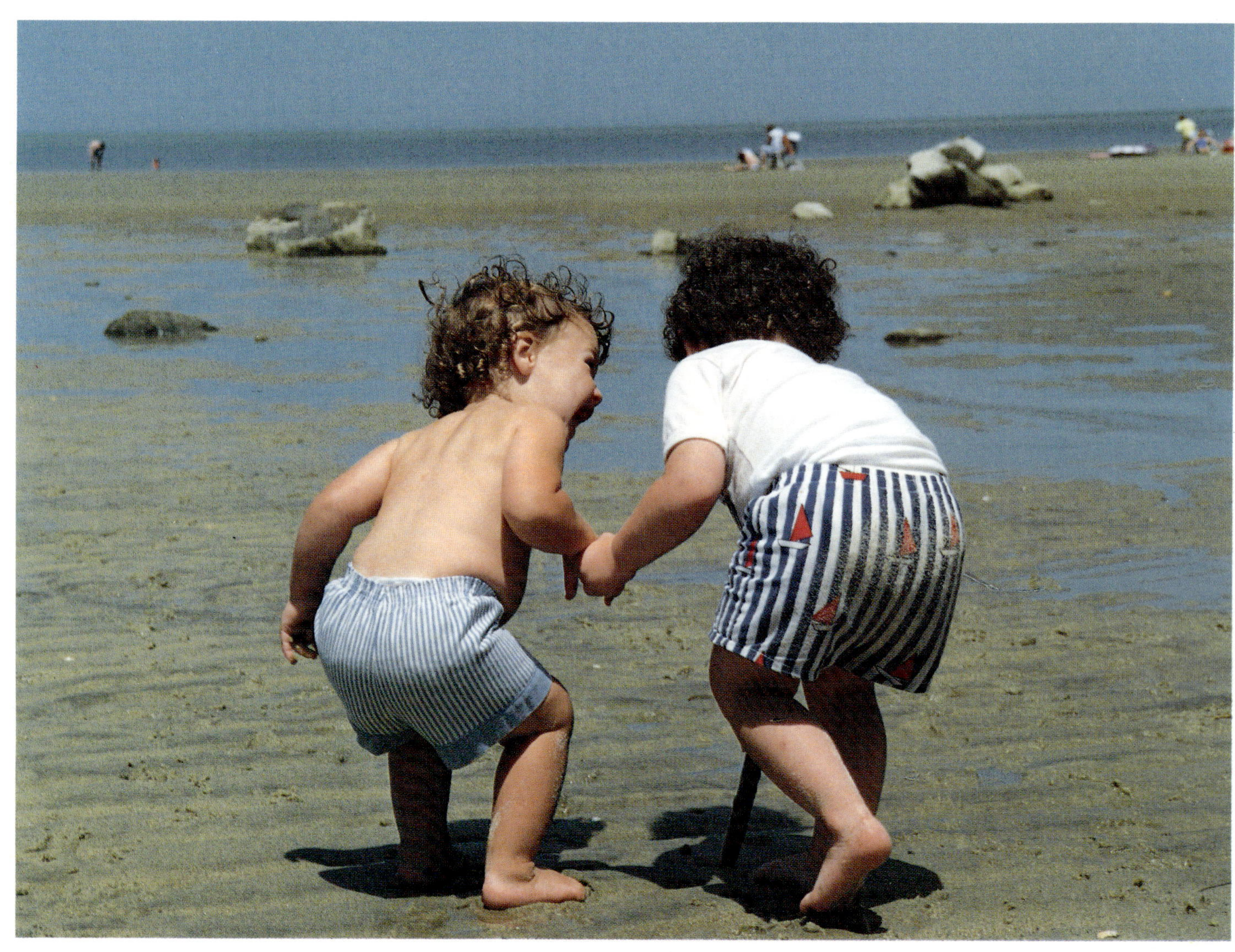

*Good Buddies: Benjamin Brewer, 2,
watches big brother Alex, 3, poking in
the sand on a beach on Cape Cod.
Photo by the boys' father, John Brewer
of Littleton, Mass.*

*Your Friendly Guide:
Kate McCartney
(right), 2, helps
brother Andrew, 1, up
a dune on Nantucket
Island, Mass. Photo
by their father, David
McCartney of Hollis,
N.H.*

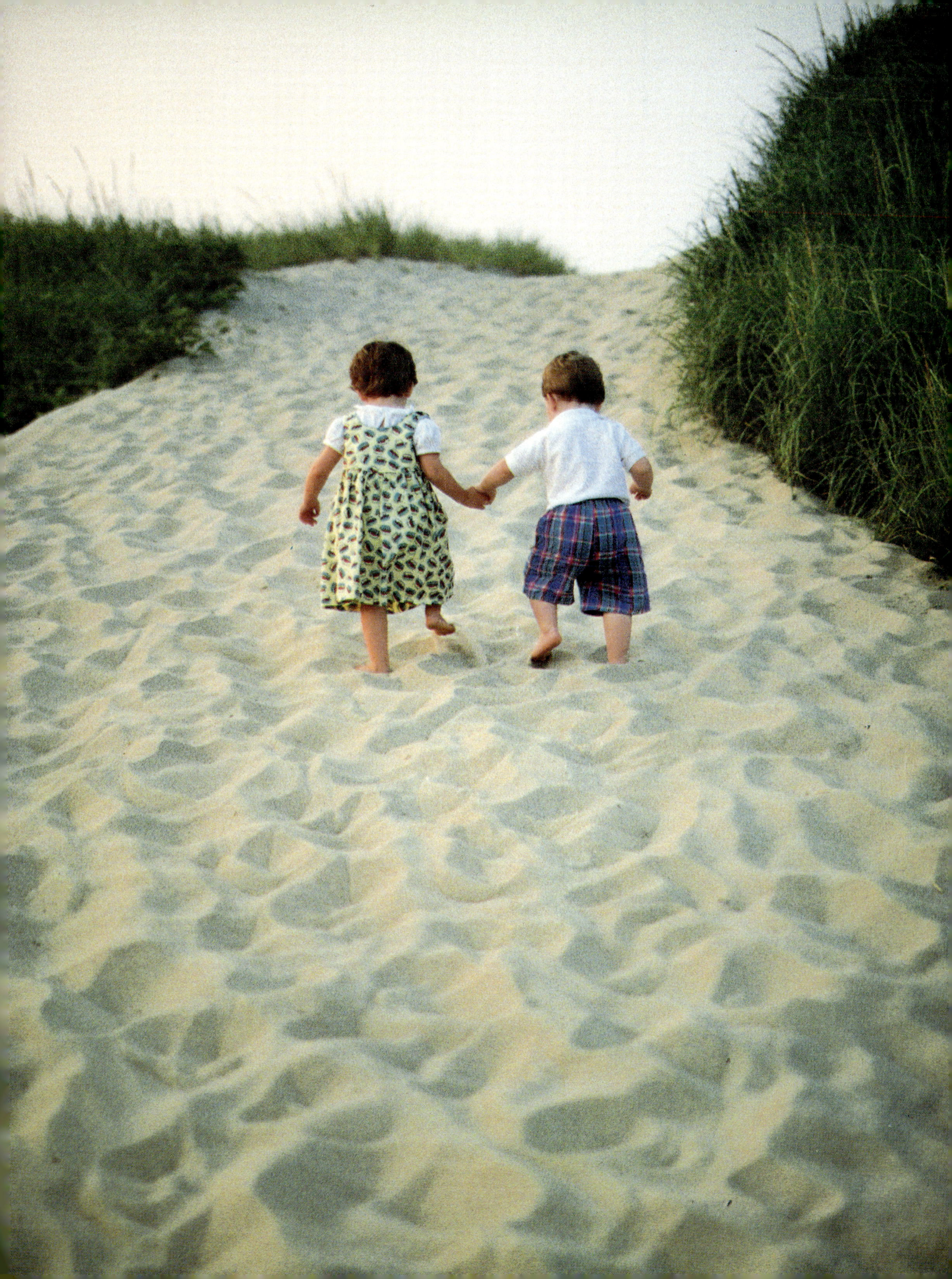

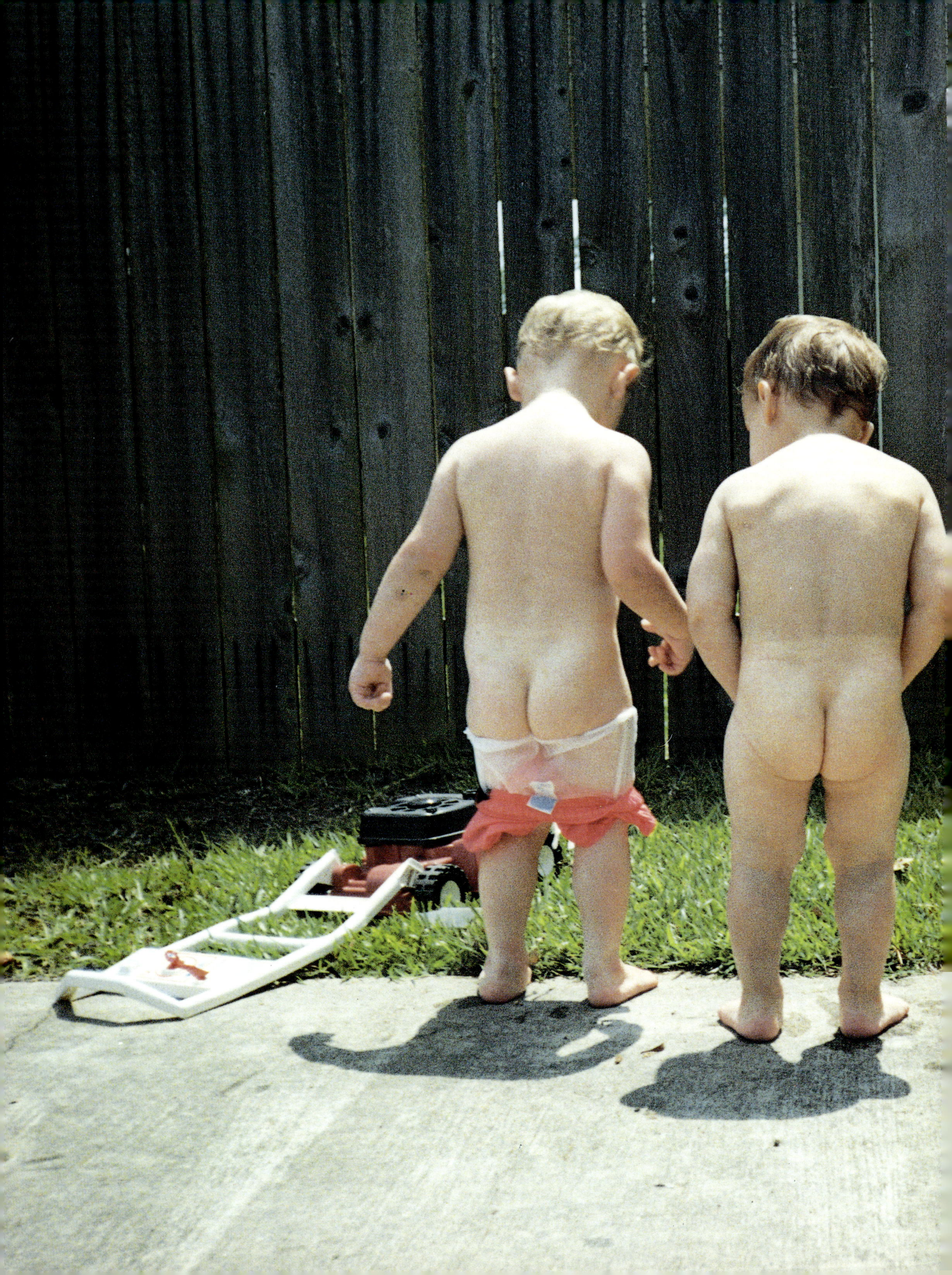

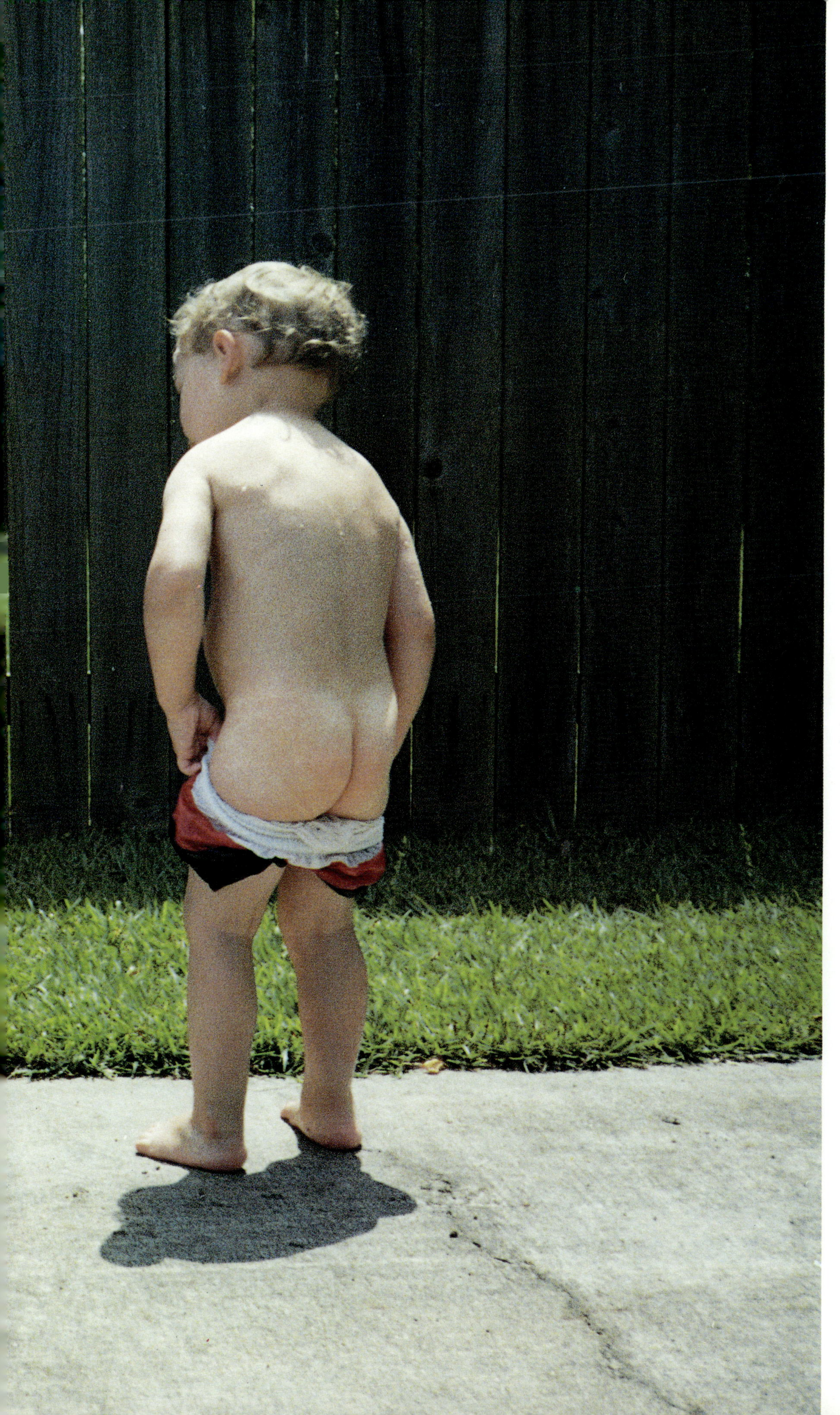

Jonathan Kearney, Ross Young and Pierre Bosley (from left), three 2-year-olds, do *everything* together, says the photographer —Jonathan's mother, Elizabeth Kearney of Baton Rouge, La.

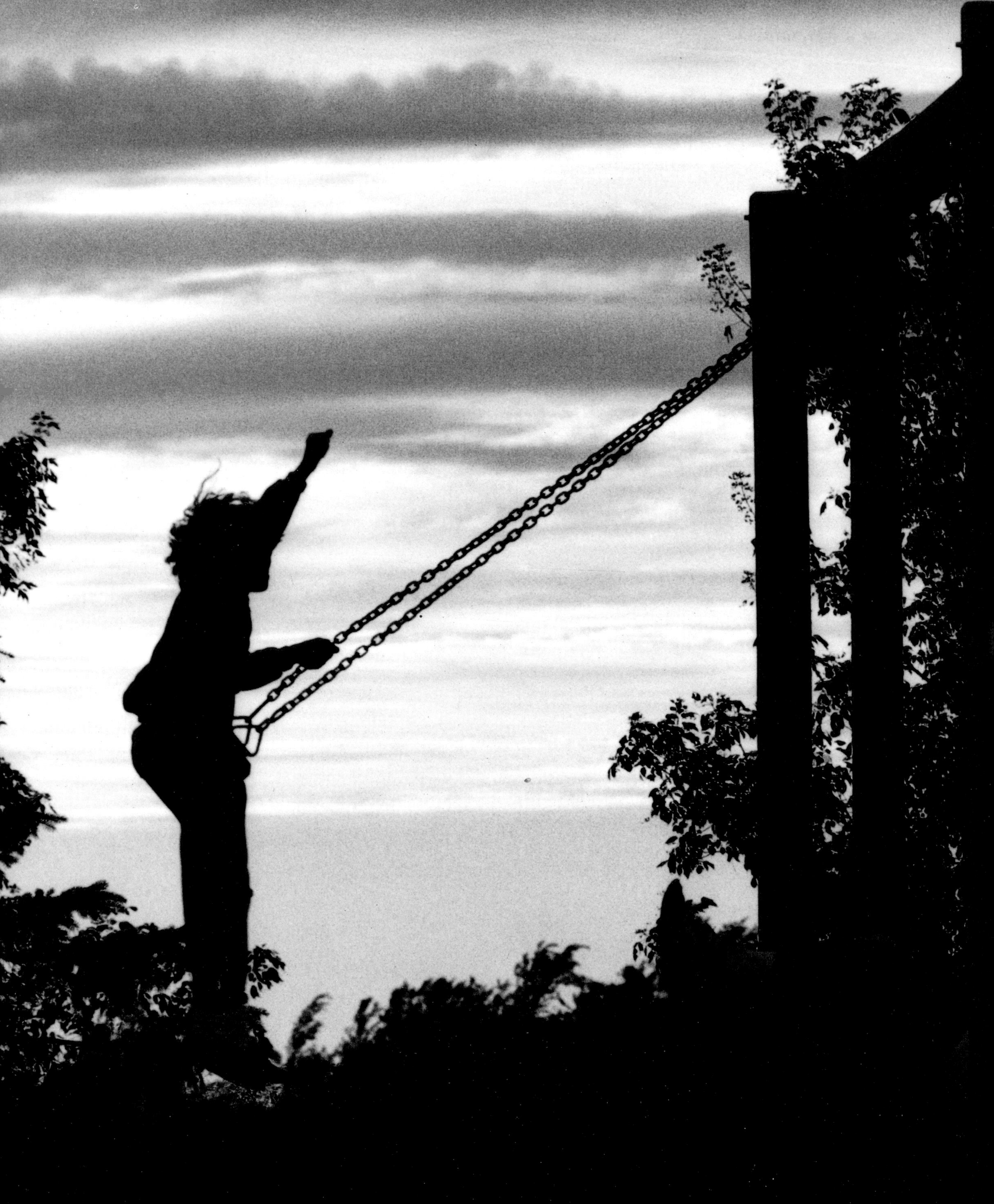

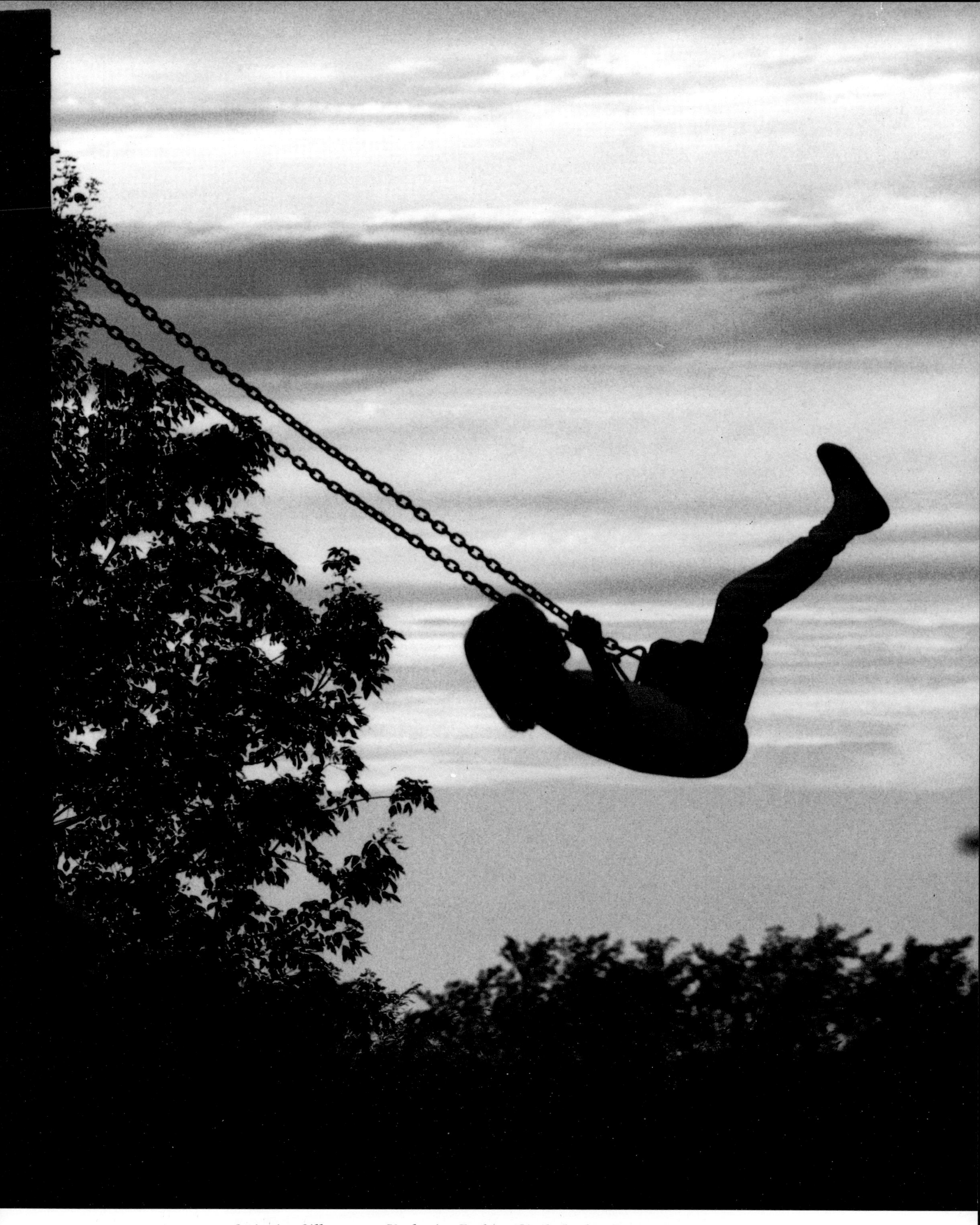

*Swinging Silhouettes: Katherine Perkins Civileth of Hudson, Wis.,
captured a scene that brought to her mind "life's pure pleasures."*

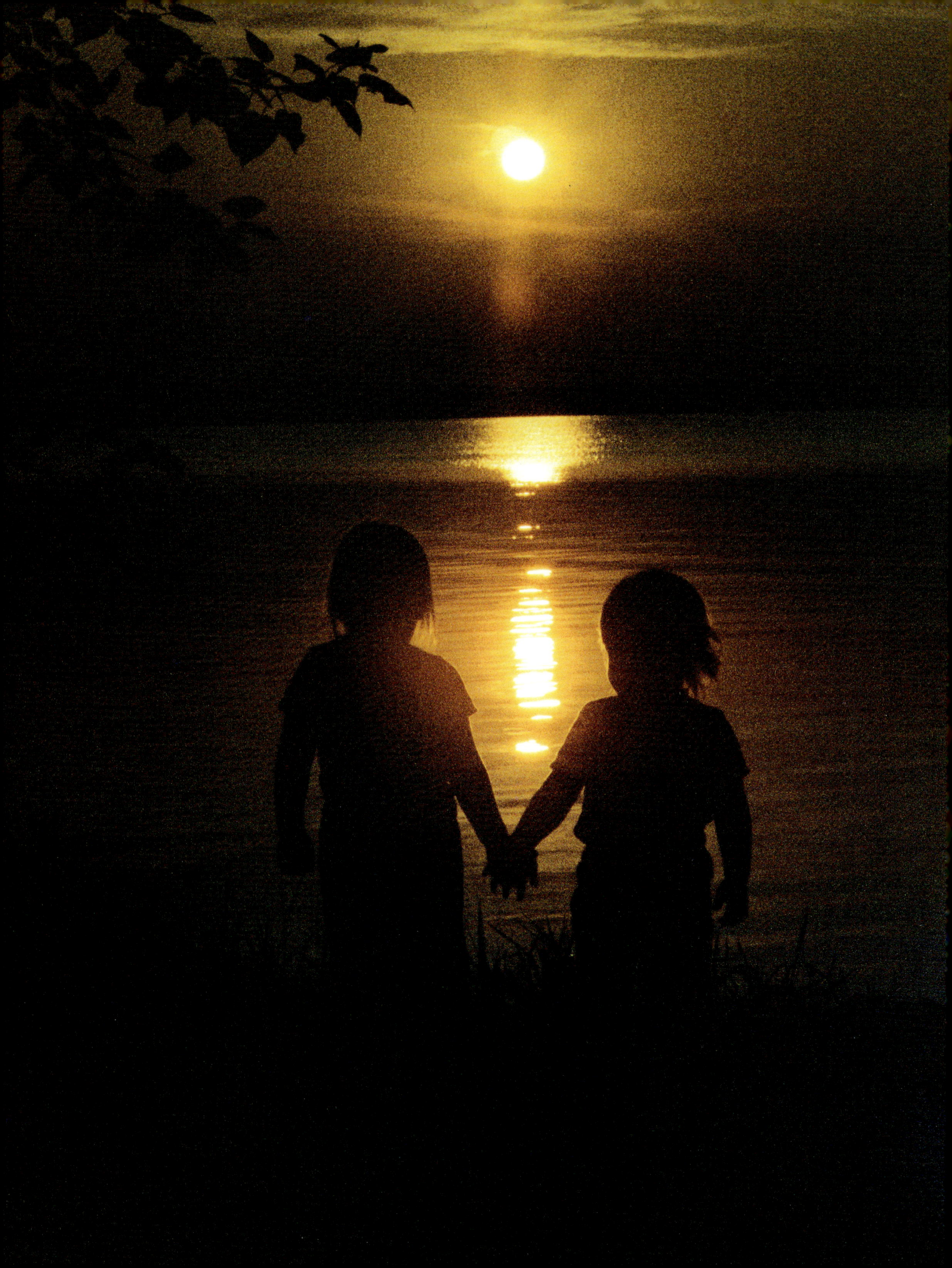

"I get by with a little help from my friends."
—John Lennon

*"In reality we are still children. We want to find a
playmate for our thoughts and feelings."*
—Dr. Wilhelm Stekhel
The Depth of the Soul

*"Wherever you are it is your own friends
who make your world."*
—William James

*"If a man should importune me to give a reason why
I loved my friend, I find it could not
be otherwise expressed than by the answer,
Because he was he, and because I was I."*
—Montaigne

*"You just call out my name, and you know wherever I am,
I'll come running…You've got a friend."*
—Carole King

*A Beginning/An Ending: New friends
(and cousins) Lisa Schreiner (left), 3,
and Stacey DeNoyer, 2, catch a still
moment at Lake Nocquebay, near
Crivitz, Wis.*

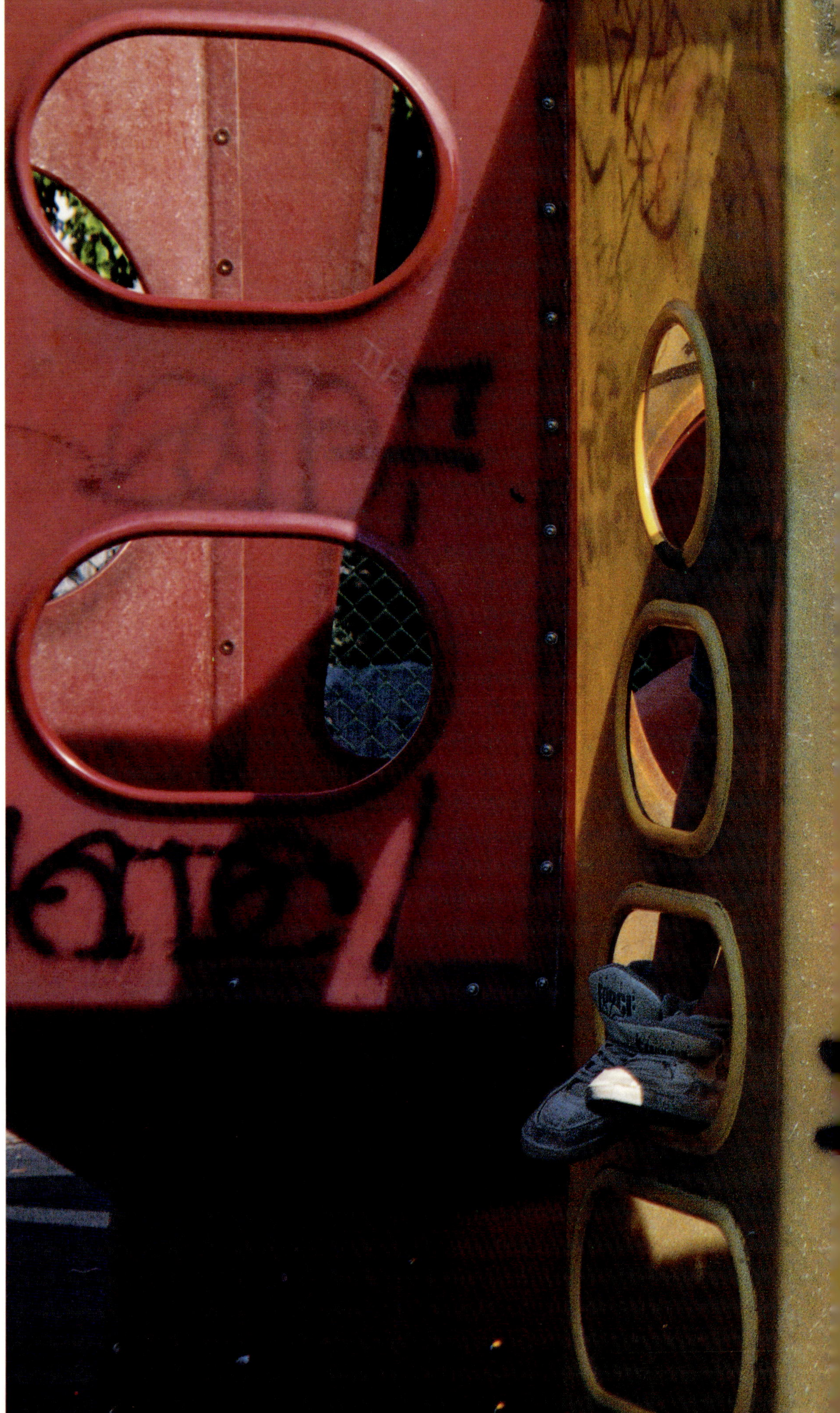

Friendly Faces: When her son and his friends turned play-sculpture to animated art at Cedar Creek Park in Seaford, N.Y., Lois Zegel preserved the moment. From top: Craig Zegel, Robbie Palazzolo, Michael DeMattio, Katelyn Piccolo and Joseph Palazzolo; standing is David Herr.

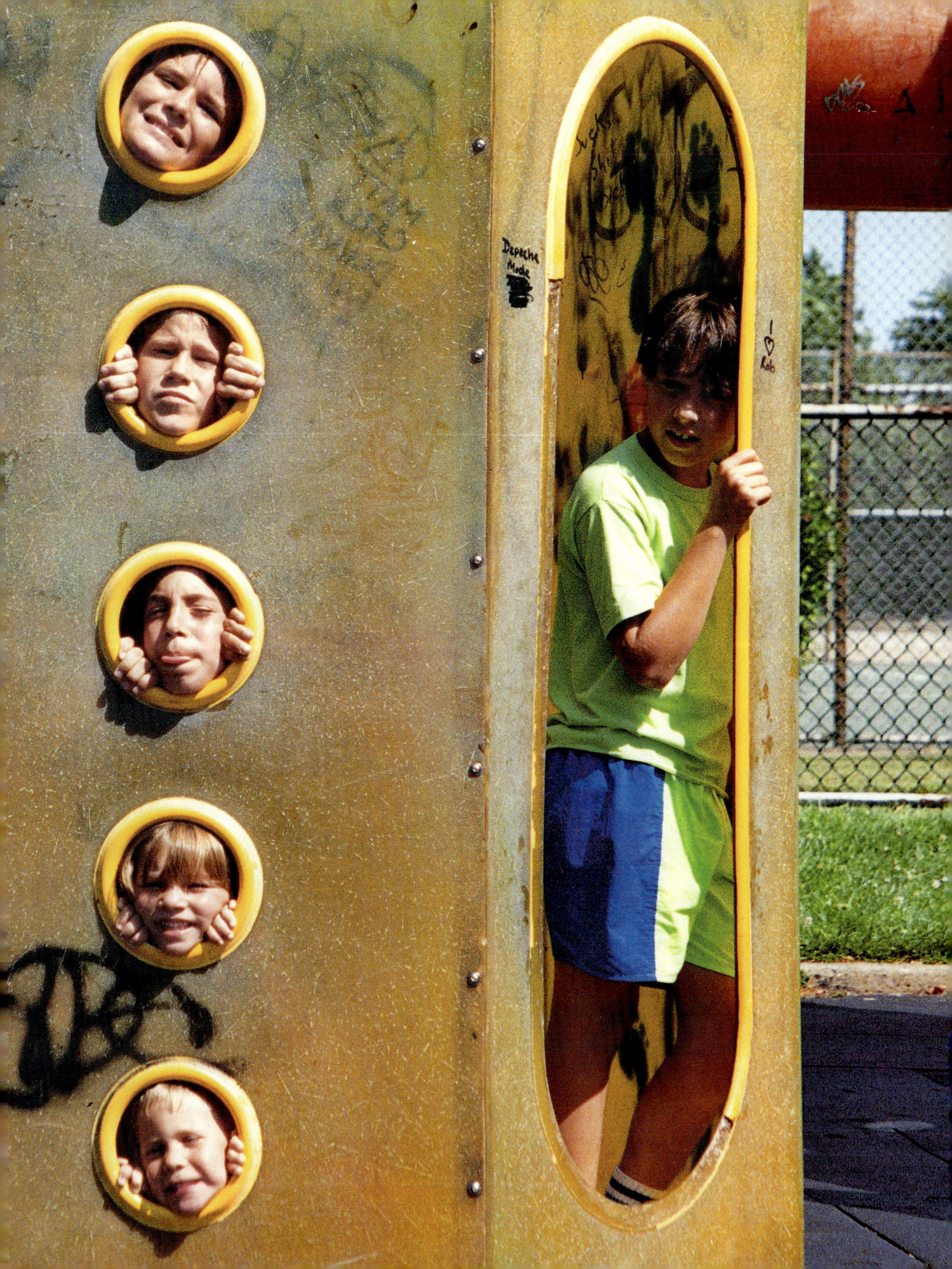

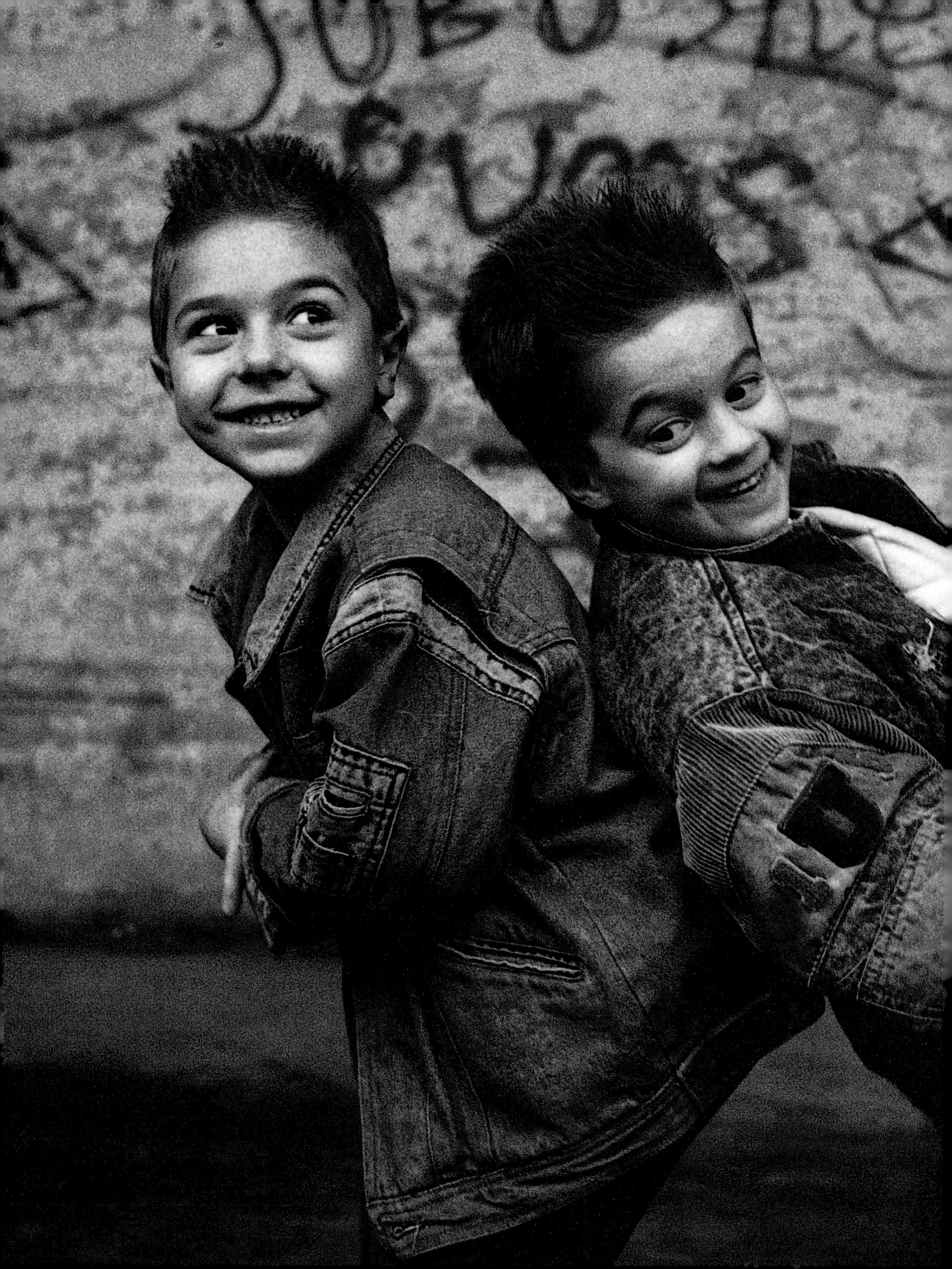

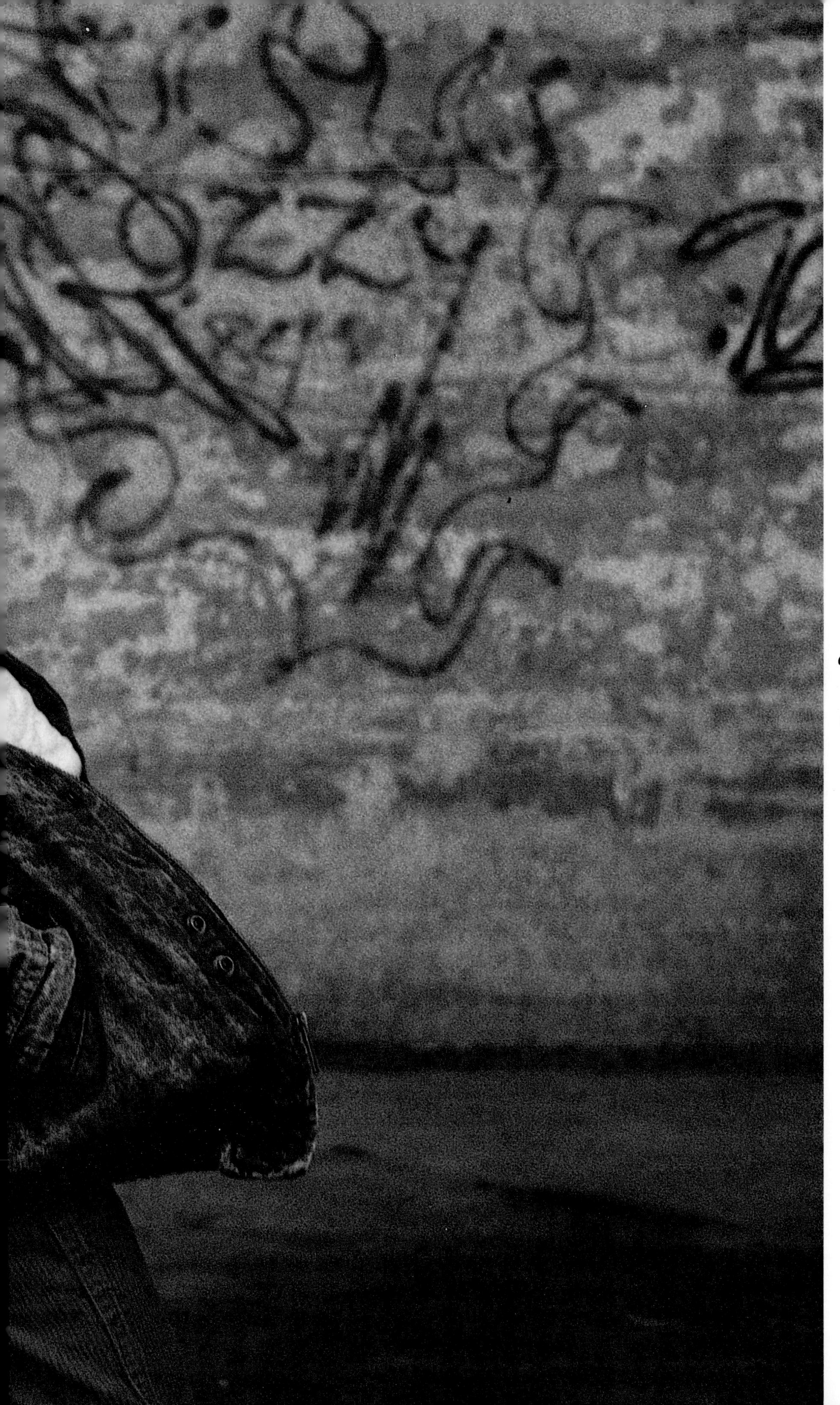

Just Fooling Around: Robbie Celani (left), 6, and his cousin Ryan Celani, 4, mug for the camera. Photo by M.K. Rynne of Nahant, Mass.

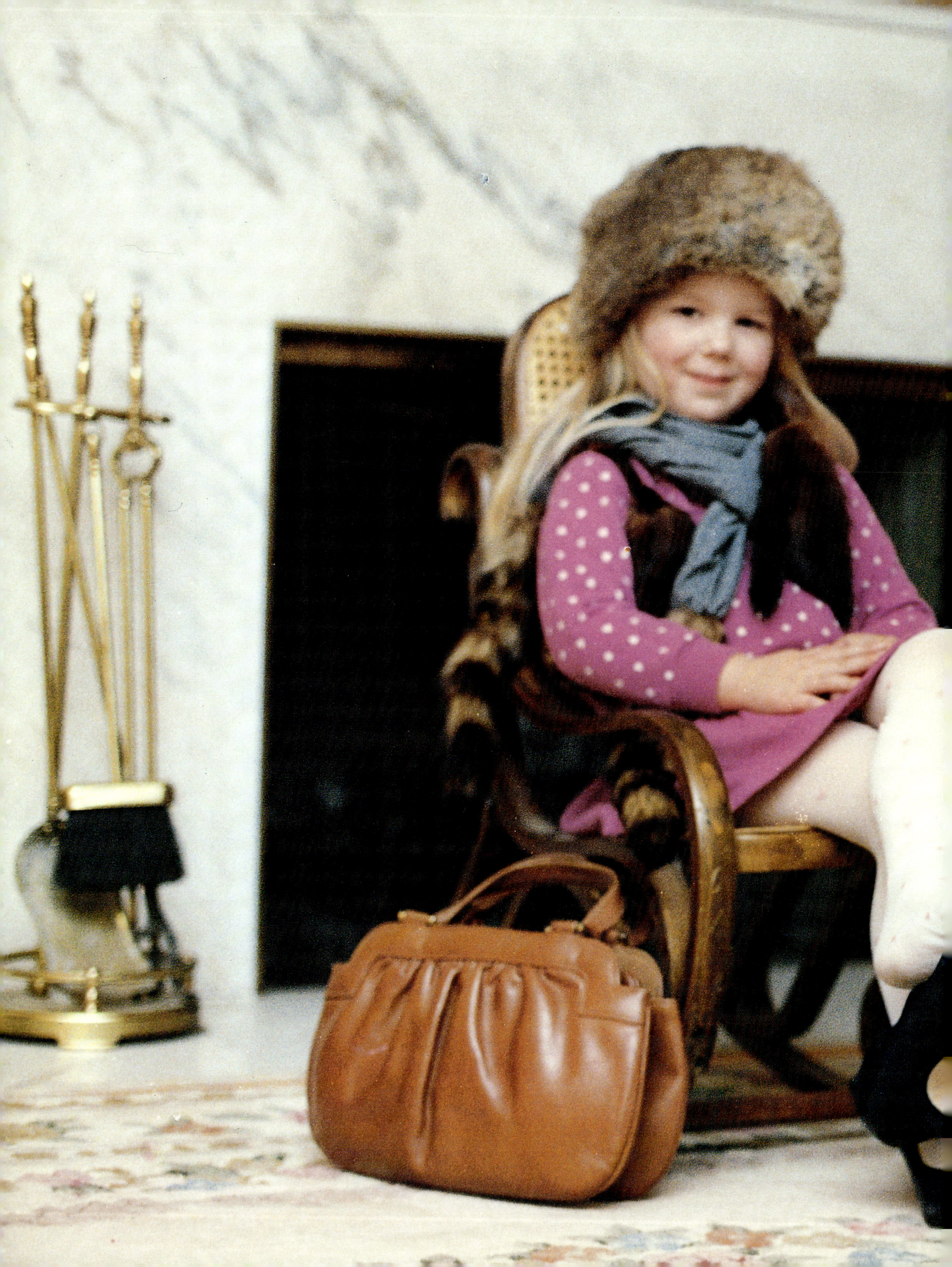

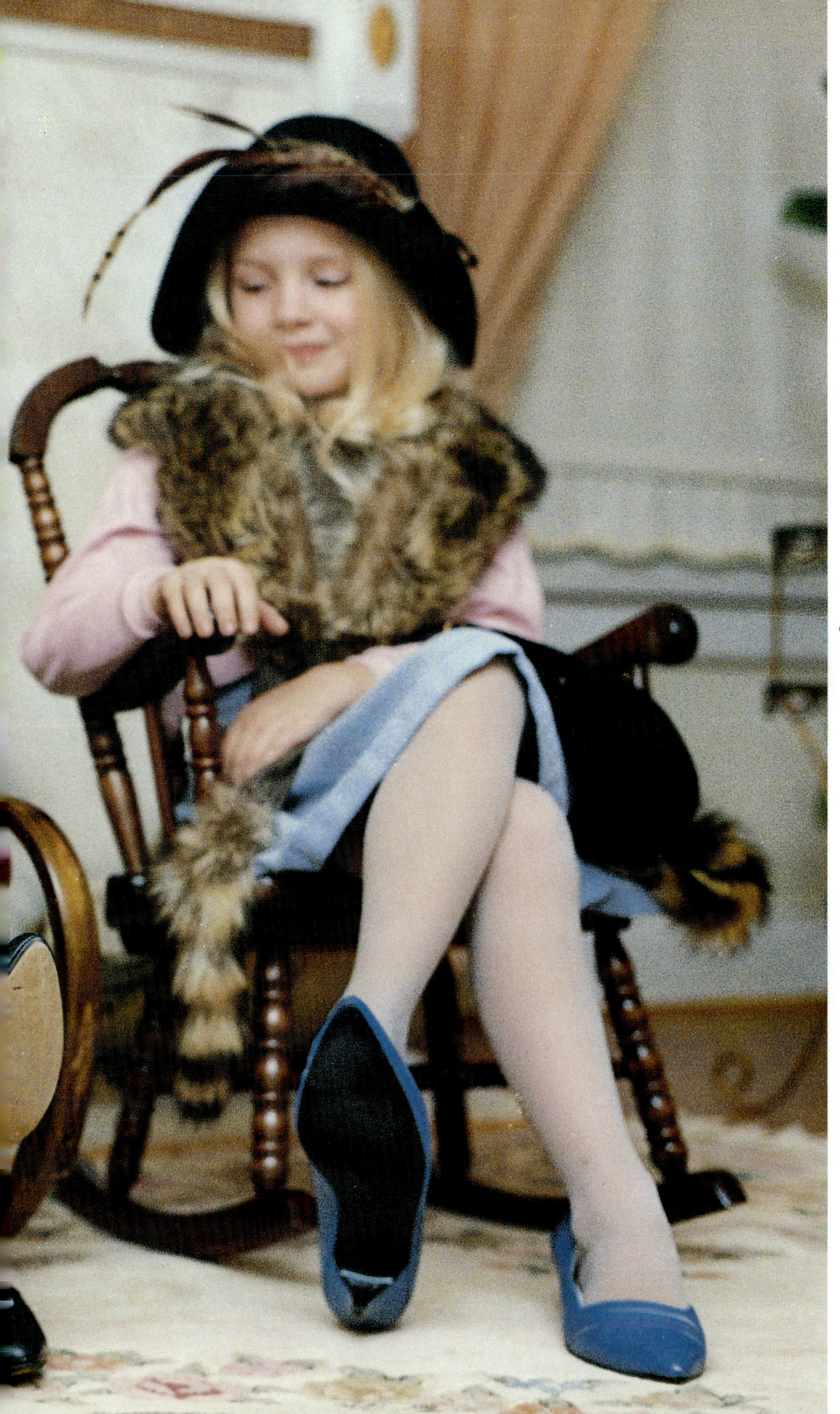

Glamour Do: Ashley Weeks, 6, and Emily Weeks, 3, puttin' on some style at home in Kansas City, Mo. Photo by their mother, Bridget.

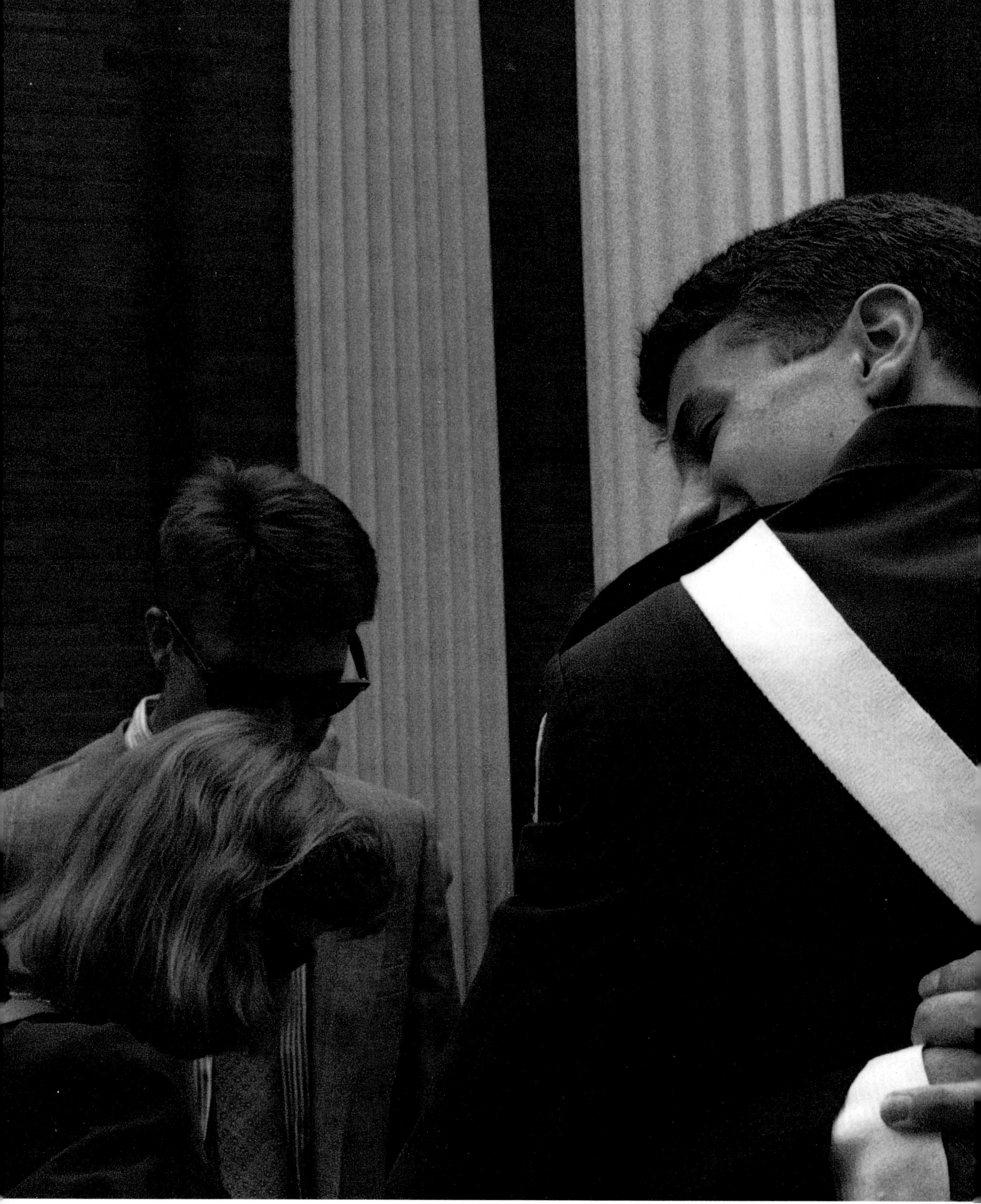

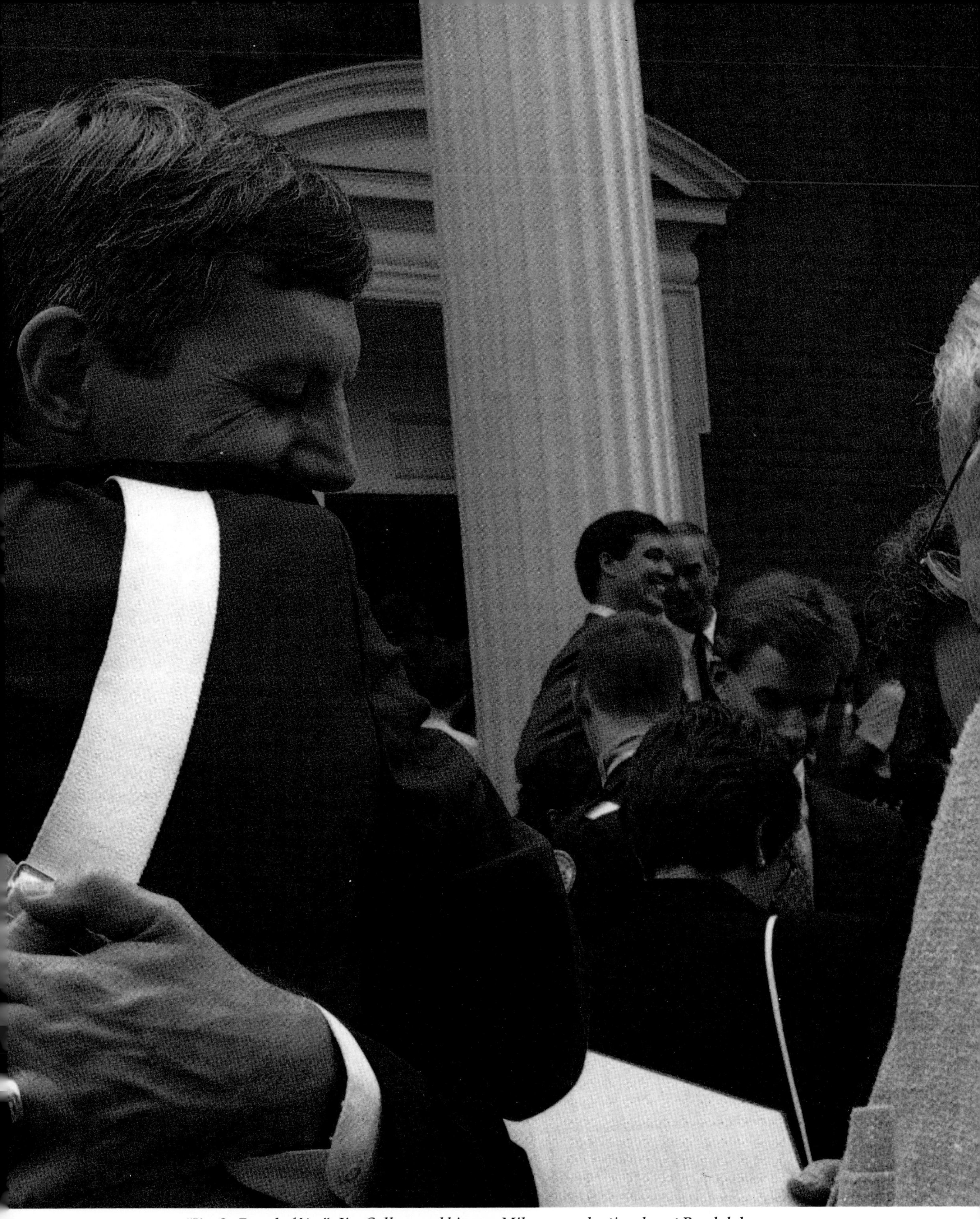

"I'm So Proud of You": Jim Cullum and his son, Mike, on graduation day at Randolph Macon Academy in Front Royal, Va. Photo by Mike's aunt, Martha Figley of Annandale, Va.

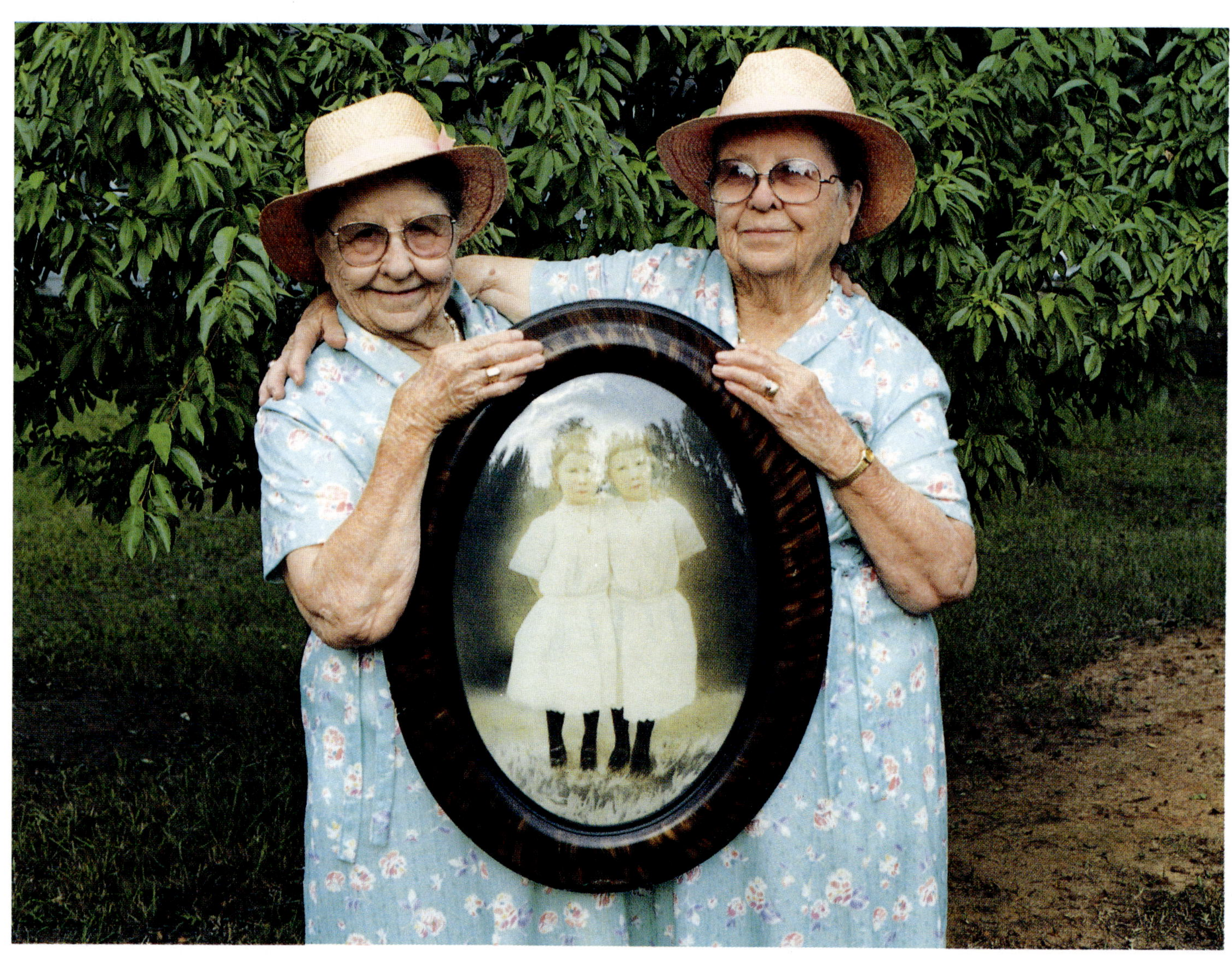

*Best Friends—But Who's Who? Elberta "Bert" Payne (left) and Elliot "Ott"
Cannon, 87-year-old twins, hold a portrait of themselves taken in 1910.
According to Mrs. Cannon's daughter—Mae C. Merrett of Montrose, Ga., who
took the photos—the two "are the cutest and sweetest ladies you will ever see.
They think alike, dress alike, and friends still get them confused."*

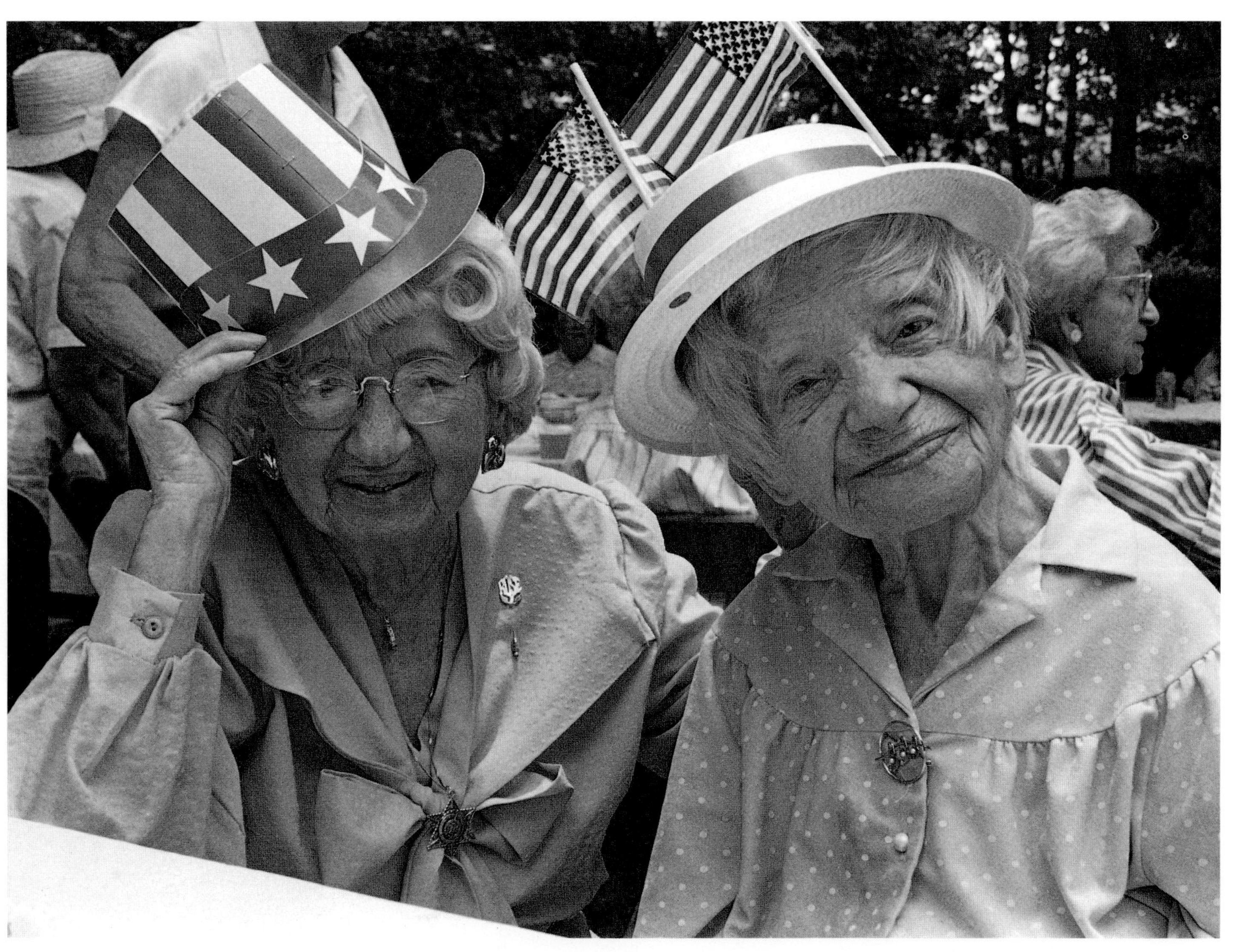

After All These Years: Sisters Rose Sims (left), 94, and Anna Fried, 101, celebrate the spirit of independence at a July barbecue. Photo by Caren Speizer of Clifton, N.J.

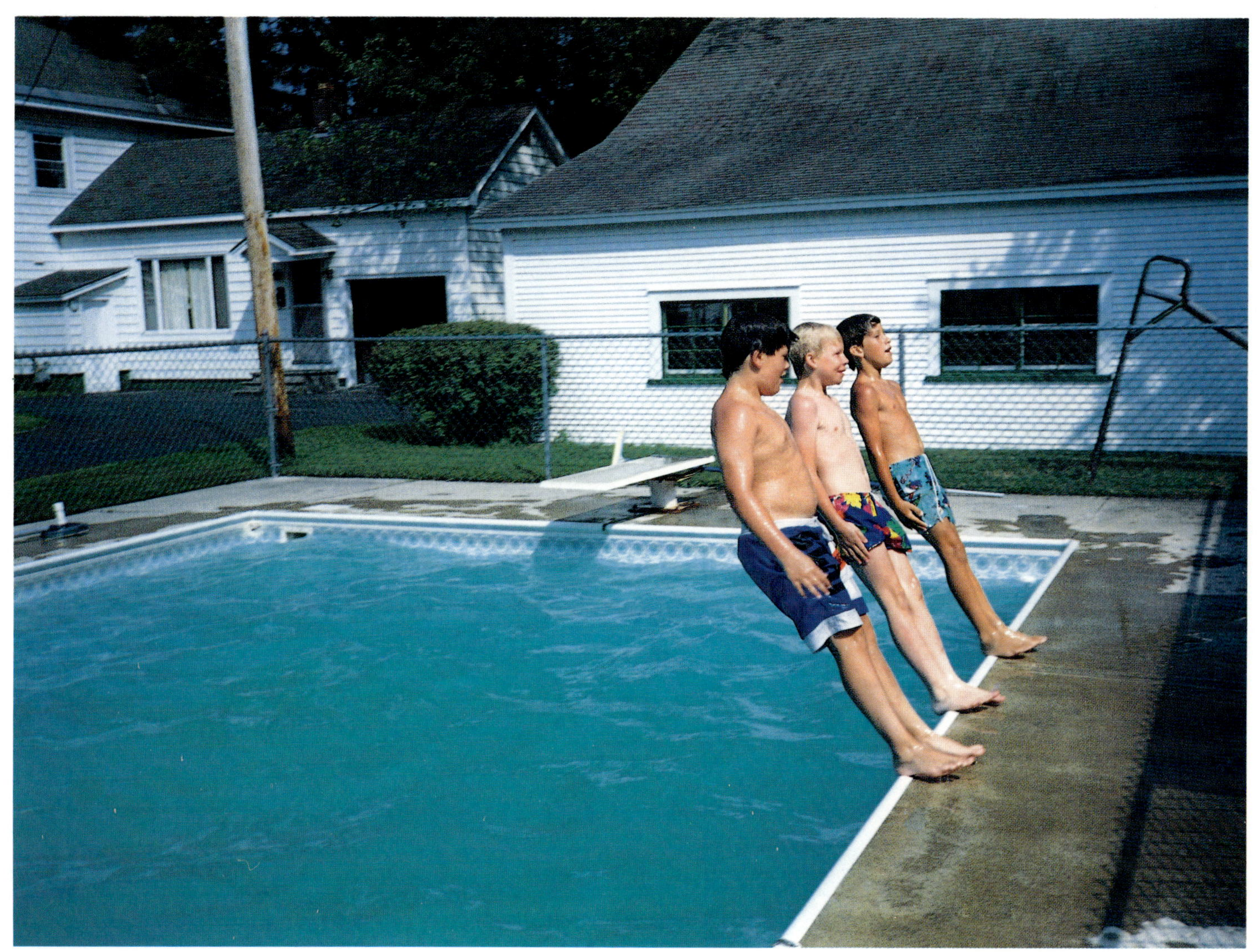

All Together Now: Justin Stimets, 10, Joshua Bullard, 9, and Daniel Wood, 9 (from left), at the pool in Swanton, Vt. Photo by Joshua's mother, Susan Bullard of Wintersville, Ohio.

Getting a Jump on Summer: David Jenkins (at front), 12, and Alexander Ellis III, 11, airborne off Marblehead, Mass. Photo by David's sister, Patricia Jenkins of Dedham, Mass.

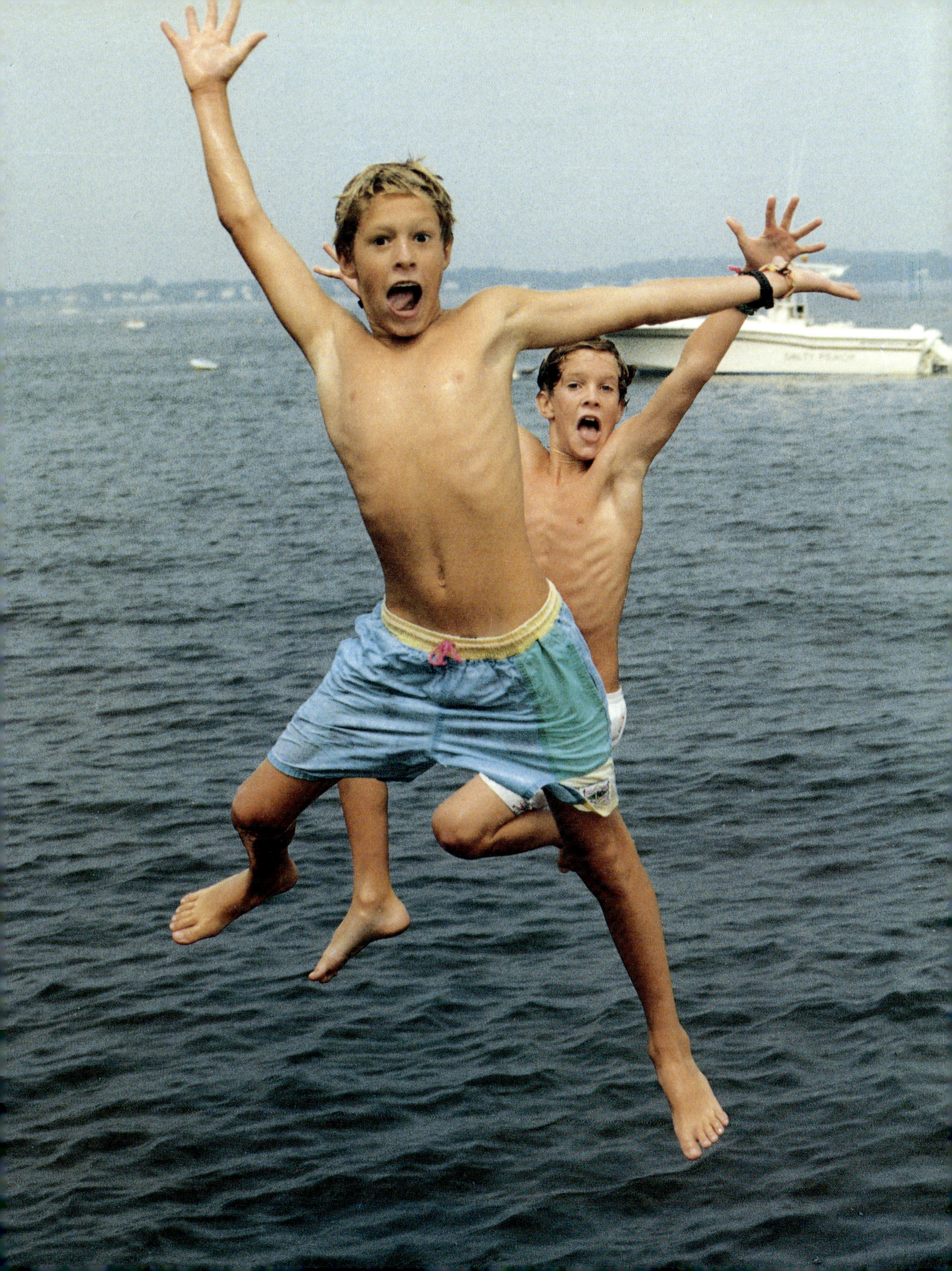

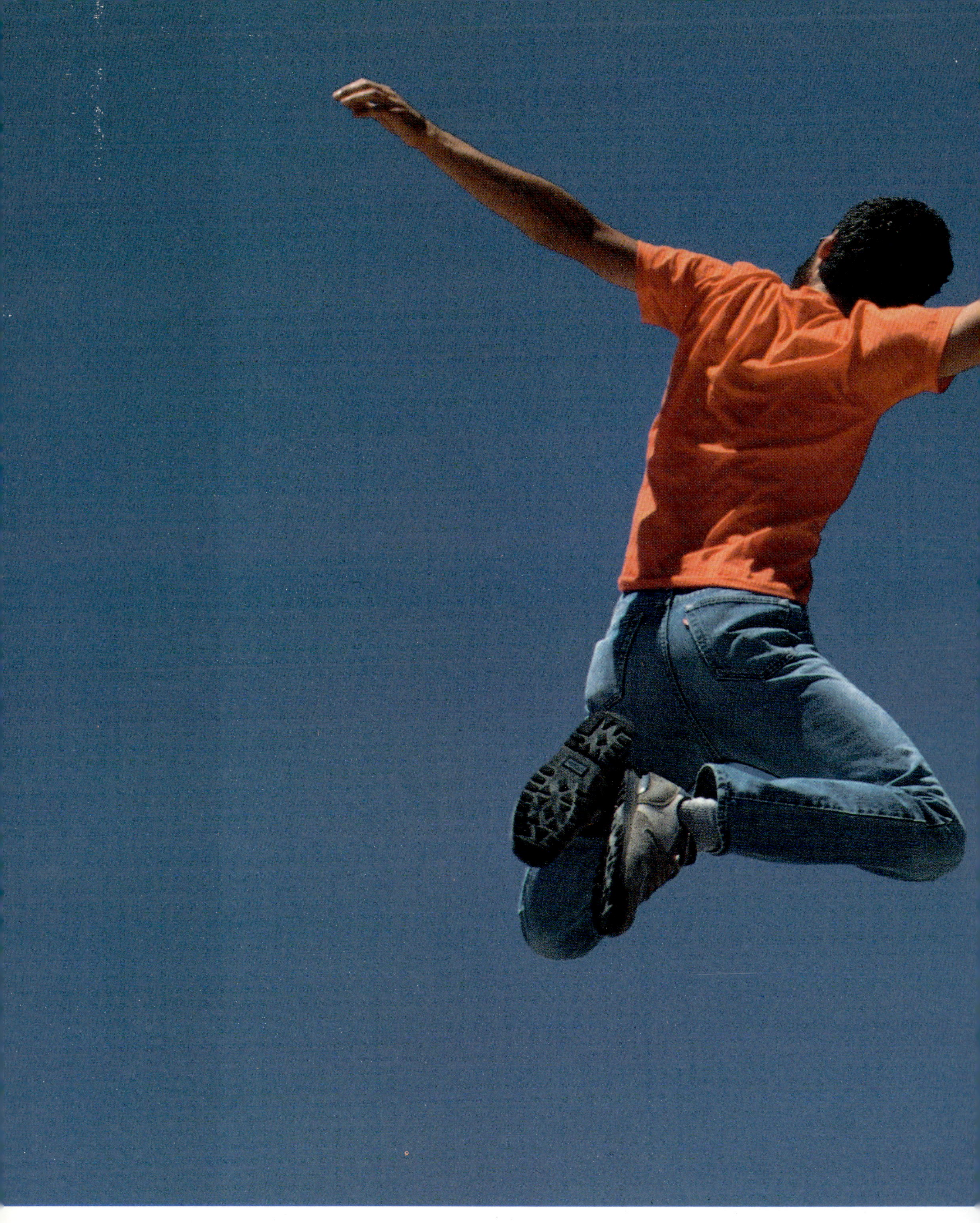

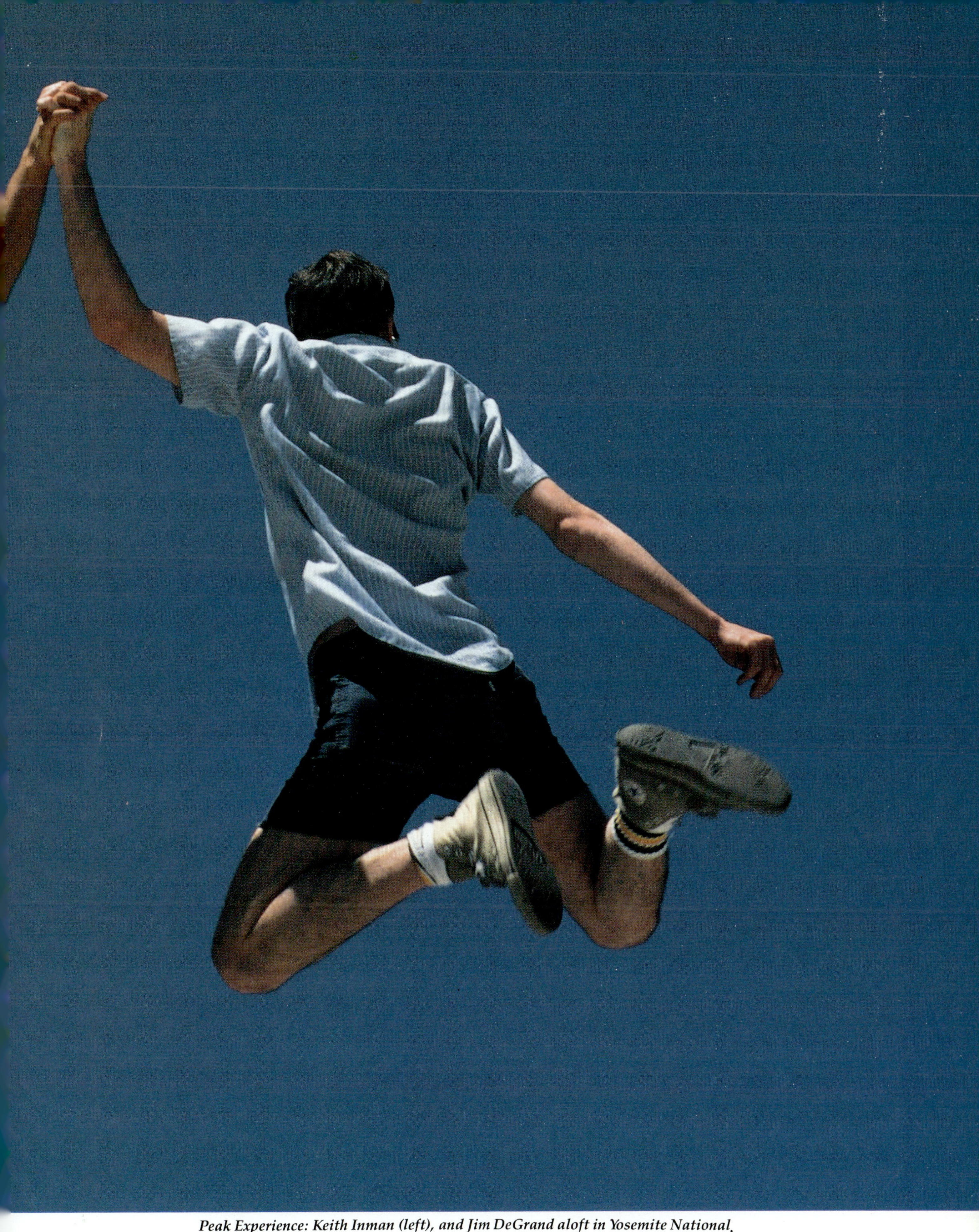

Peak Experience: Keith Inman (left), and Jim DeGrand aloft in Yosemite National Park, Calif. Photo by Jim's wife, Cynthia DeGrand of Bloomington, Ind.

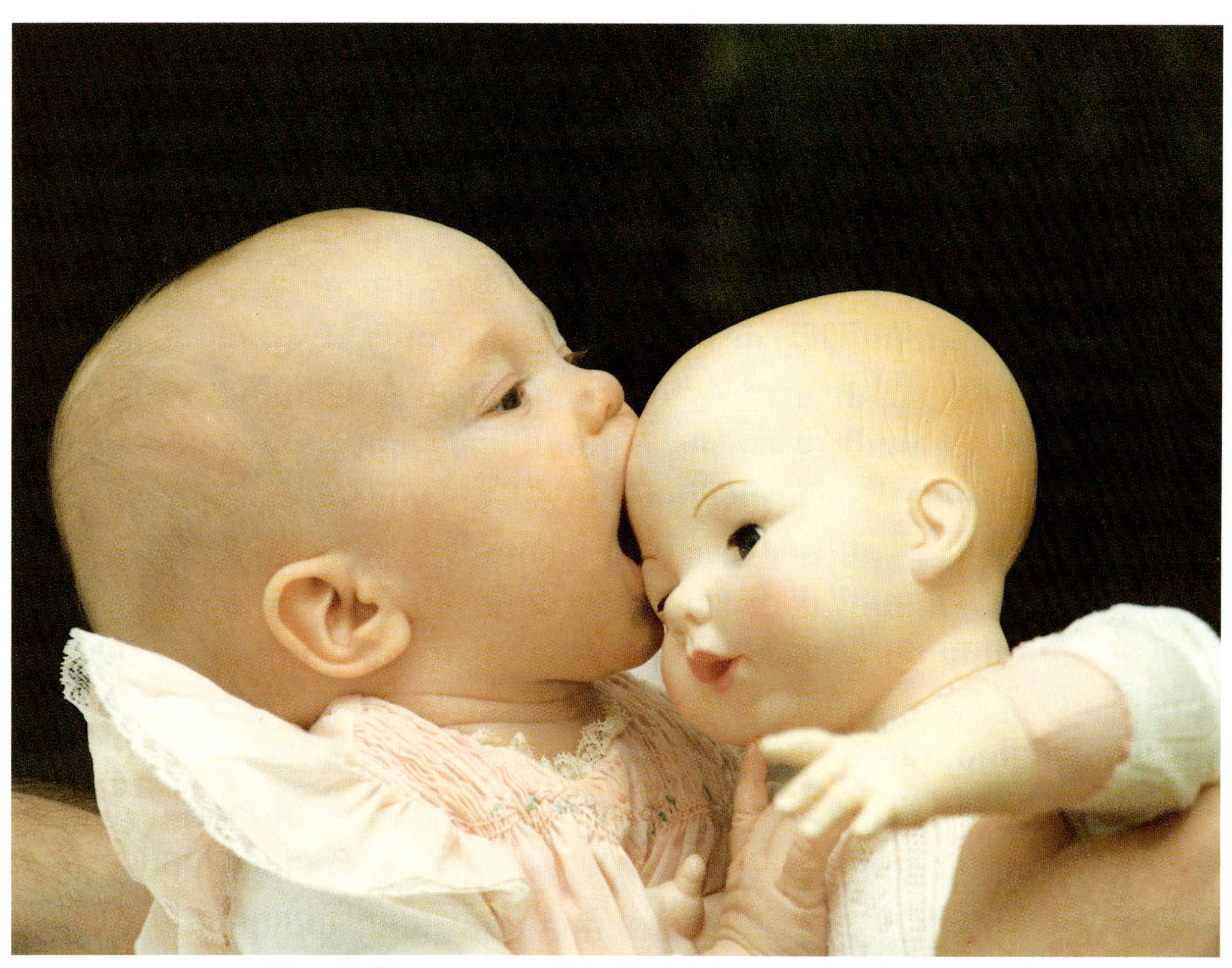

What a Doll! For some reason, Claire Elizabeth Ross, 4 months, feels a special closeness for Rosie. Photo by Claire's father, Ken R. Ross of Reidsville, N.C.

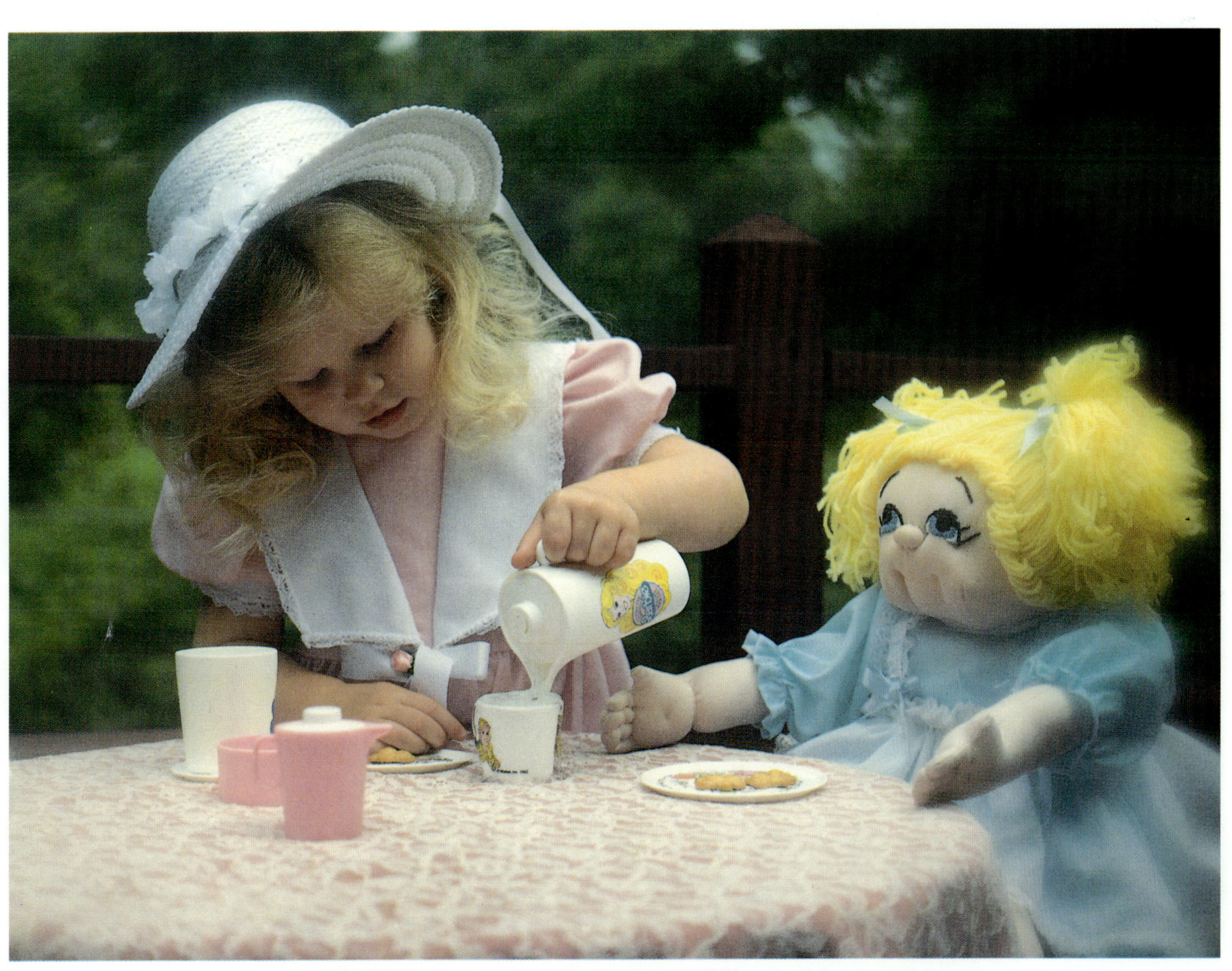

Carol Ann Smolka, 2, pours for Emma, a real doll, in a celebration of a new tea set. Carol Ann's mom, Teresa C. Smolka of Youngstown, Ohio, took the picture.

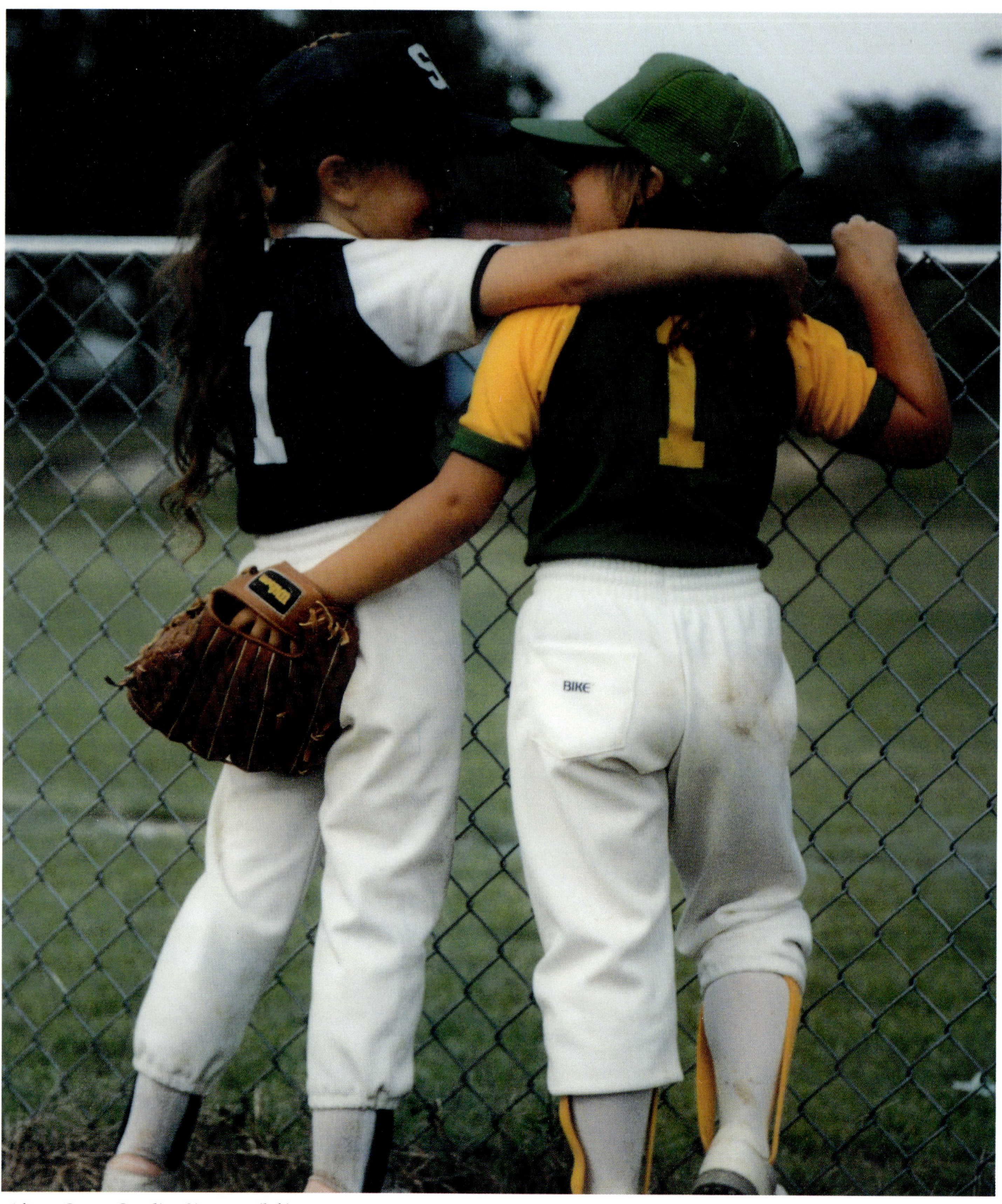

After a Game: Caroline Simmons (left) and Karen Leslie, both 7—best friends since they were 3—were rivals on the softball field in Crewe, Va. Photo by Charlotte H. Leslie, Karen's mother.

Batting Gloves and Pony Tails: Scott Halleran of Oldsmar, Fla., shot this picture of a pair of Little Leaguers who were among six girls on a coed team in Santa Monica, Calif.

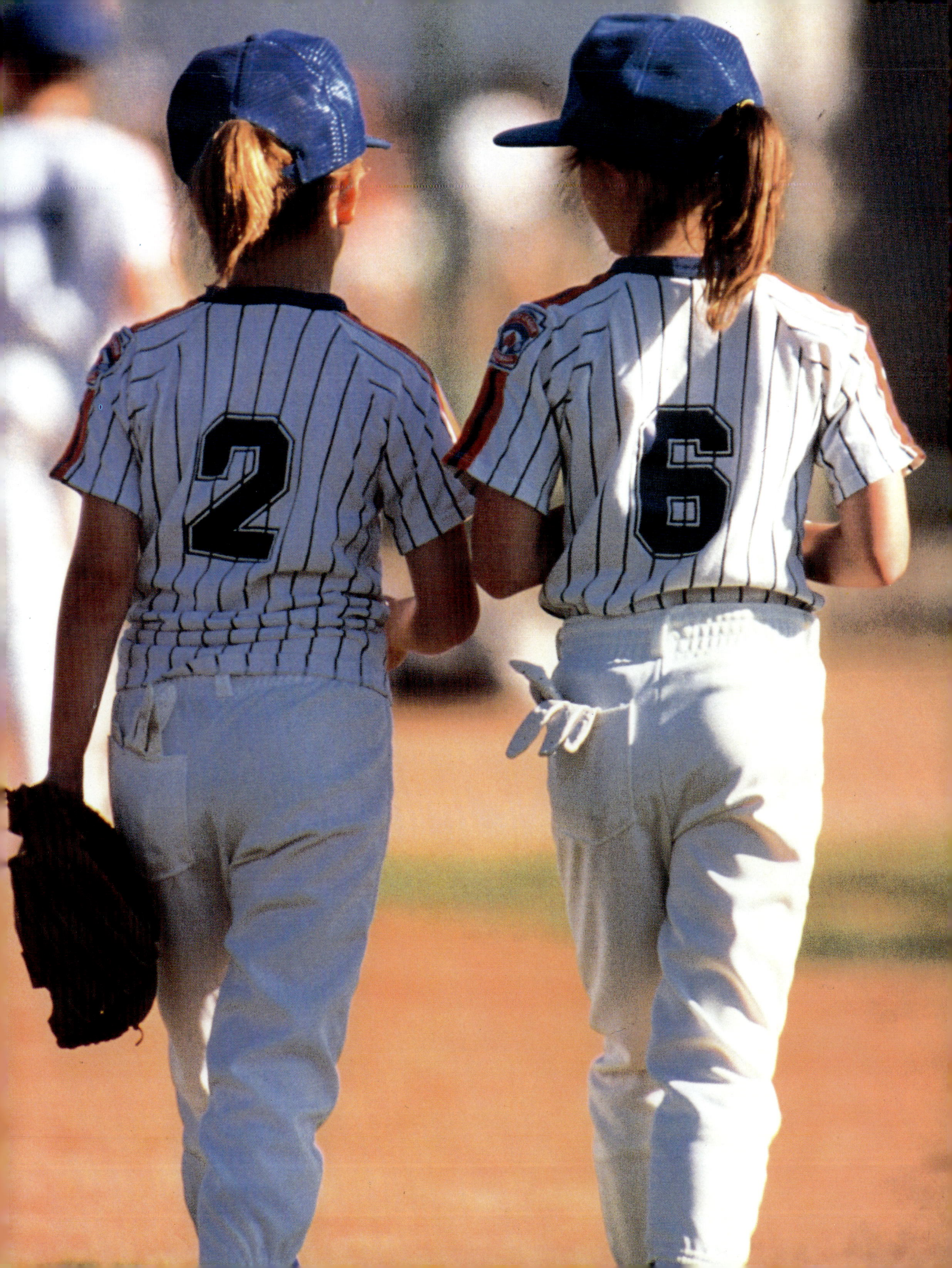

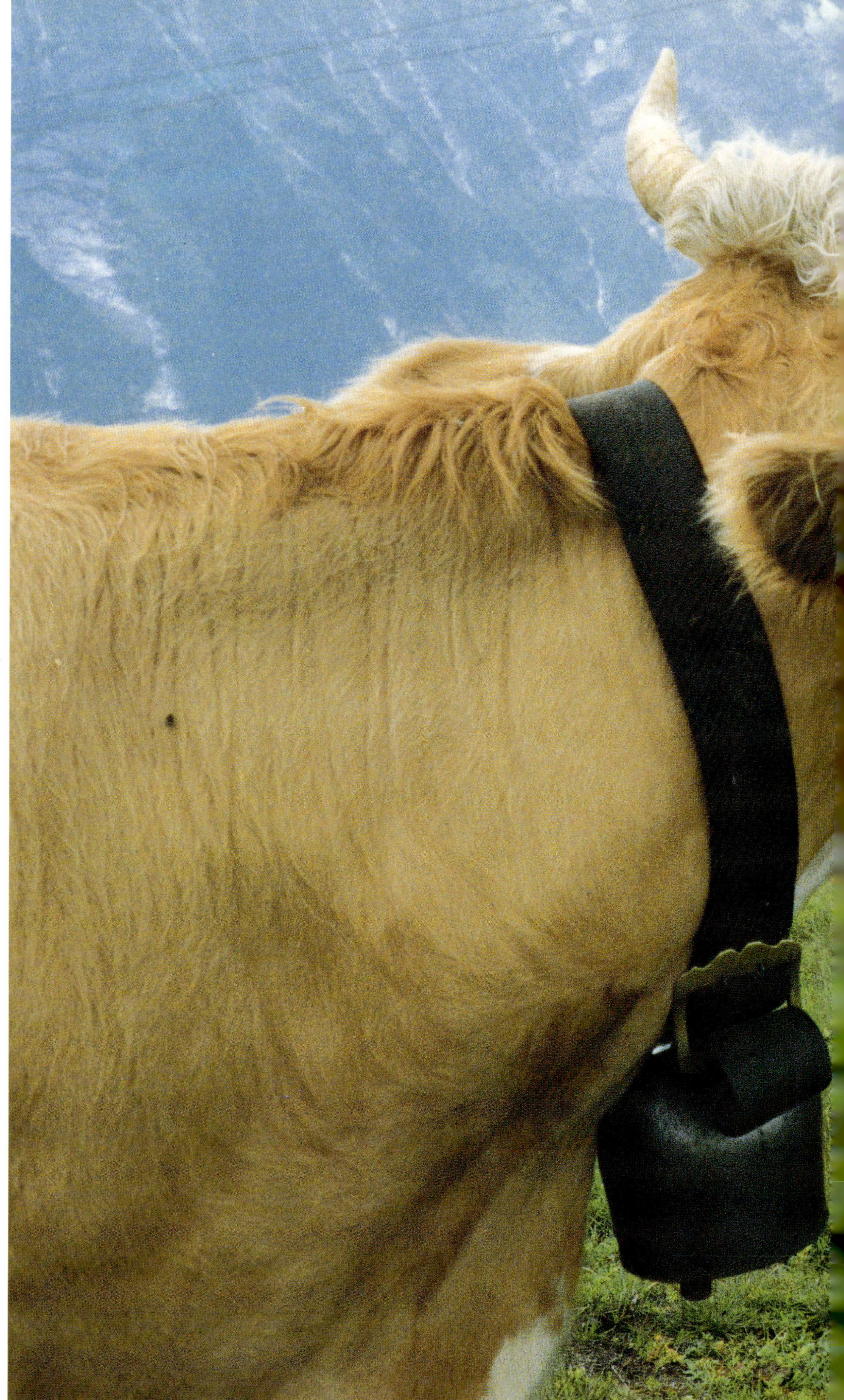

A Buss From Bossy: Two cows get friendly in a meadow near the top of the ski lift at Grindelwald, Switzerland. Photo by Doris E. Muir of Shrewsbury, Pa.

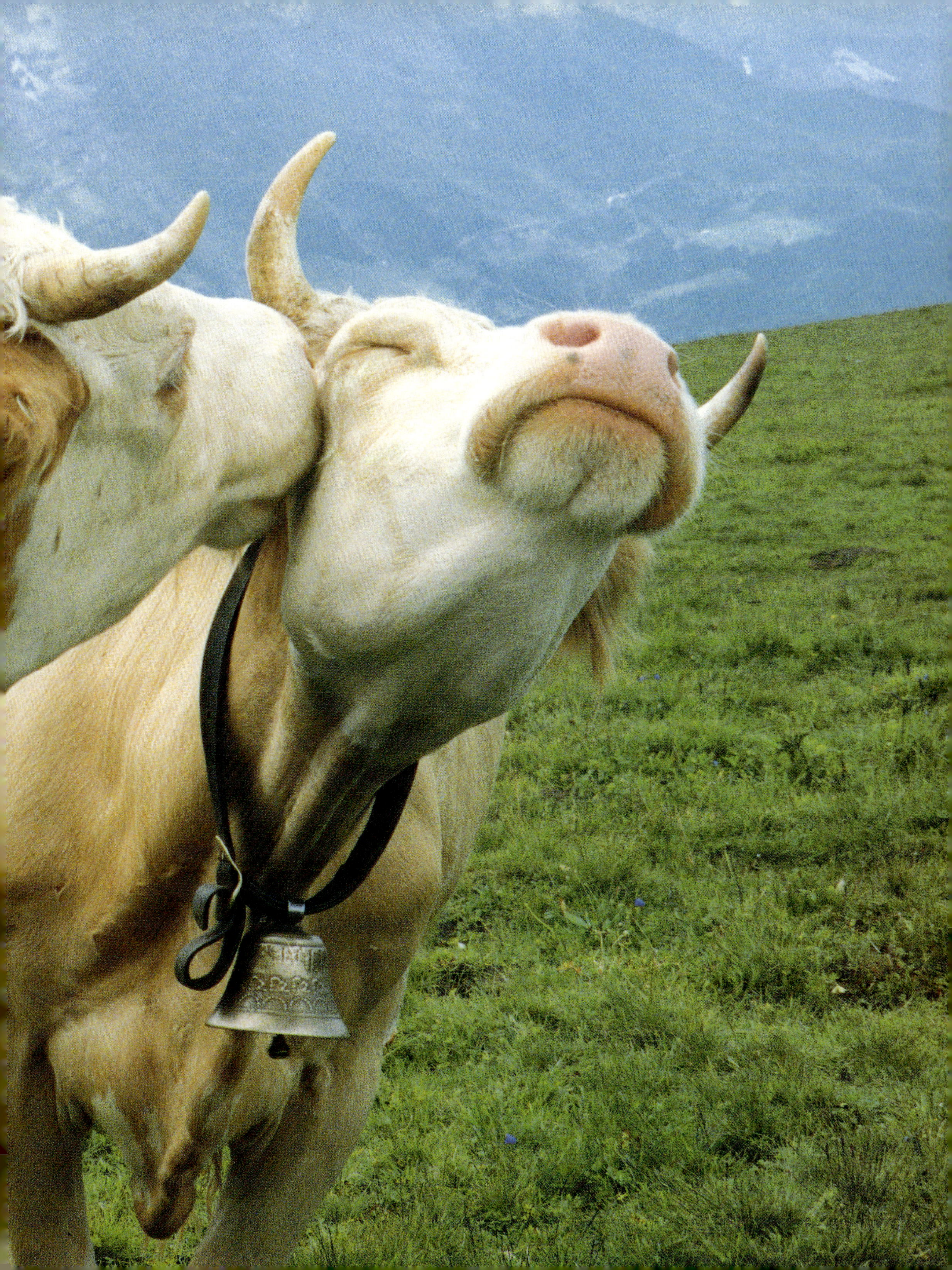

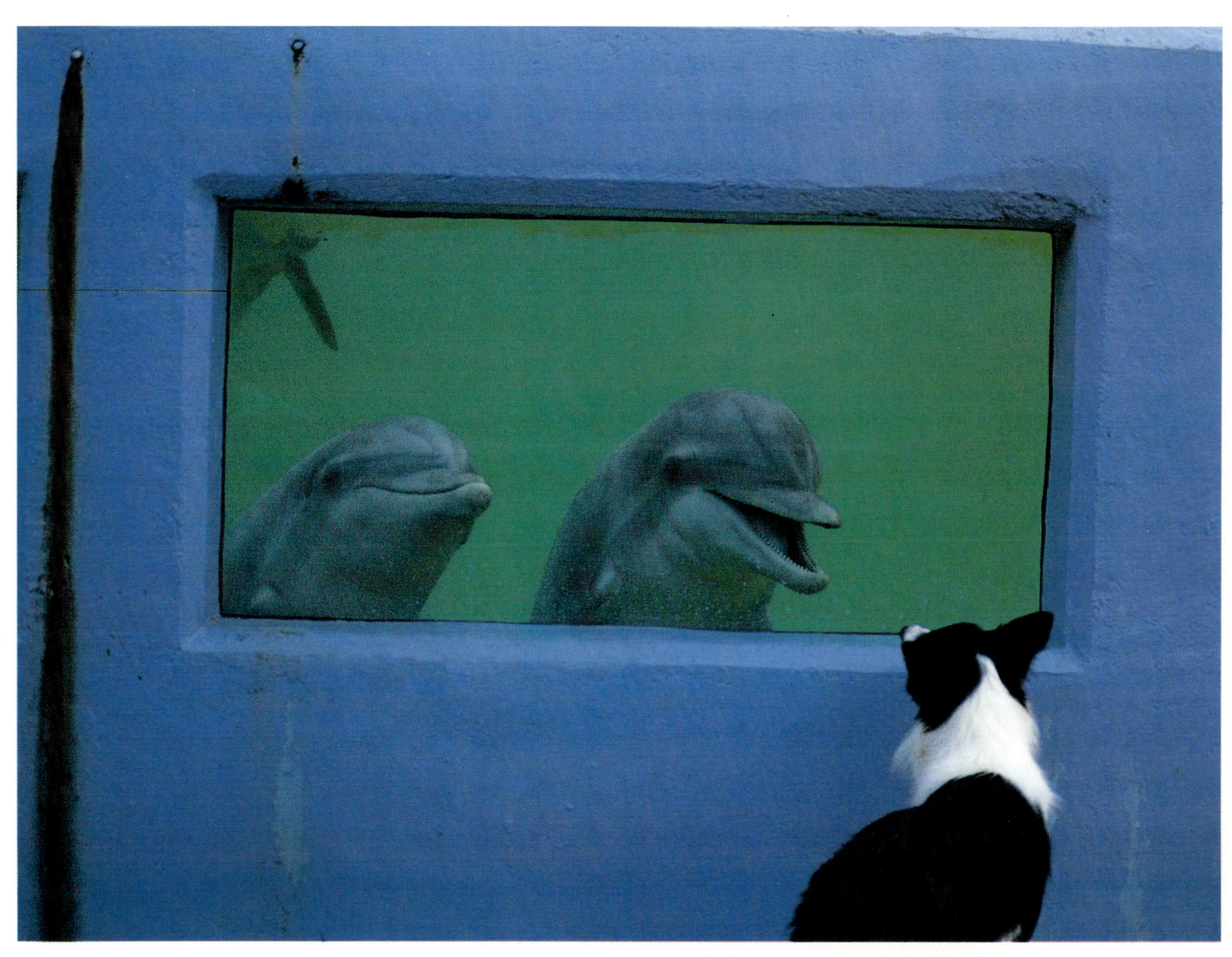

One Talks, the Other Just Smiles and Listens: Rikki the dog meets Mauka and Makai, the dolphins in Hawaii. Photo by Harry Katz of Cambridge, Mass.

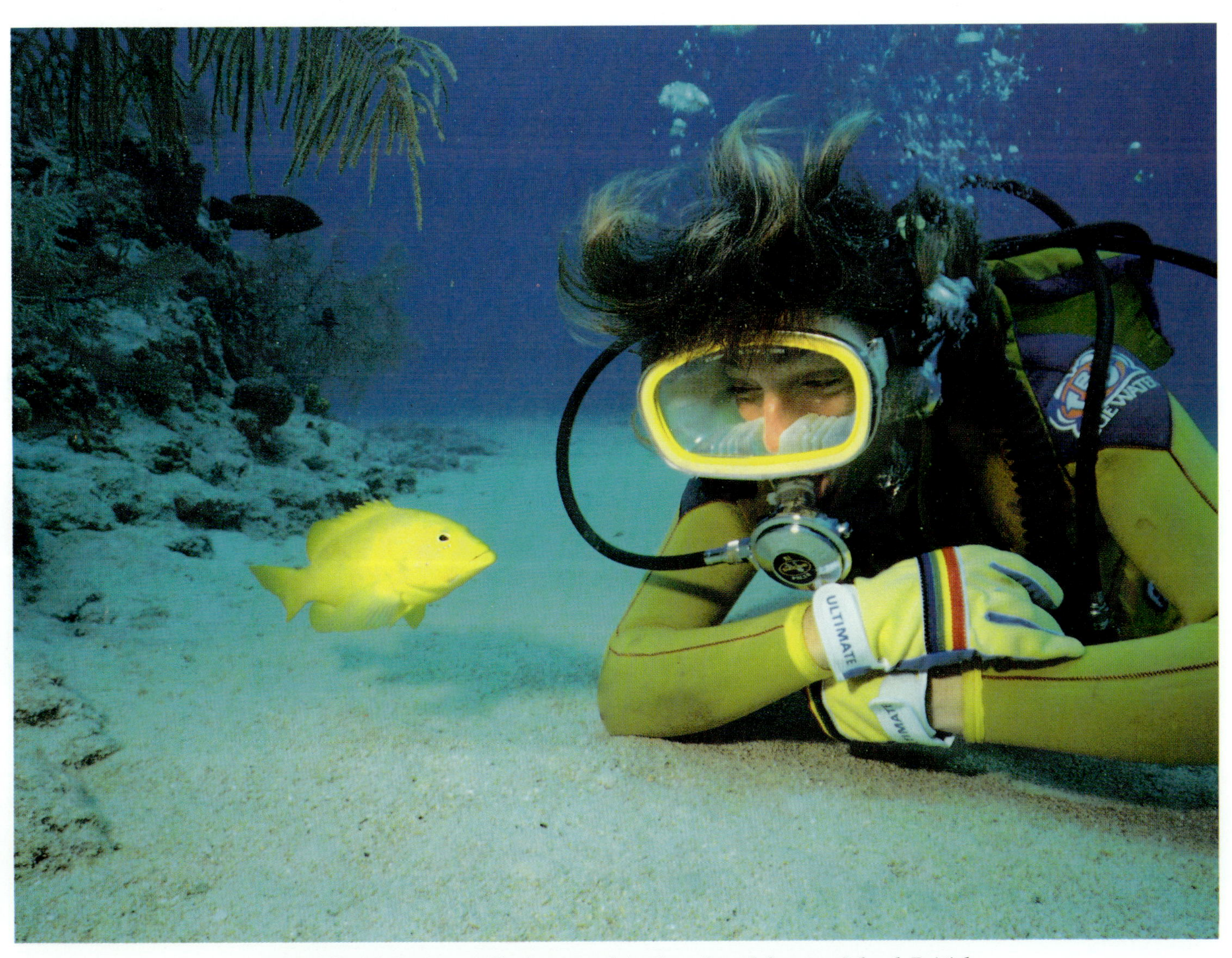

Cathy Church finds a really deep new friend on Grand Cayman Island, British West Indies. Photographer is Heidrun Grell Faulconer of San Diego.

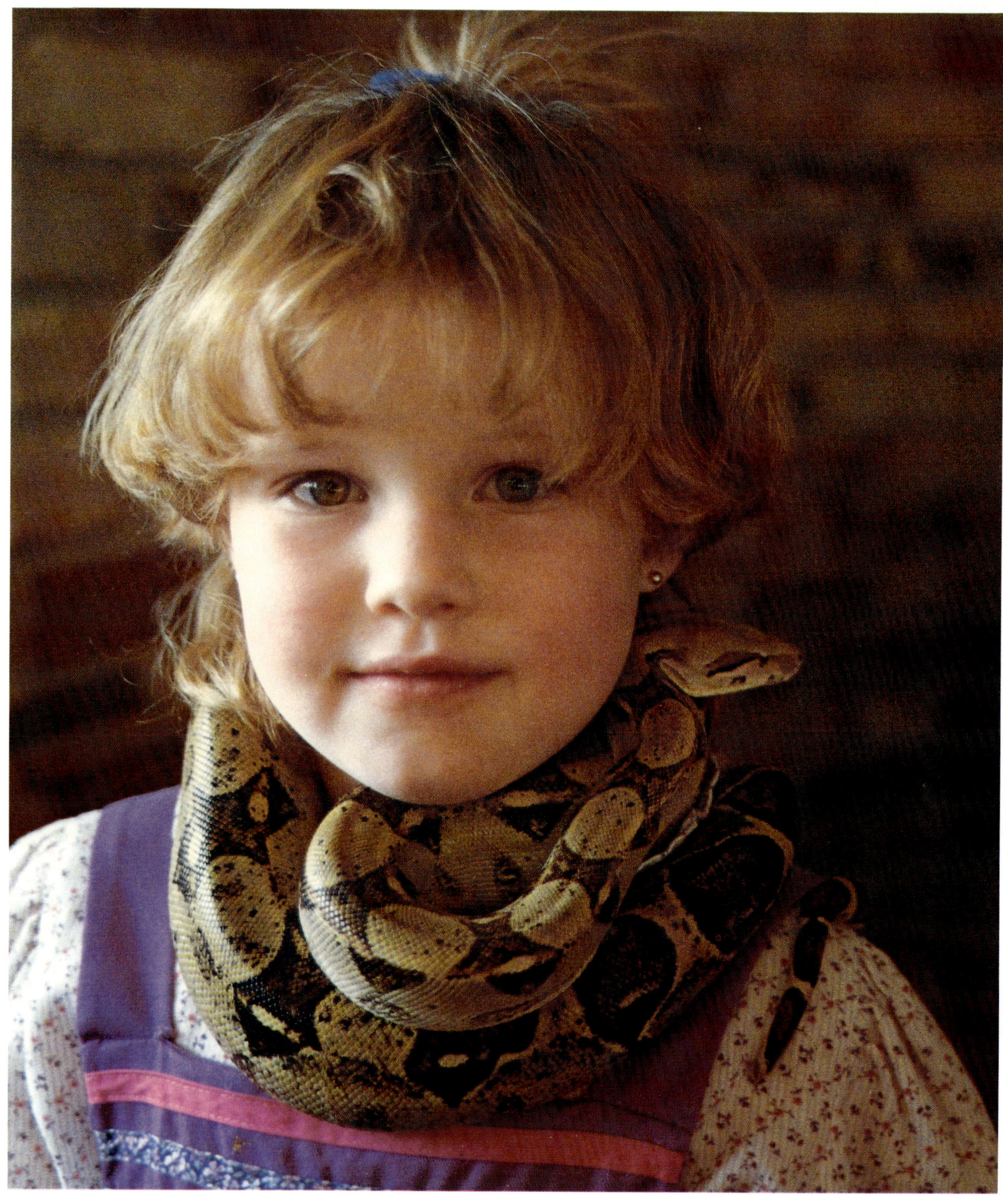

They're Very, Very Close: Nicole Loyet, 4, and "Snakey". Photo by Nicole's father, Mikell Loyet of Richmond, Utah.

A Close "Family" Relationship: Vanessa Valbuena, 9, with her housemate, Coby, 5. Photo by Vanessa's mother, Gini Valbuena, who raises chimpanzees at home in Clearwater, Fla.

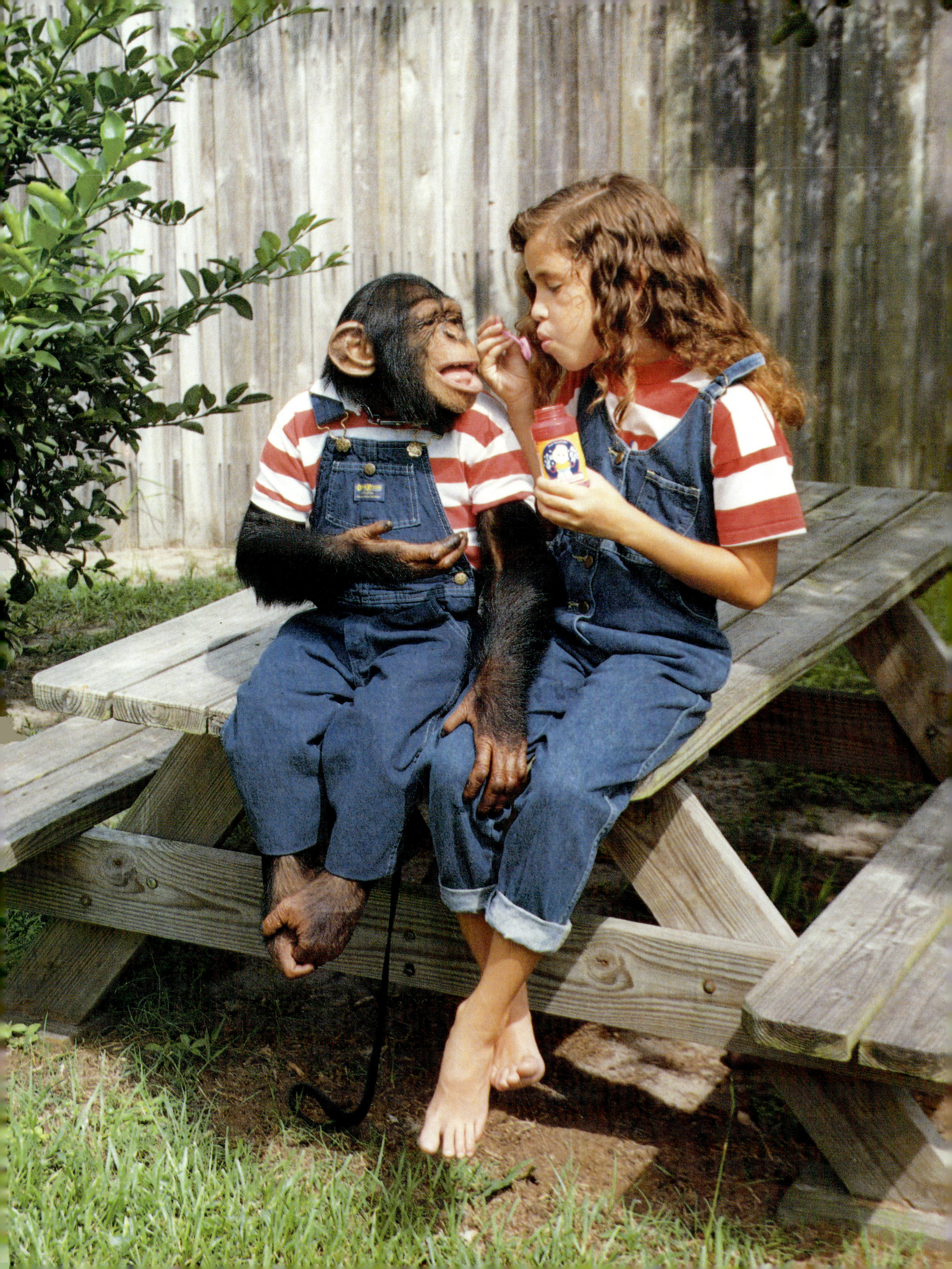

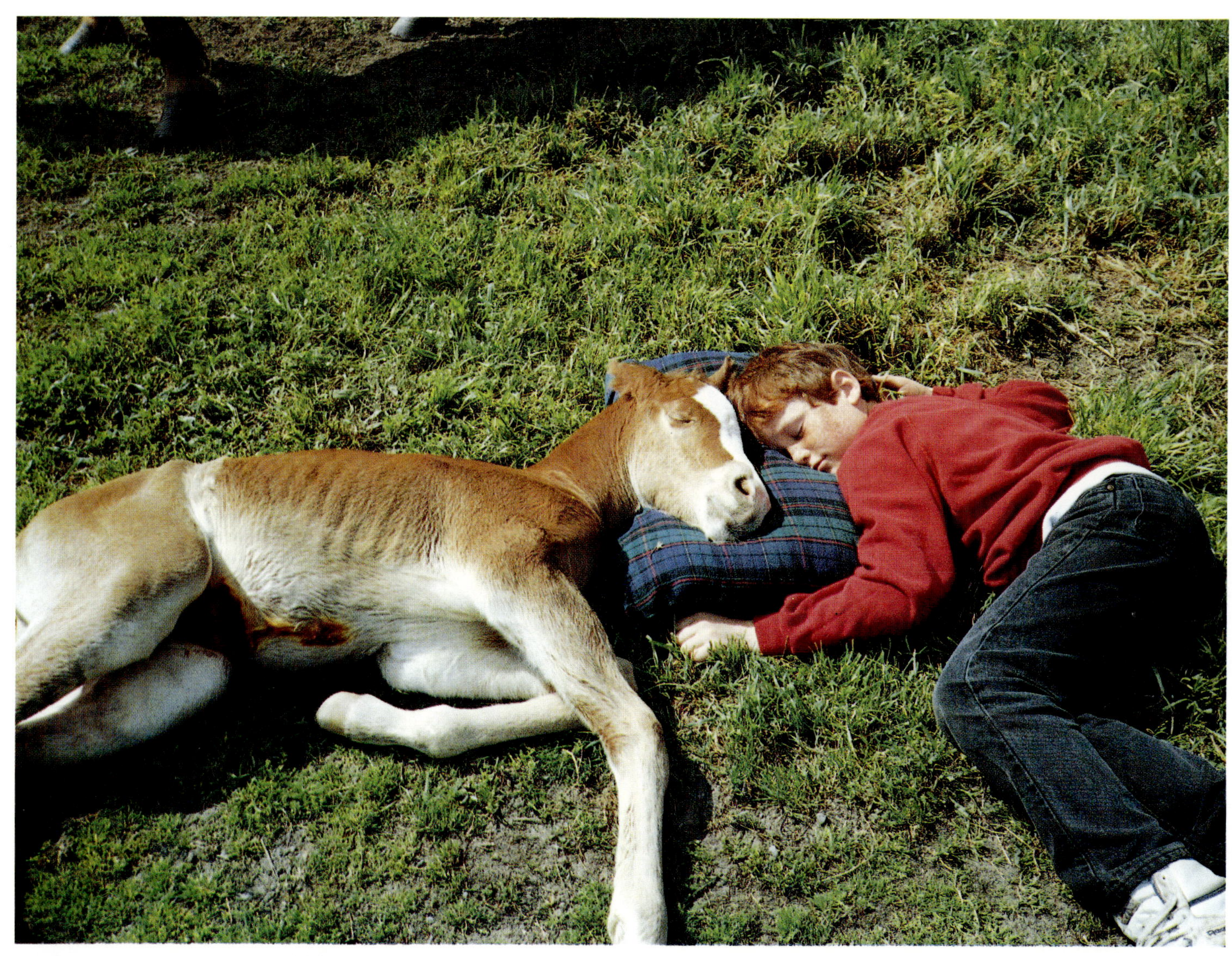

Do Not Disturb: Nine-year-old Ross Koplen, son of a rancher, snuggles down for an afternoon nap with his colt. Ross' mother, Linda Koplen of Santa Rosa, Calif., snapped the photo.

How About a Little Peck? Jill Reger took this photo of Mariano Tripi, 76, a retired baker in Santa Barbara, Calif., as part of a class assignment on love.

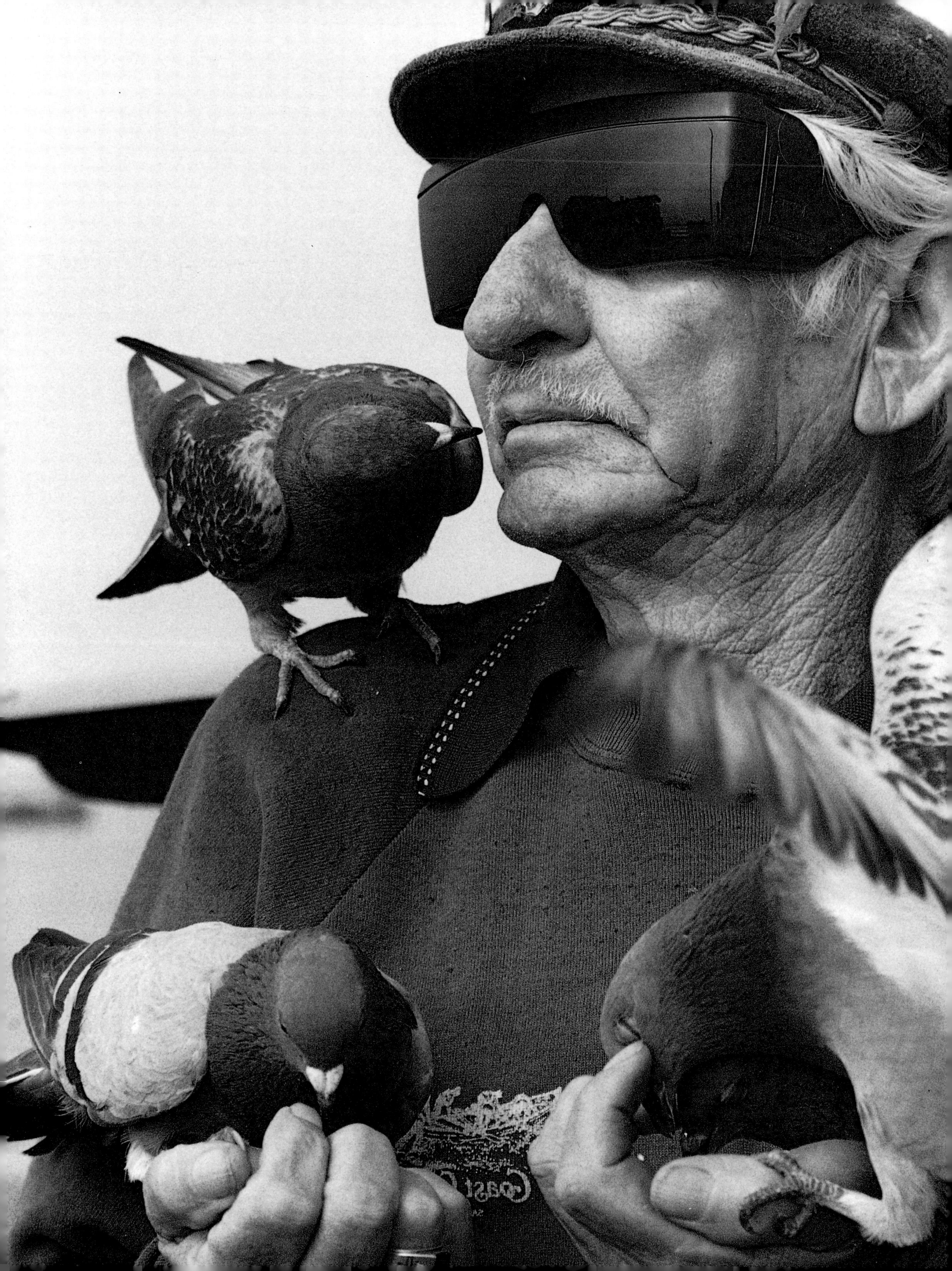

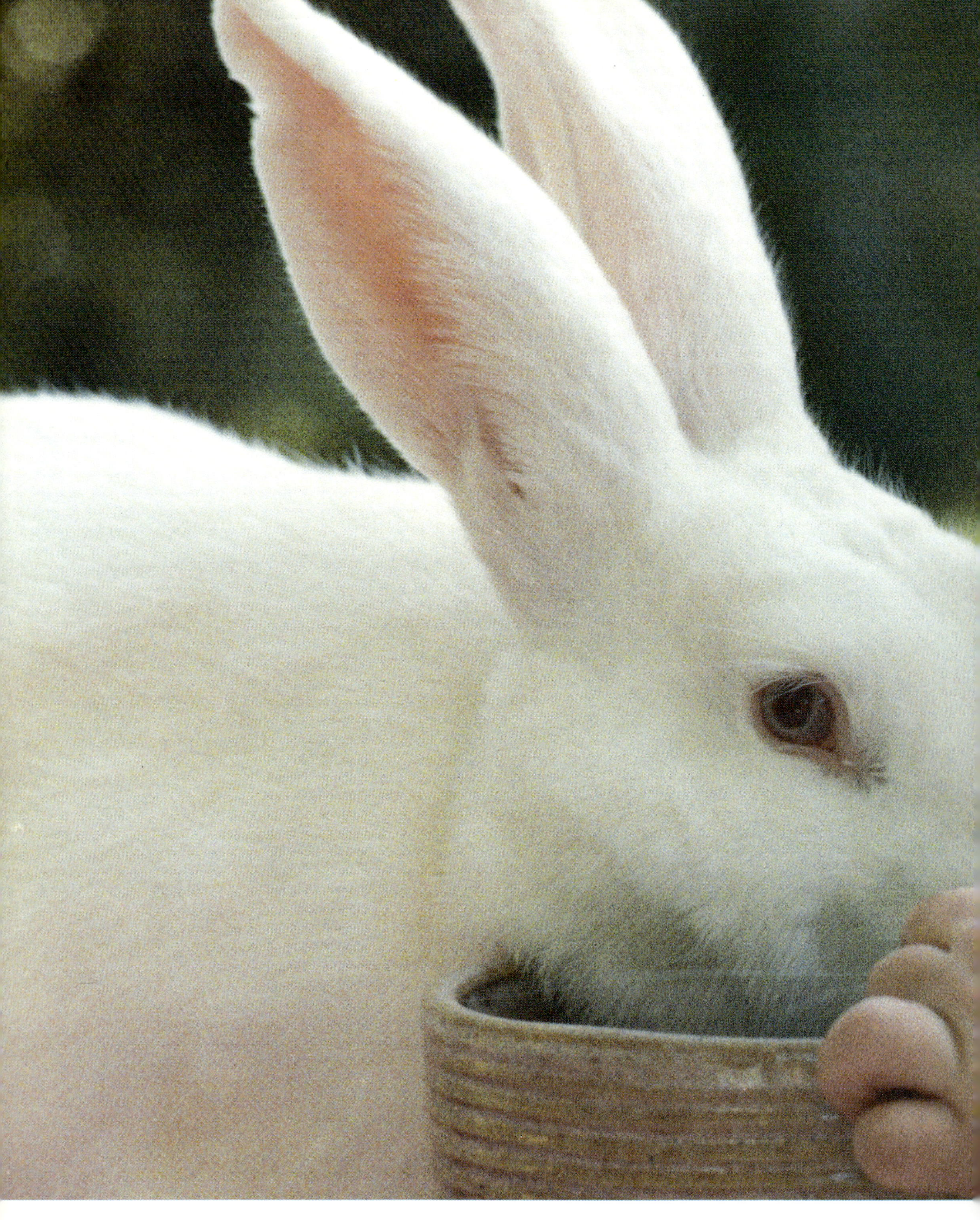

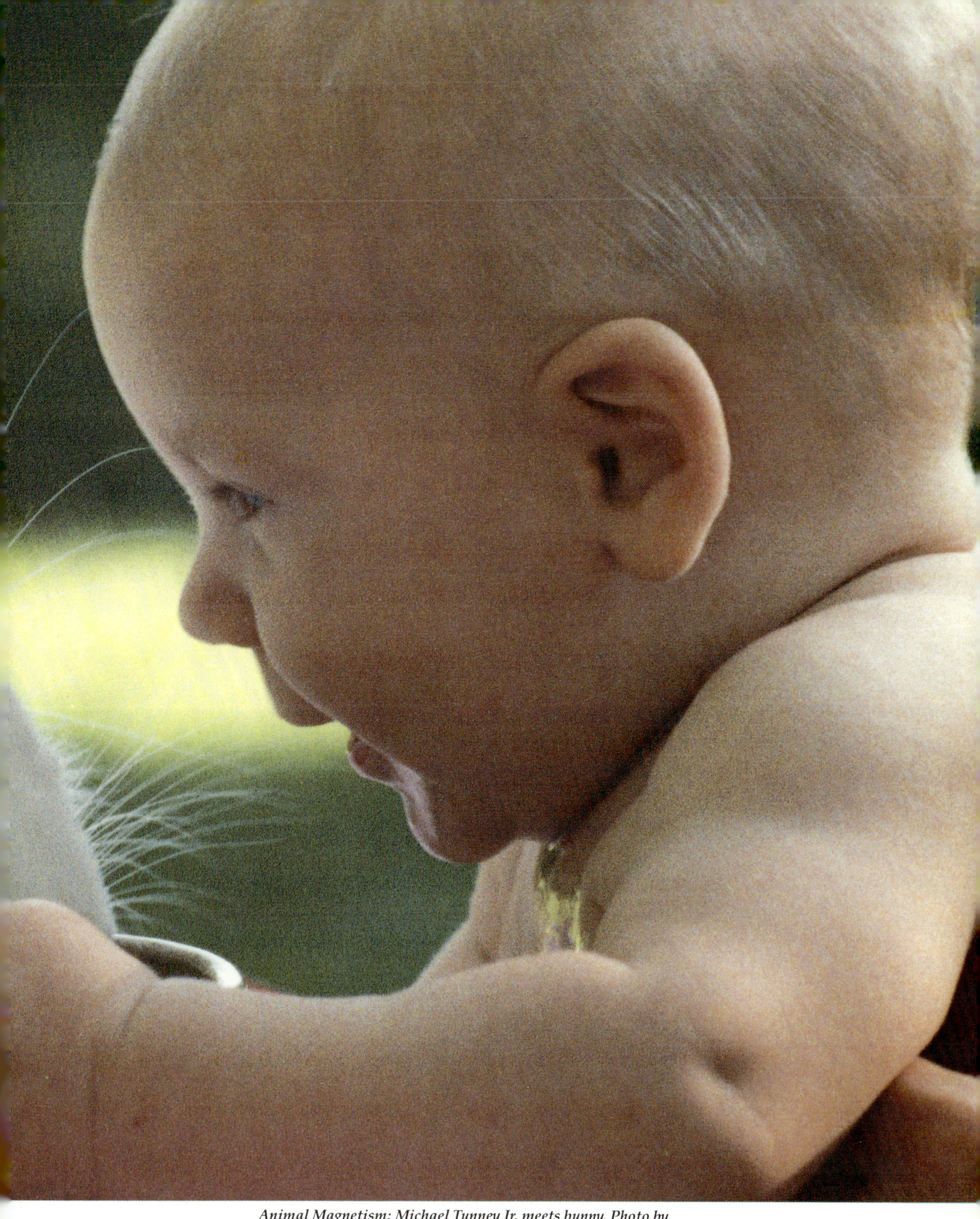

*Animal Magnetism: Michael Tunney Jr. meets bunny. Photo by
Michael Tunney Sr. of Deltaville, Va.*

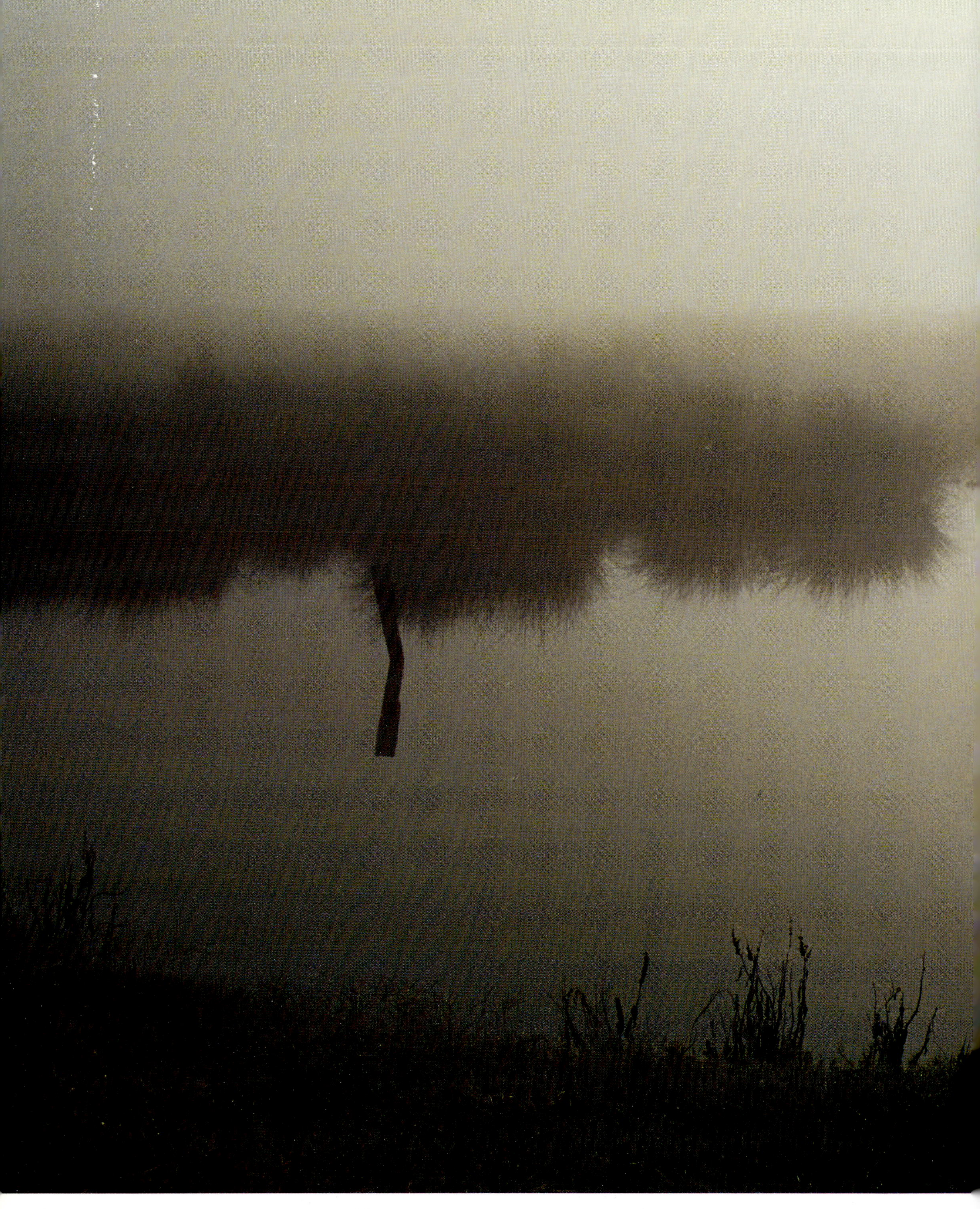

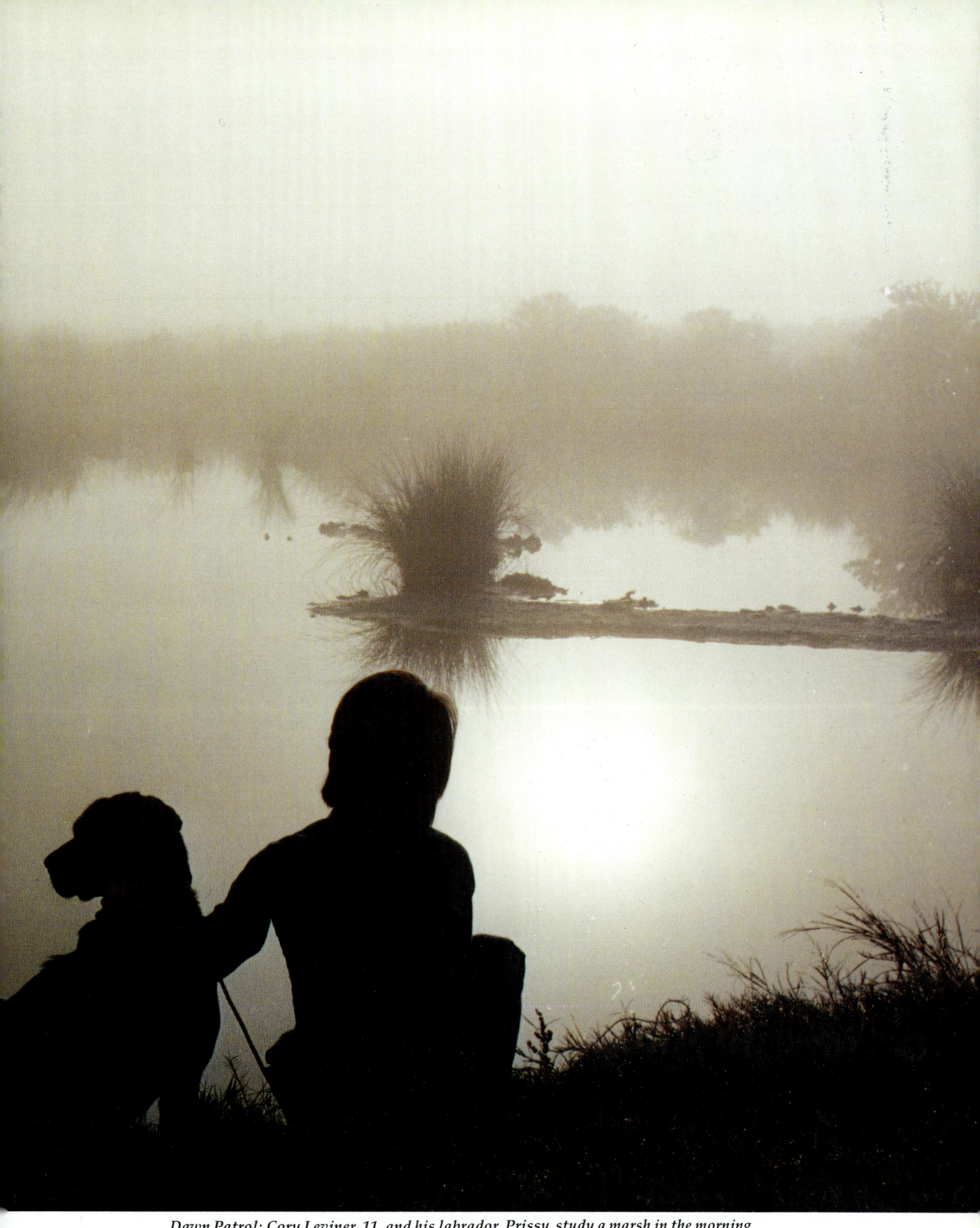

Dawn Patrol: Cory Leviner, 11, and his labrador, Prissy, study a marsh in the morning mist near Cameron, La. Photo by Cory's uncle, Jon Nutt of Lake Charles, La.

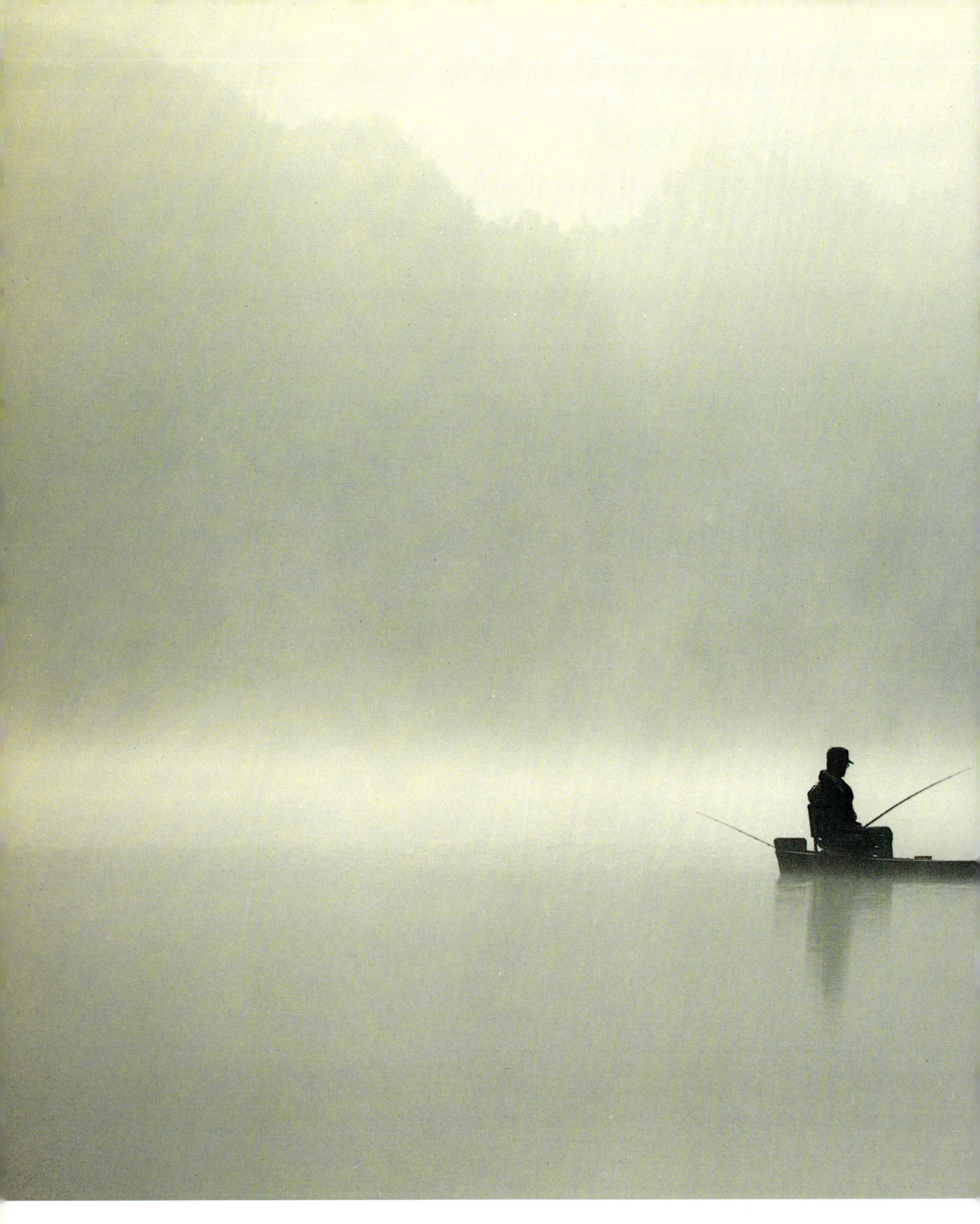

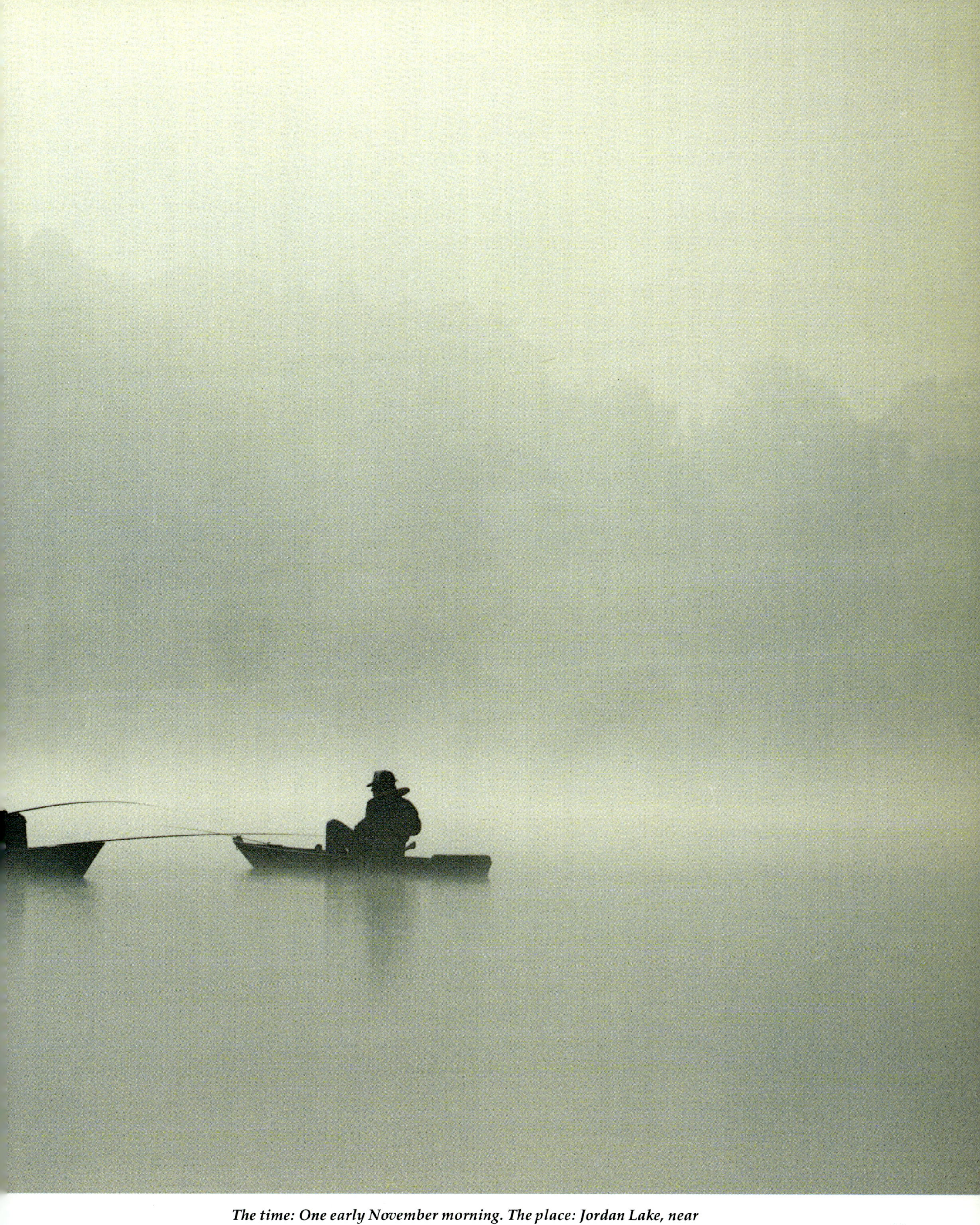

The time: One early November morning. The place: Jordan Lake, near Chapel Hill, N.C. The photographer was Don Pound of Newark, Ohio.

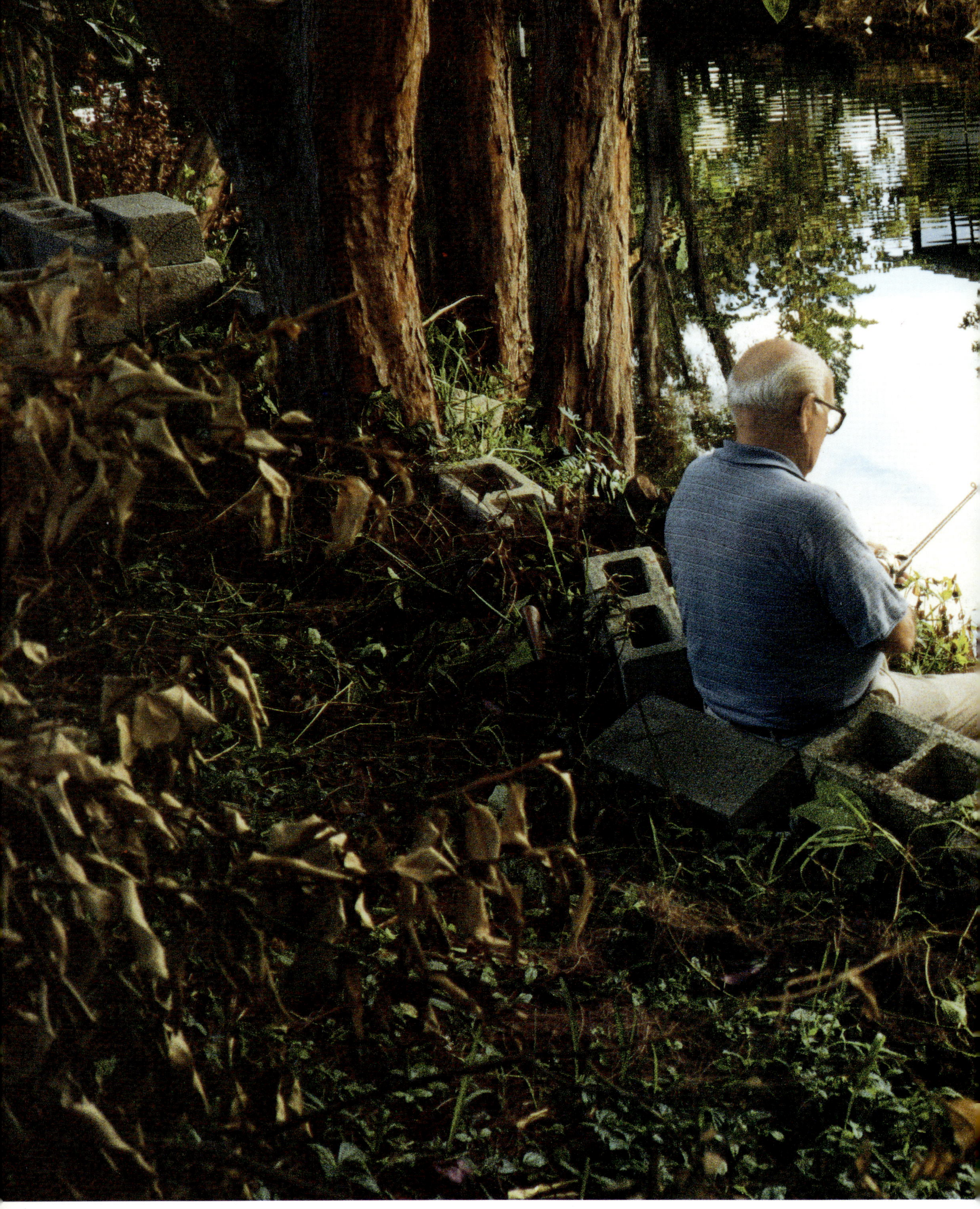

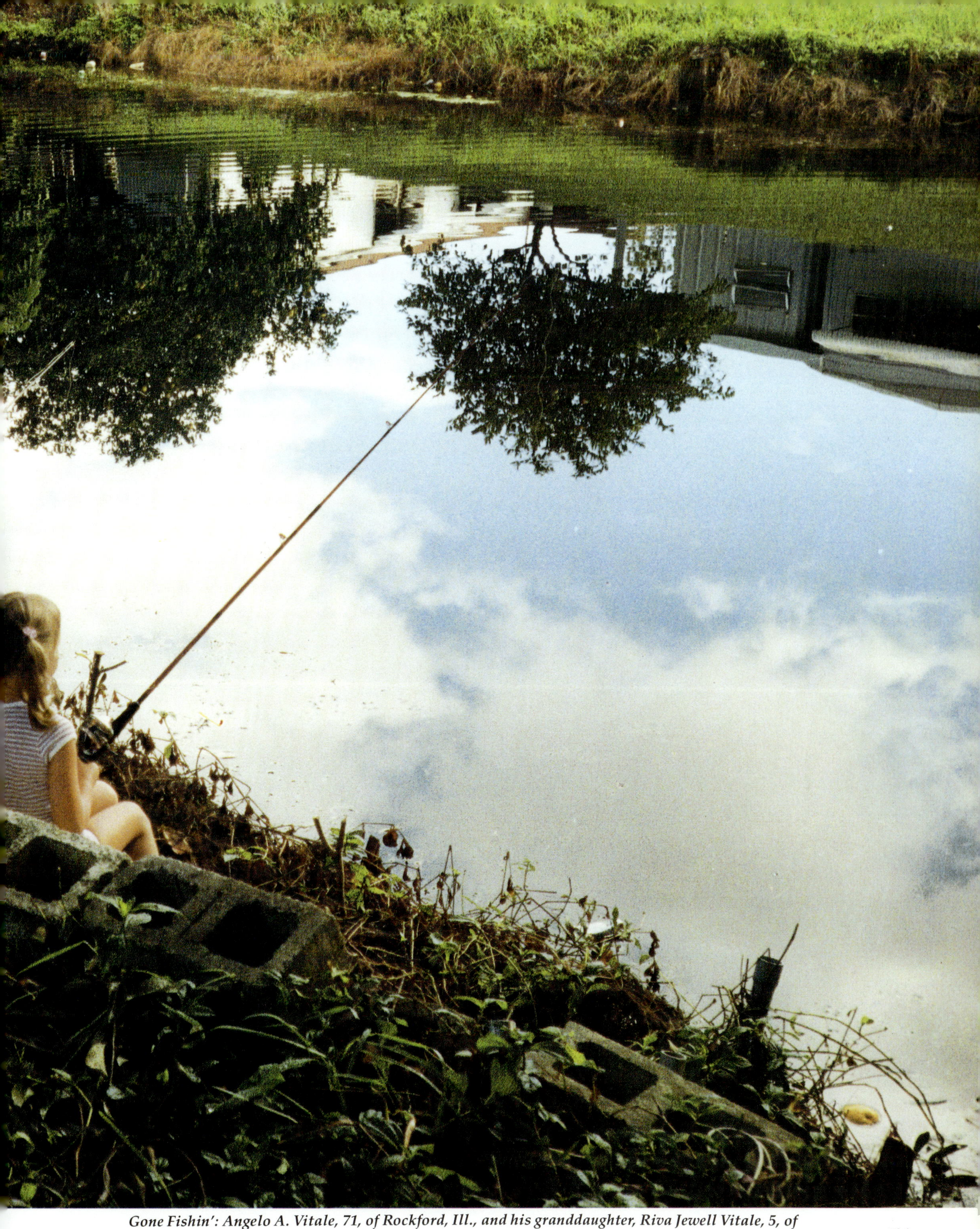

Gone Fishin': Angelo A. Vitale, 71, of Rockford, Ill., and his granddaughter, Riva Jewell Vitale, 5, of Dubuque, Iowa, have bait, will wait. Riva's mom, Jane Jewell-Vitale, took this photo in Boca Raton, Fla.

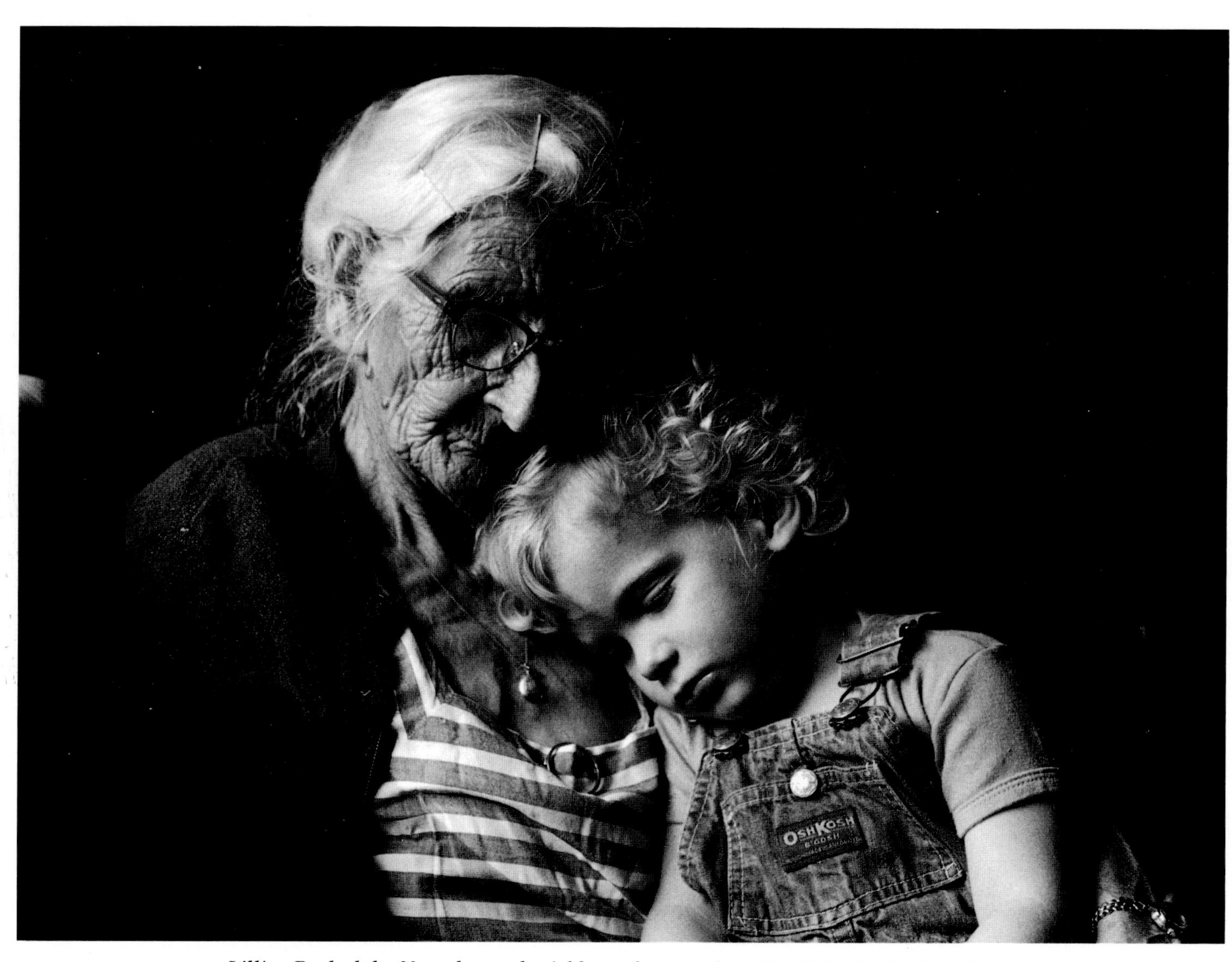

Lillian Backsdale, 89, and a good neighbor —her grandson, Jim Kalergis, 3—don't feel the need to talk. Photo taken by Jim's mother, Mary Kalergis of Charlottesville, Va.

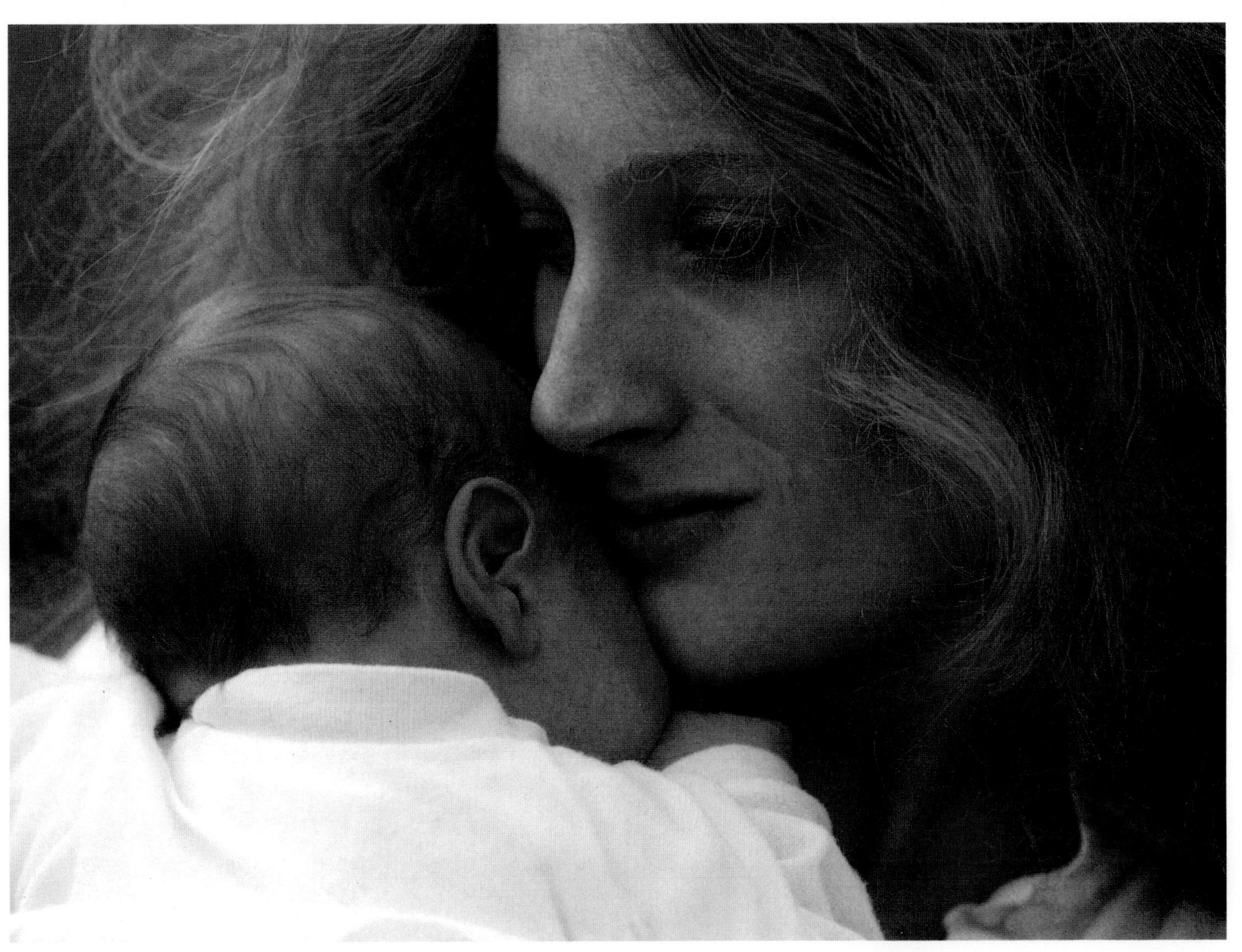

A Mother's Love: Melissa Payne— cuddling her 2-week-old son, Halsey— celebrates her first Mother's Day. Photo by the proud papa, Bryan Payne of Gaithersburg, Md.

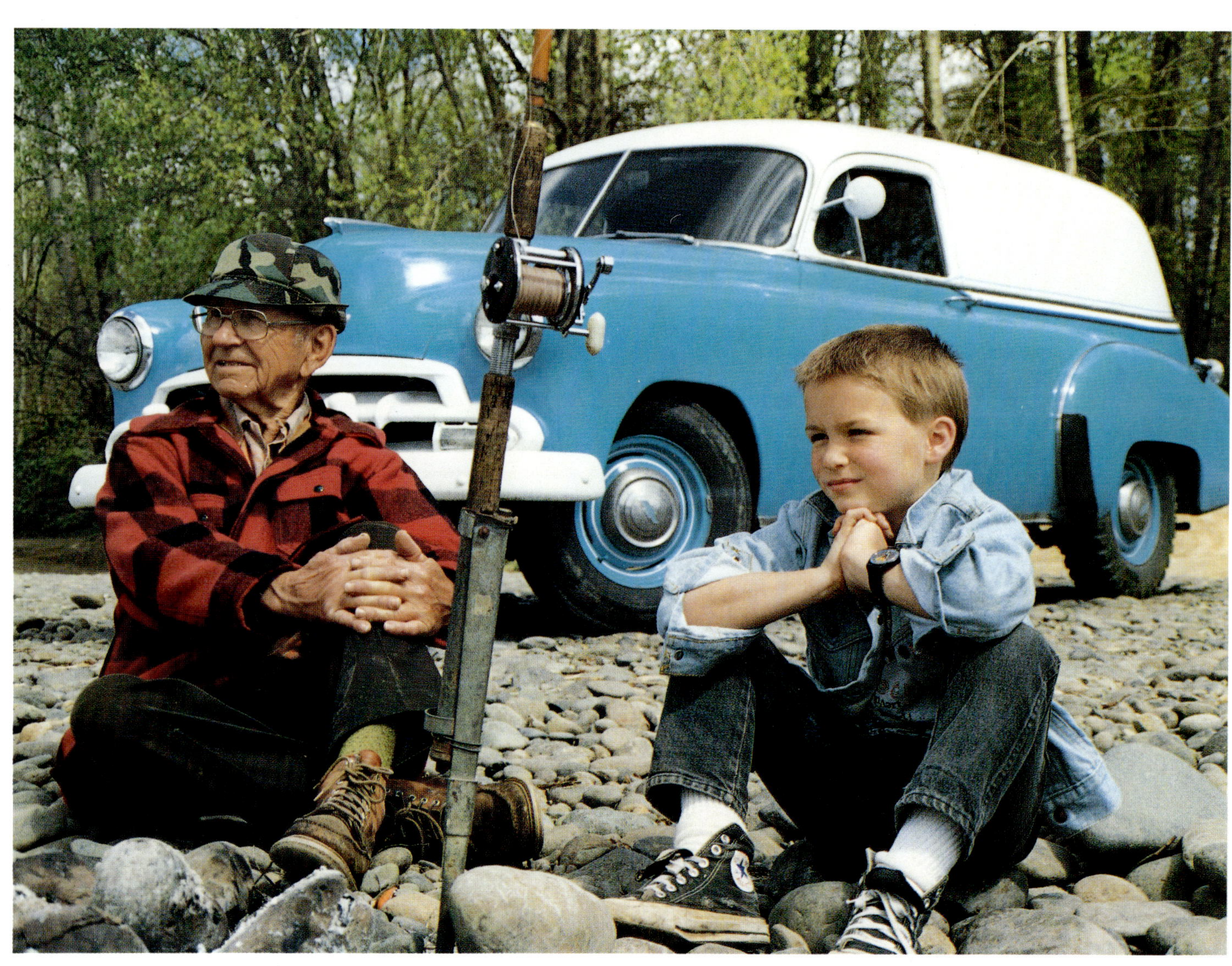

Byron Hess, 87, and his great-grandson Michael, 11, do what fishermen from time immemorial have always done: sit and wait. Photo by Hollis Hess—son of Byron and grandfather of Michael—of Gladstone, Ore.

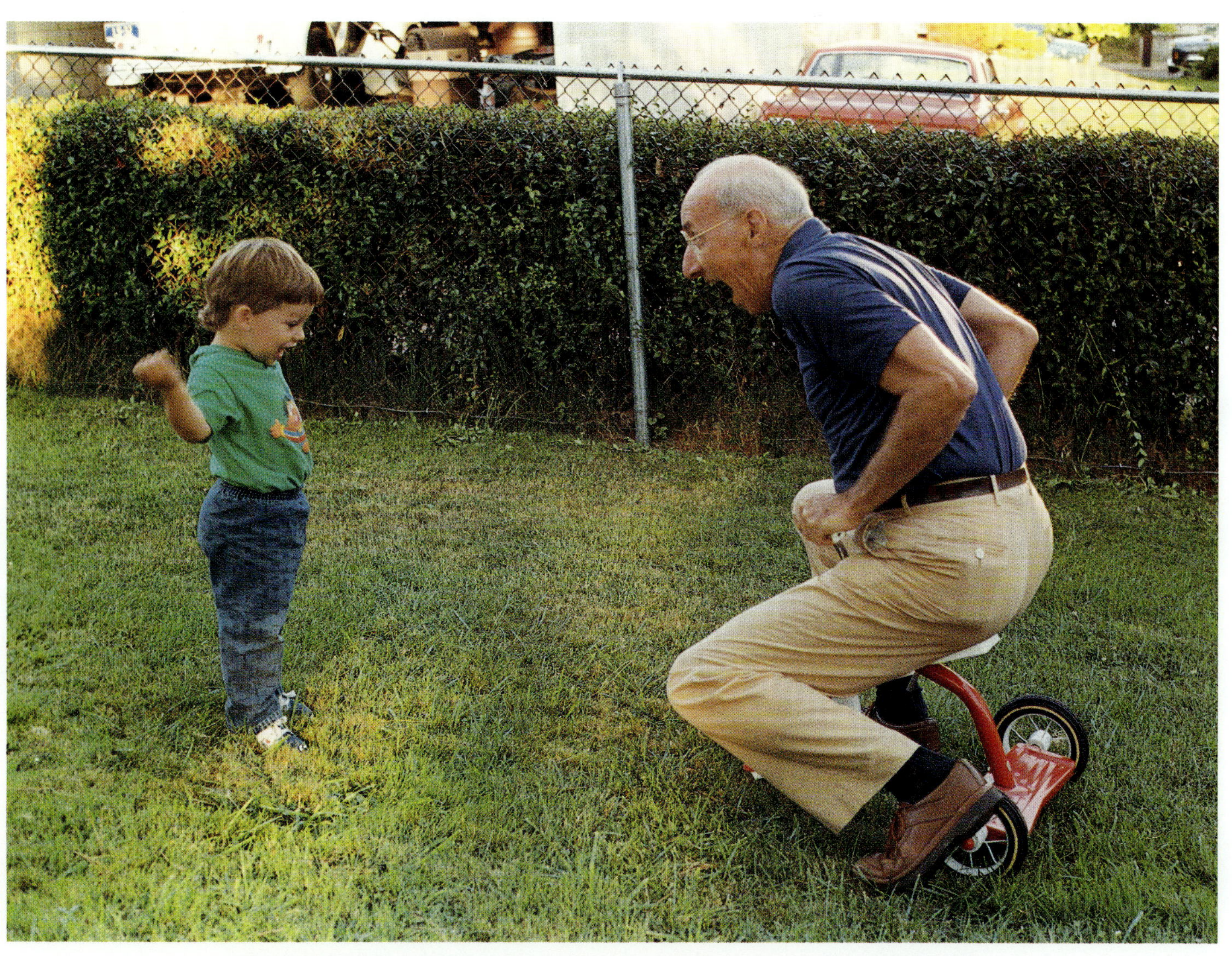

'Tain't Fittin'! Trying this tyke's trike amused Walter S. Krater, 72, but his grandson and best buddy, Willie, 2, said: "You no fit, Pop-Pop! You no fit!" Willie's mom, Kathleen Anthony, caught the moment in her backyard in Irwin, Pa.

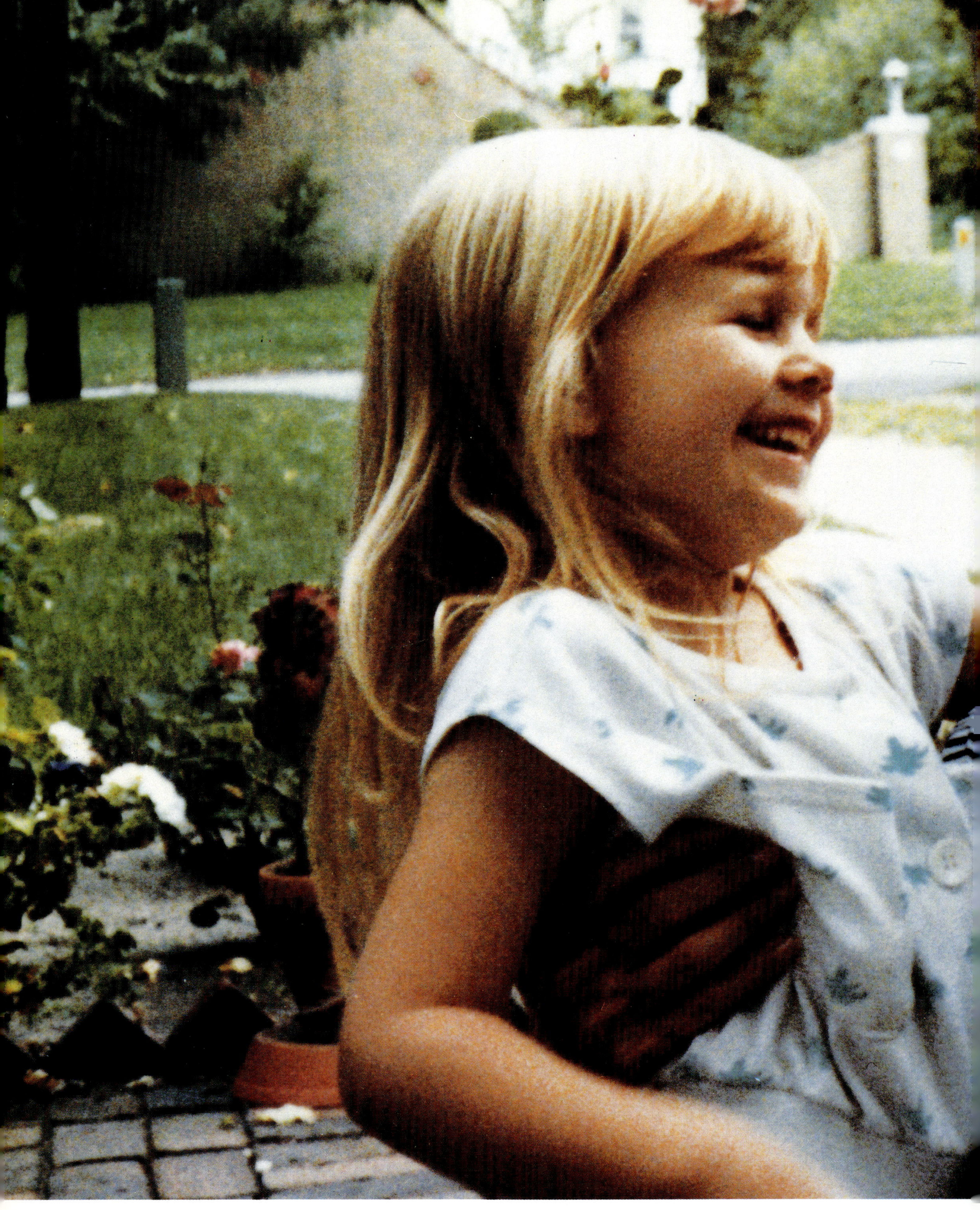

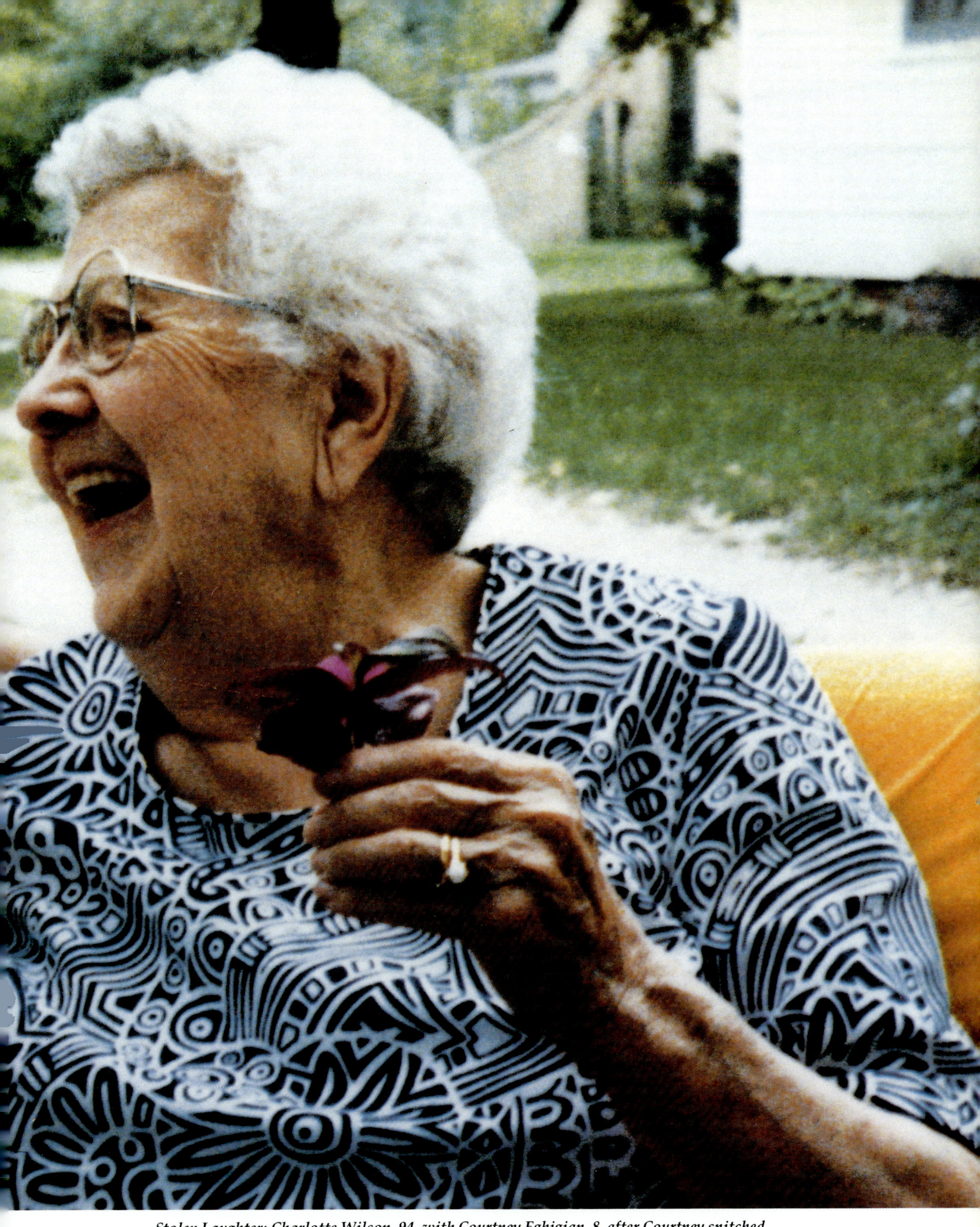

Stolen Laughter: Charlotte Wilson, 94, with Courtney Eghigian, 8, after Courtney snitched a blossom from her uncle's garden. Photo by Tracy Wilmsmeyer of Edwardsville, Ill.

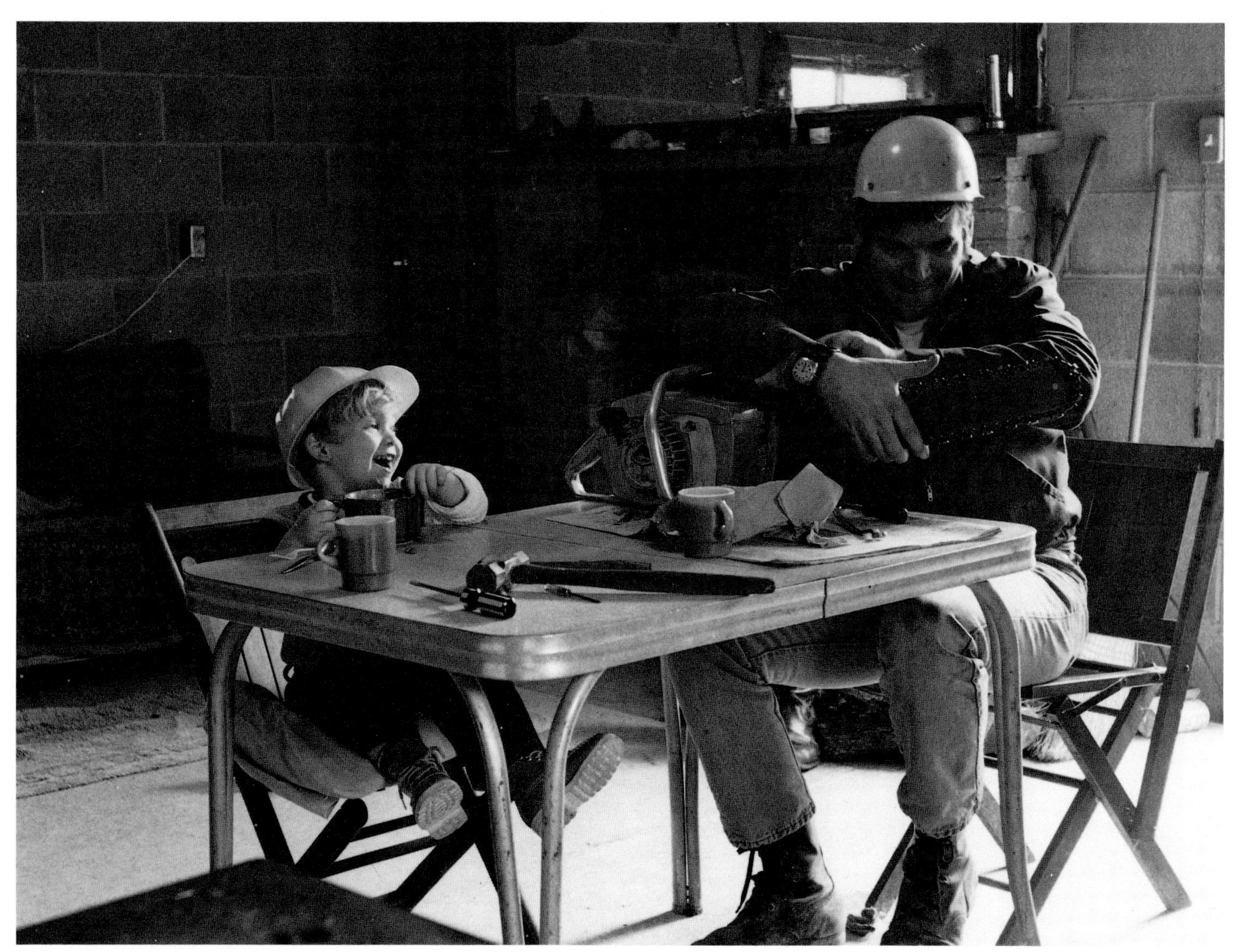

Two-year-old Robbie Munro—hard hat, boots and all—gets ready to go cut wood with his father, Robert, in West Virginia. Photo by Roxie Munro of New York City.

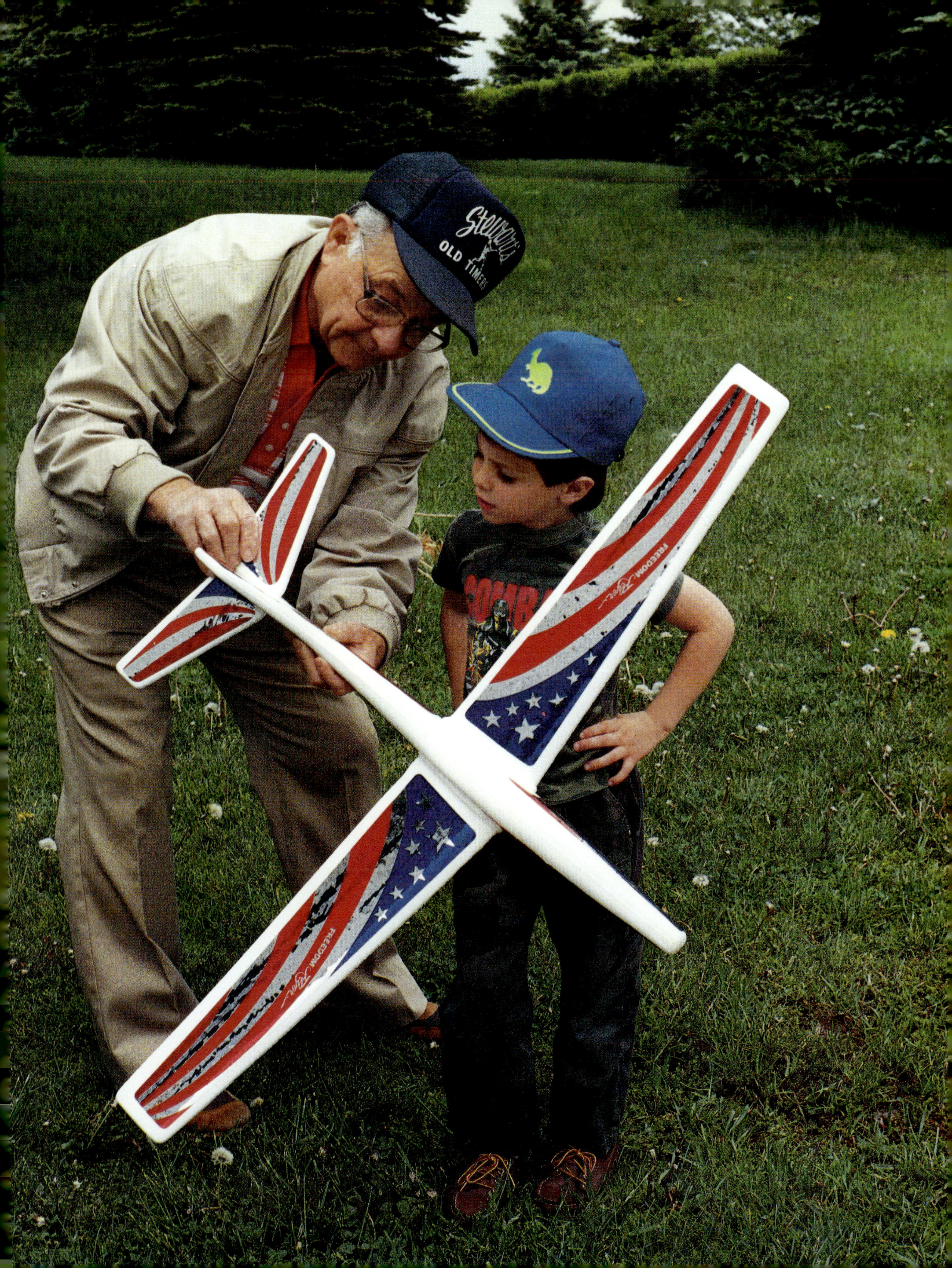

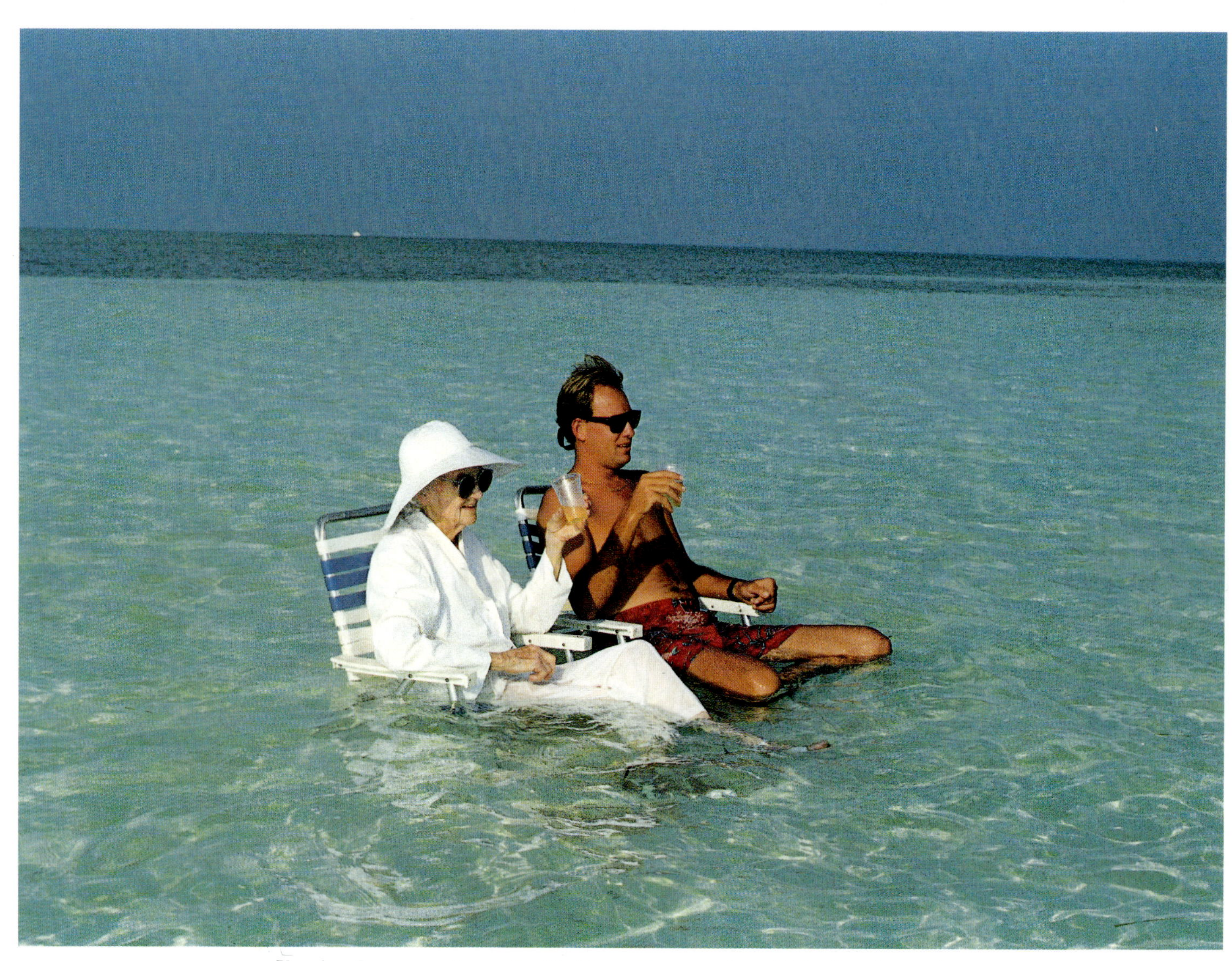

Keeping Company: Laura Smith, 90, and her grandson Kirk, 30, relax in the Florida Keys. Photo by Kirk's wife, Paula Smith of Gainesville, Fla.

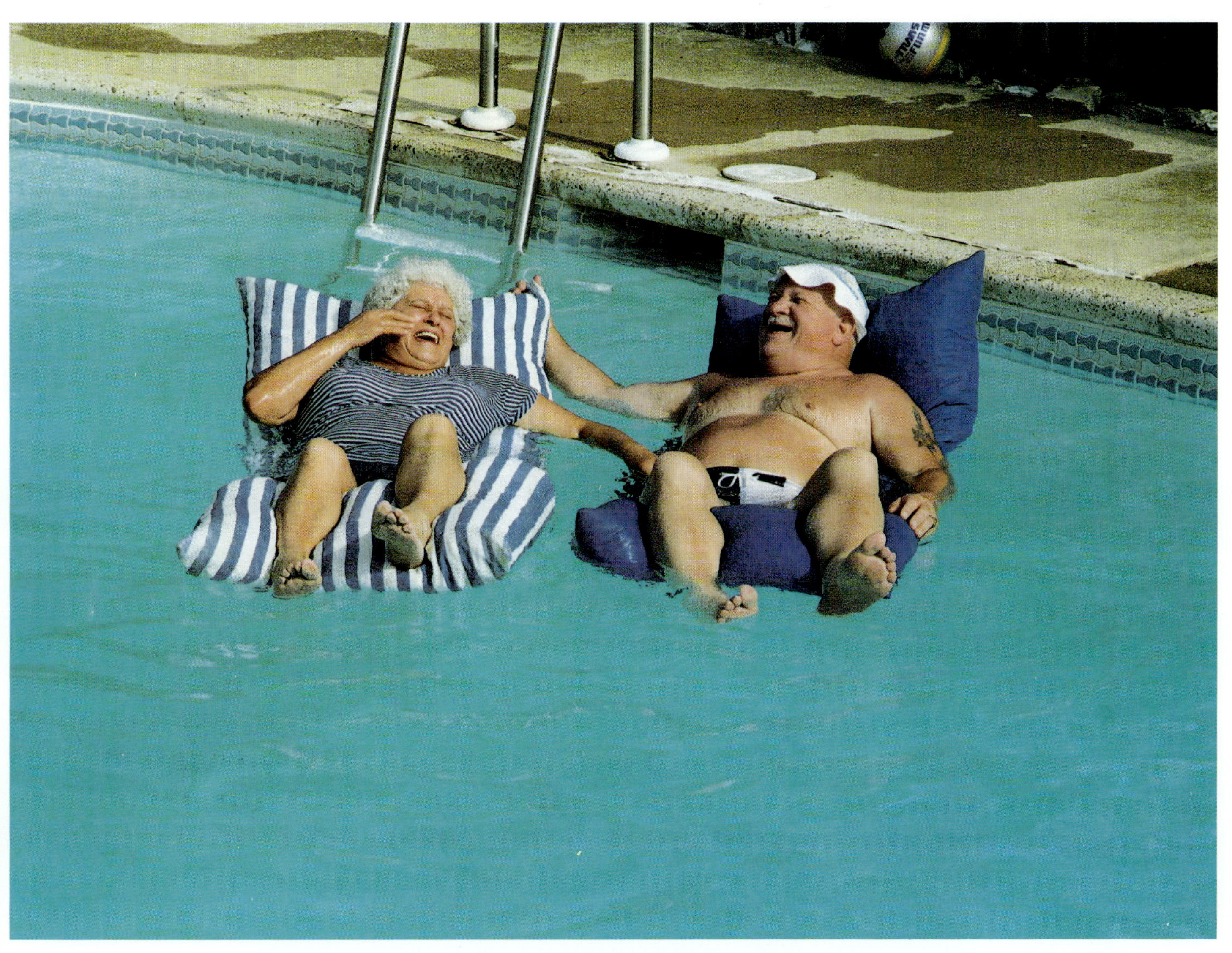

*What a Hoot! Riding high at a family get-together are Helen T. Yeager and her
husband, Robert, both 66, during a family reunion in Finksburg, Md. Photo by
Ron Yeager of Woodbridge, Va.*

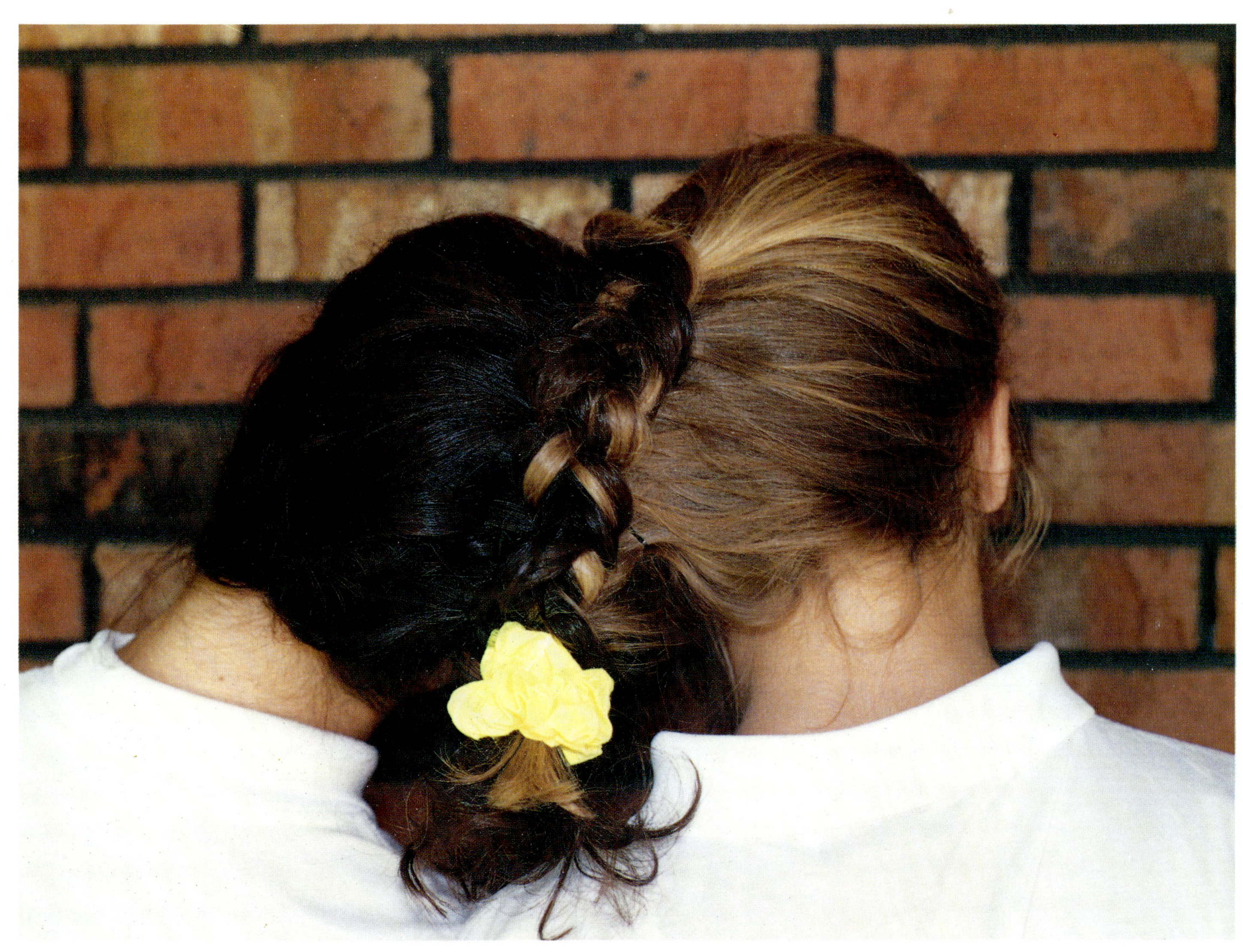

Fit To Be Tied: Amy Marie Fazalare, the brunette, gets braided with her good friend, Nicole Marie Stump, the blonde, in Weirton, W.Va. Both girls were 13. The photographer was Marie Fazalare, Amy's mother.

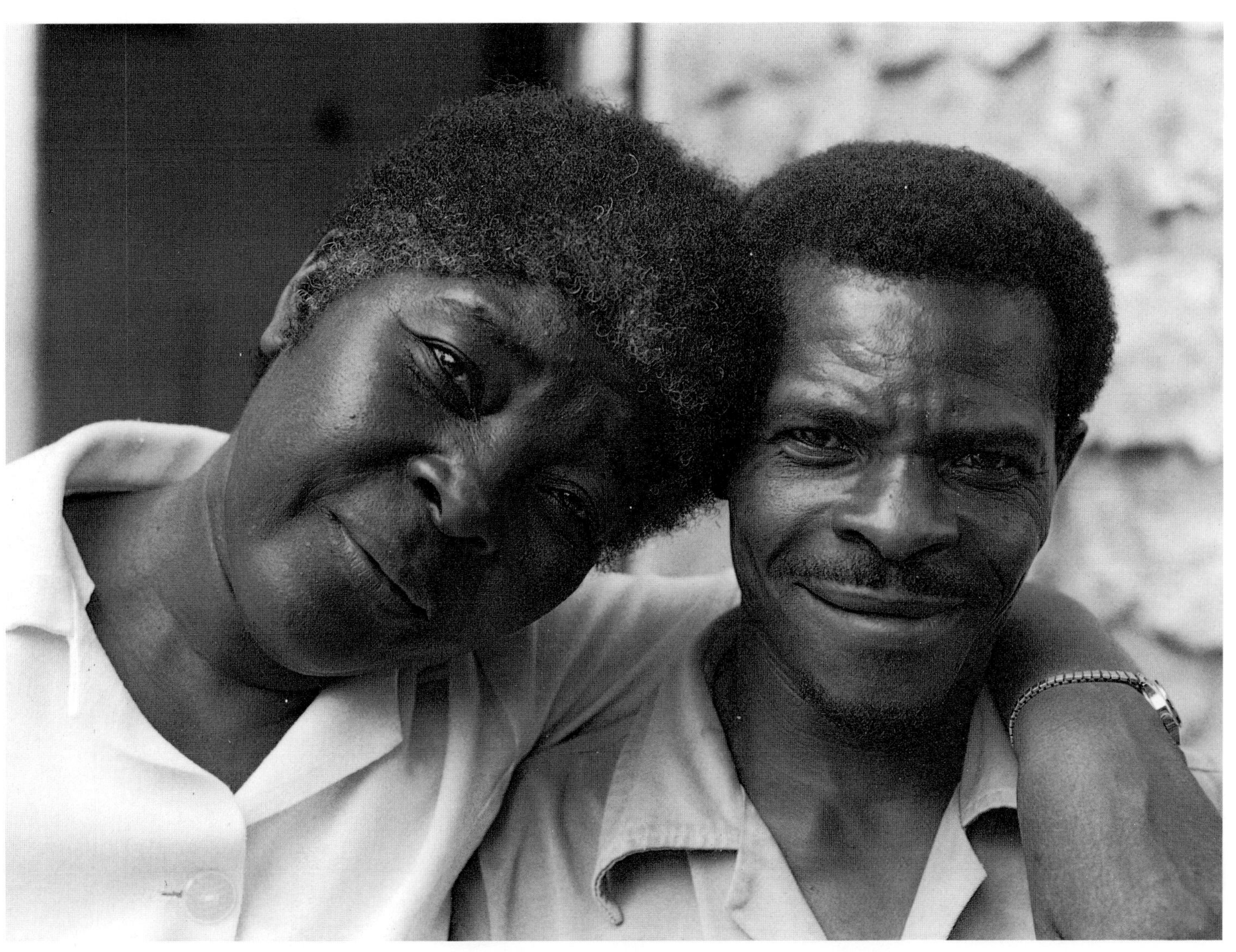

Longtime Friends: Marguerite Paul and Joseph Pamphile in their hometown of Port-au-Prince, Haiti. Photo by Stephan Kenn of New York City.

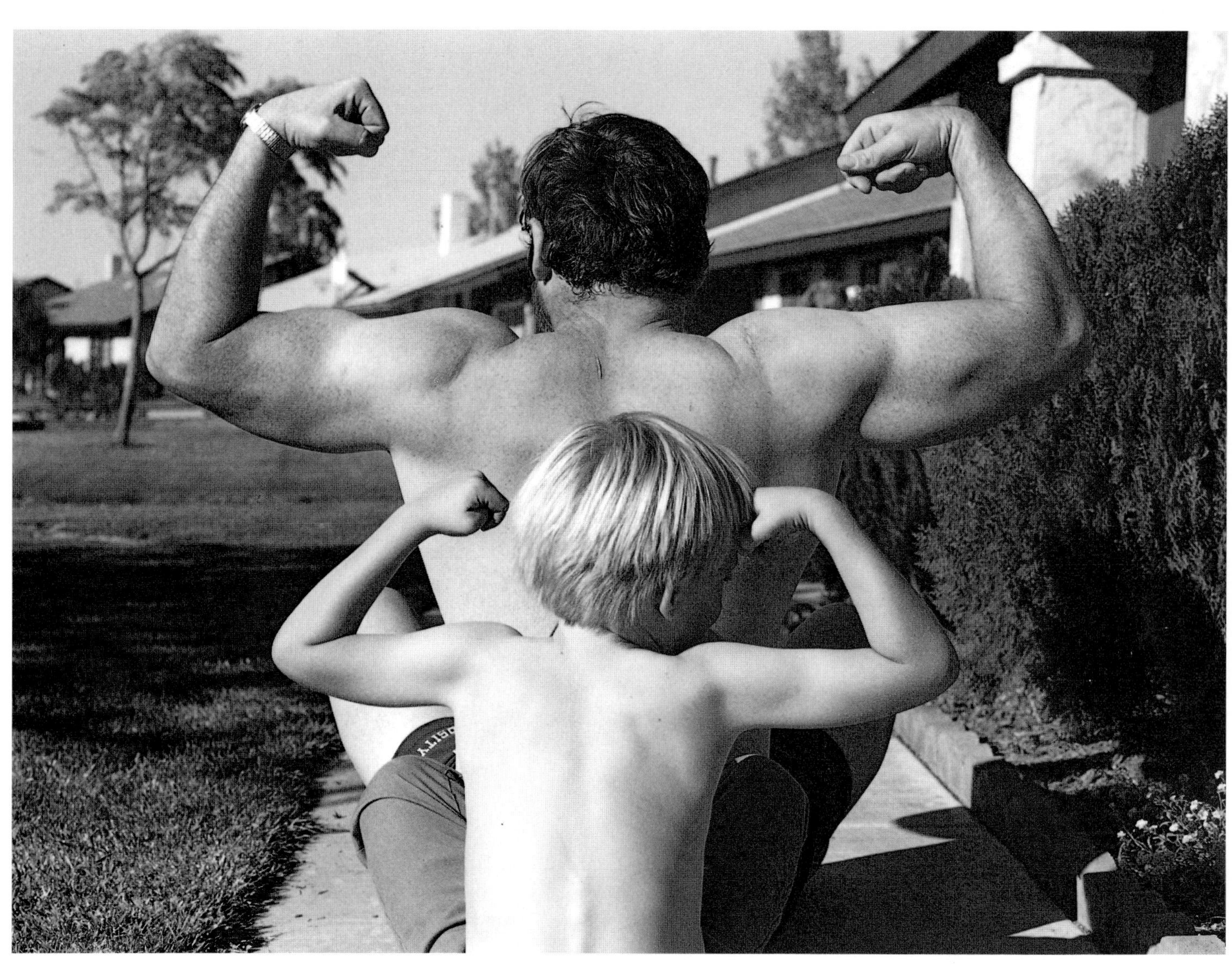

Look at All Those Muscles: Christopher Ferguson, 5, shows off with dad, Gregory, in Victorville, Calif. Photo by mom, Cynthia.

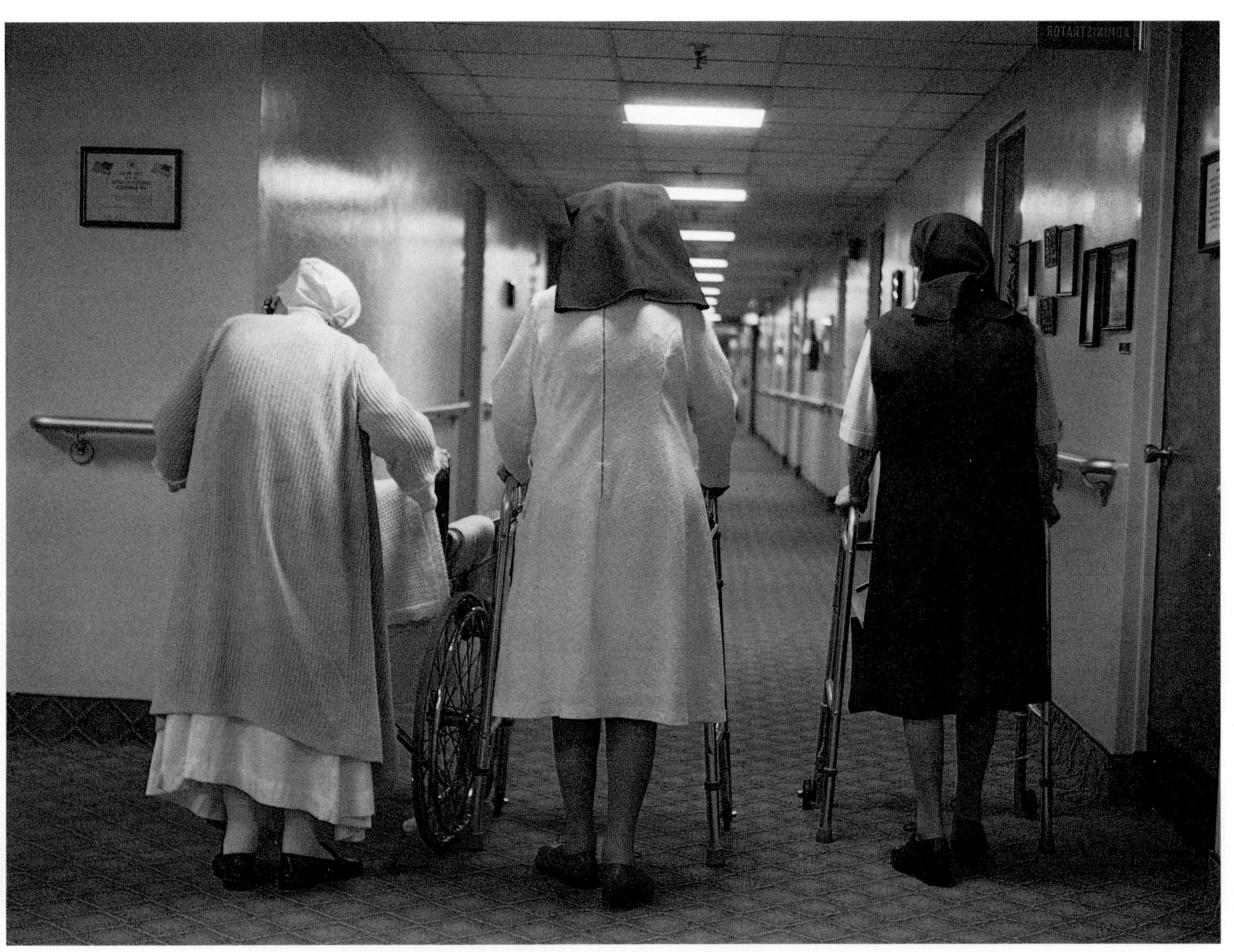

Sharing Faith: Sisters Margarite, Serraphine and Madeline Evangelemax (from left), all in their 90s, reside at the Saint Francis Infirmary in Tampa, Fla. Candice A. Morrow, who used to work there as an RN, took the photo.

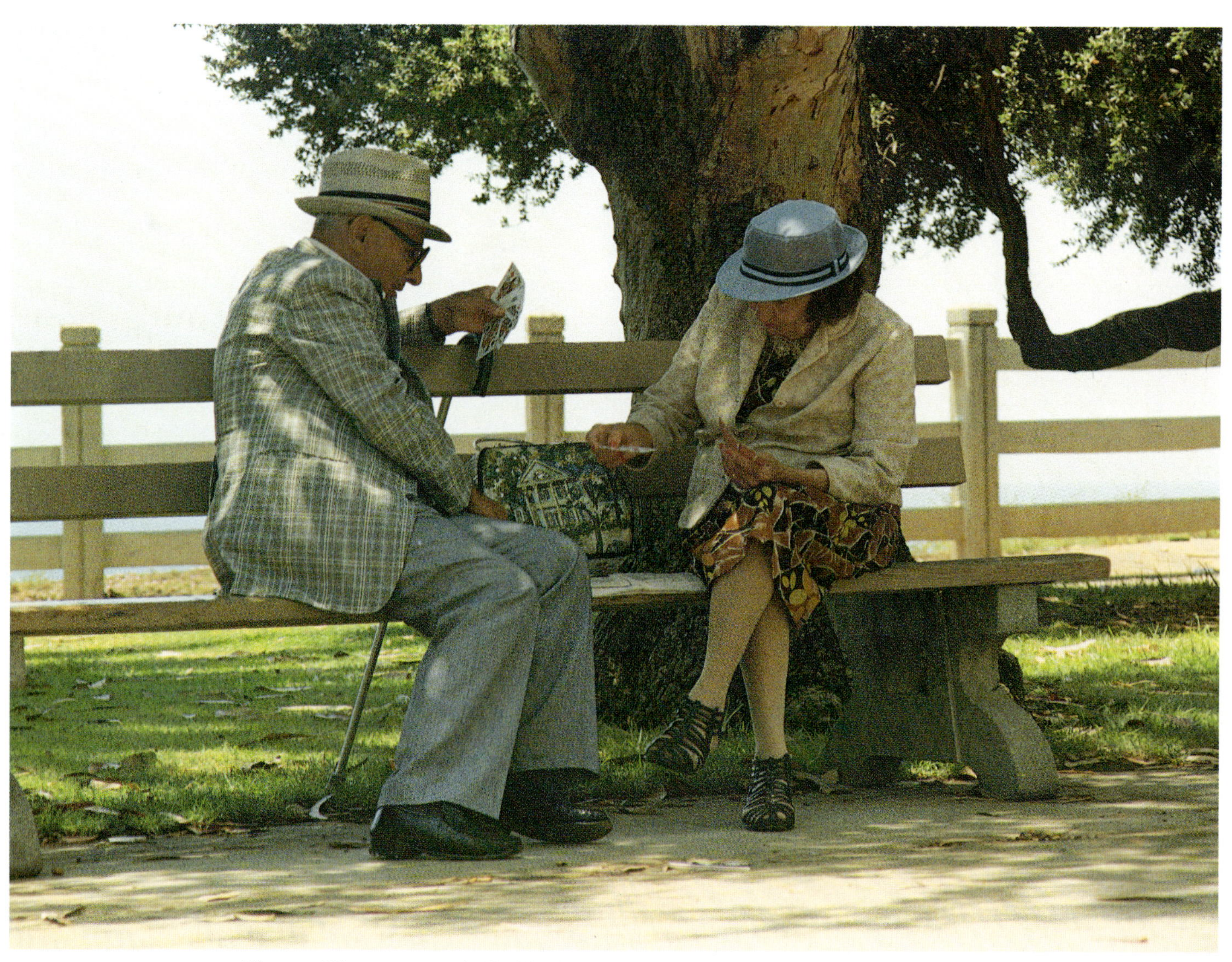

Herman Klepper, 74, and Gladdys Brighton, 71, stay cool in the summer shade as they play a friendly game of cards. Photo by Harricklia Maria Hadjian of Canton, Ohio.

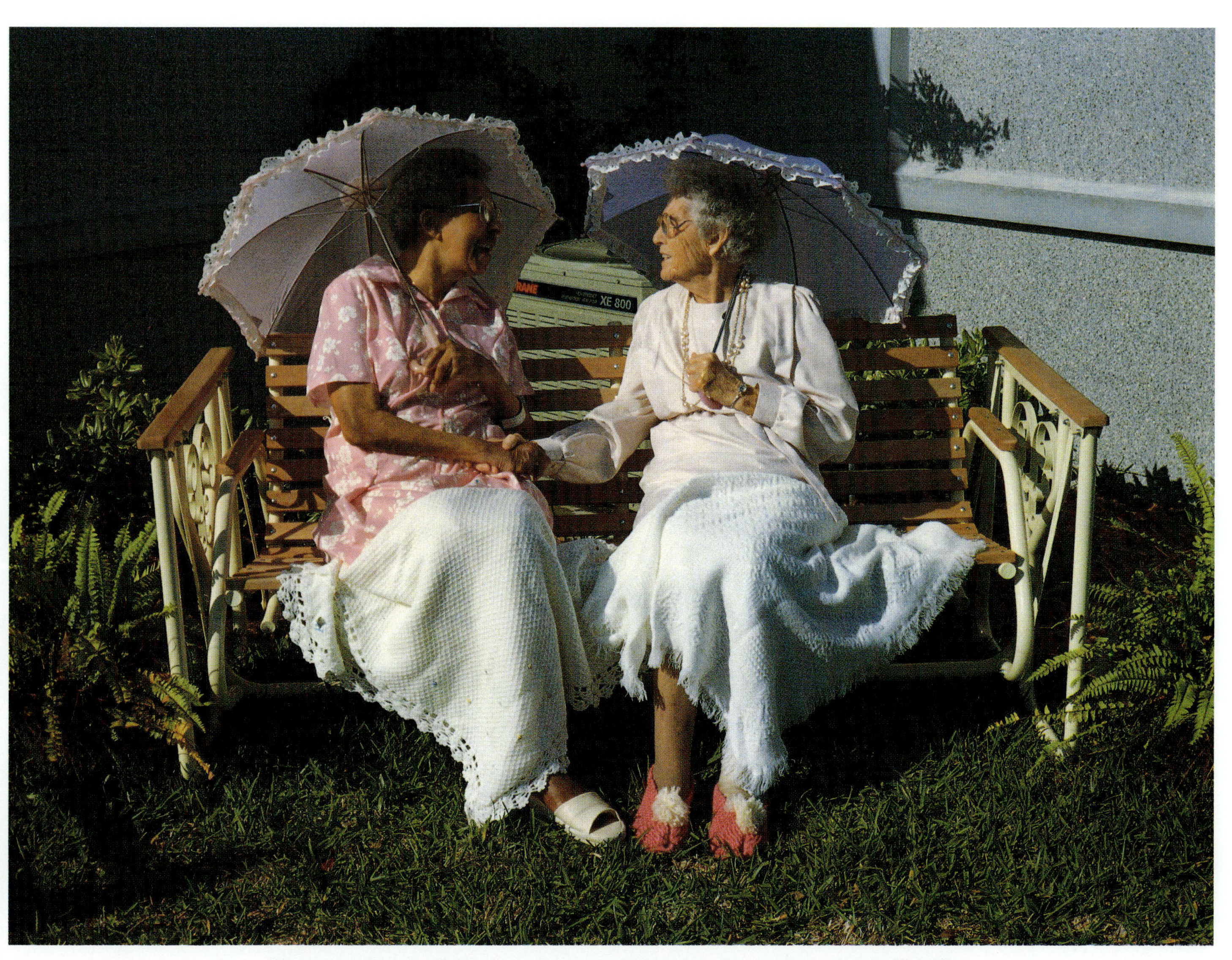

*Altamease Harris (left), born Sept. 4, 1910, takes the sun in Jacksonville, Fla.,
with her good friend Loucinda Crews, who was born May 3, 1899. Photo by
Debra Scott of Jacksonville.*

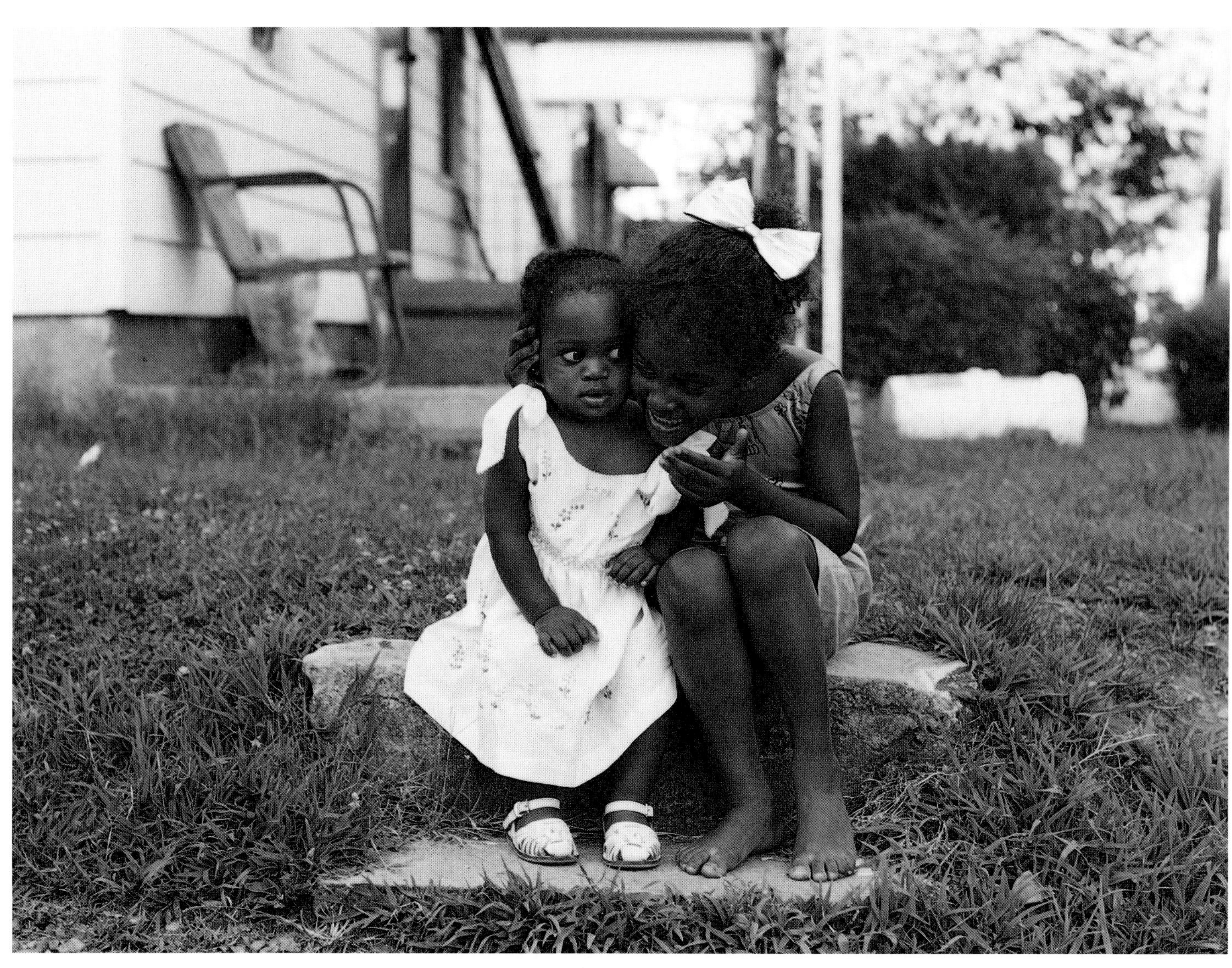

Sharon Pearson, 4, cajoles Tierra Lawrence, 18 months, on a summer day in Memphis. Photo by Leslie D. Settles.

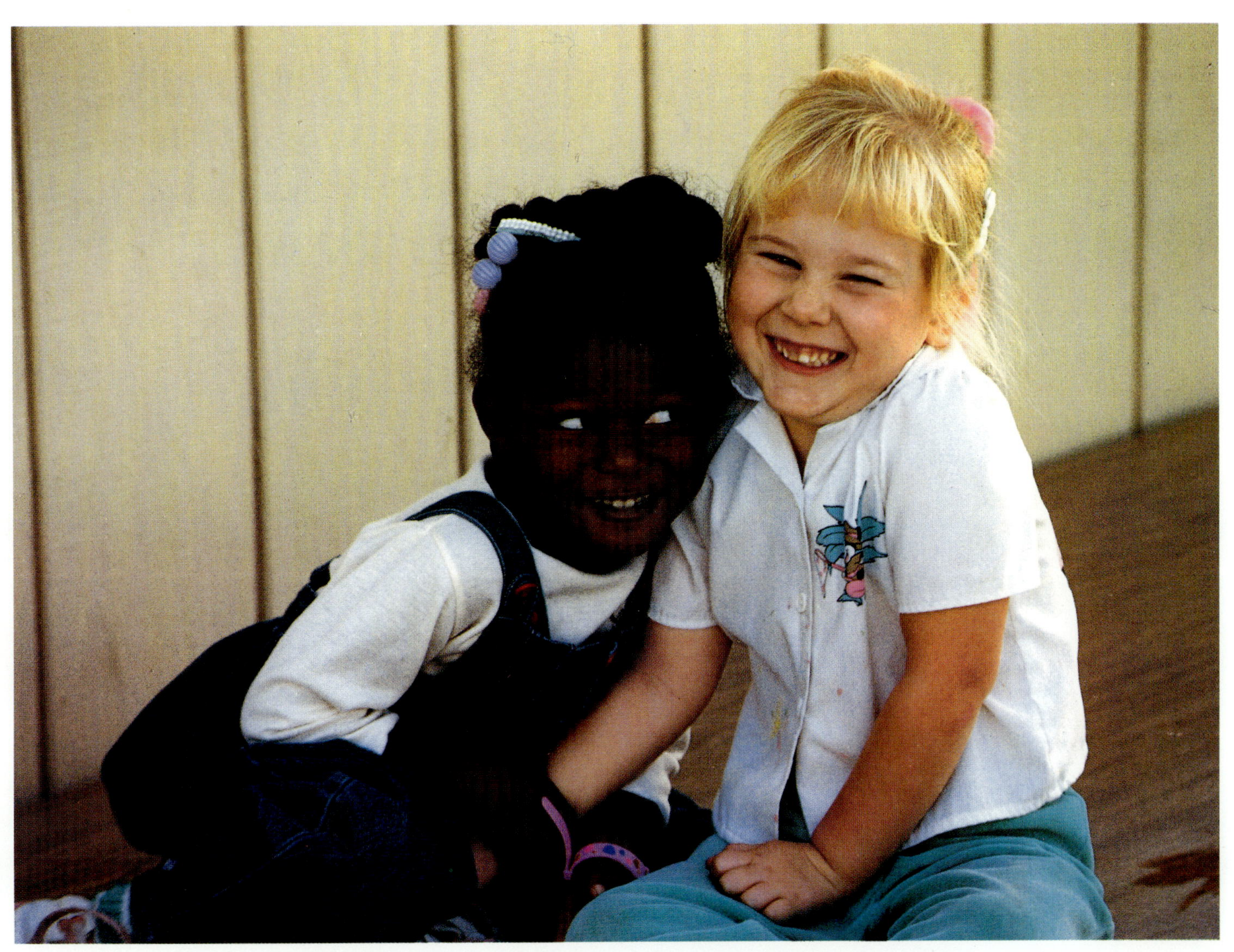

Inseparable: Natasha Park (left) and Melanie Riffle, both 4, share a giggle. "They're almost always together," says the photographer, Chris Penning, a teacher's aide in their pre-school class in Fresno, Calif.

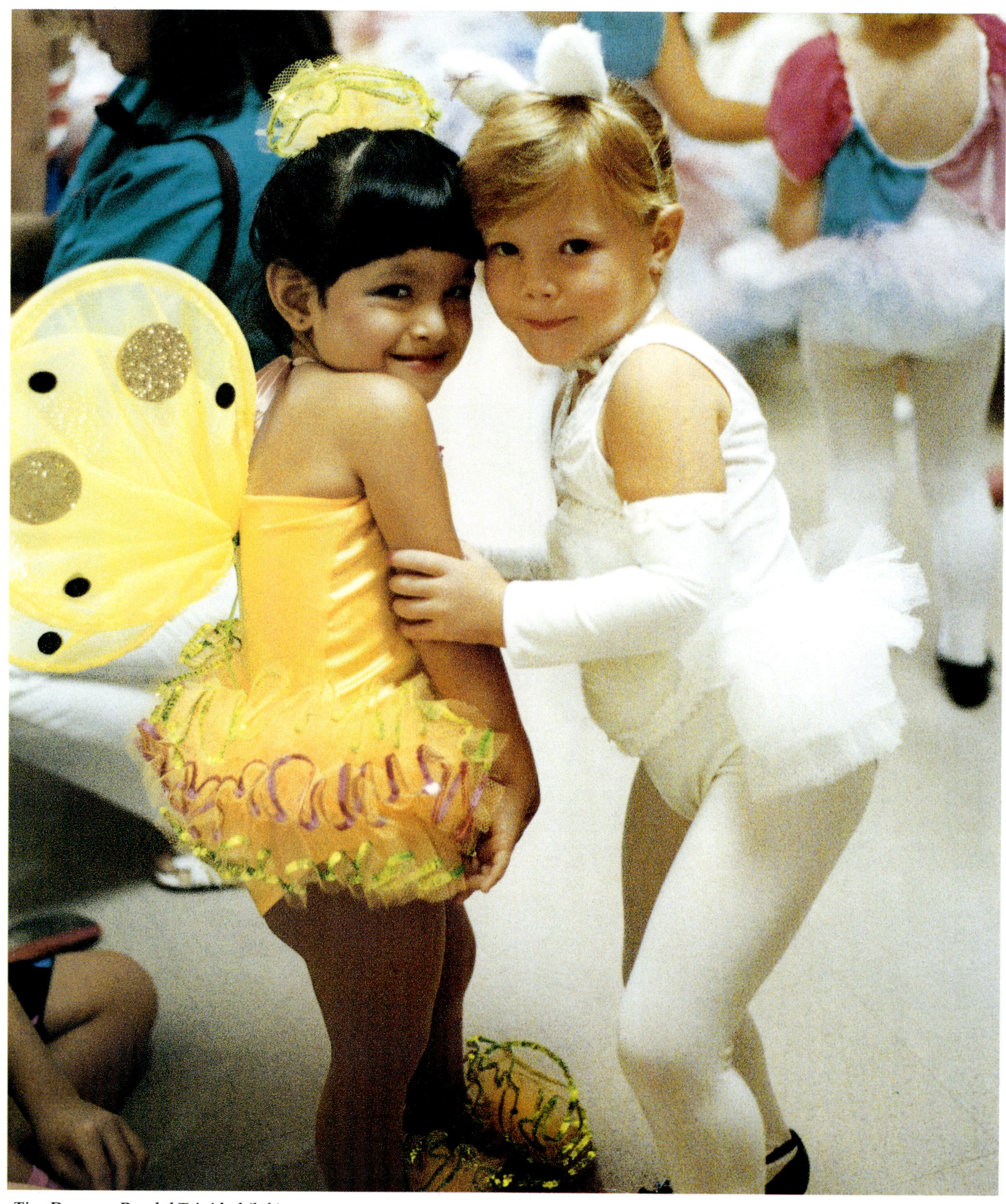

Tiny Dancers: Randal Trinidad (left), 3, and Heather Williams, 4, backstage at their first dance recital. Photo by Randal's mother, Linda Olivarri de Trinidad of Jacksonville, Fla.

New Easter duds draw smiles from the Illig boys—Nicholas (left), 6, and Christopher, 5—of Portland, Ore. Photo by "Aunt Ivy" FrancesP, a friend of the boys' mom, Mary Kay Illig.

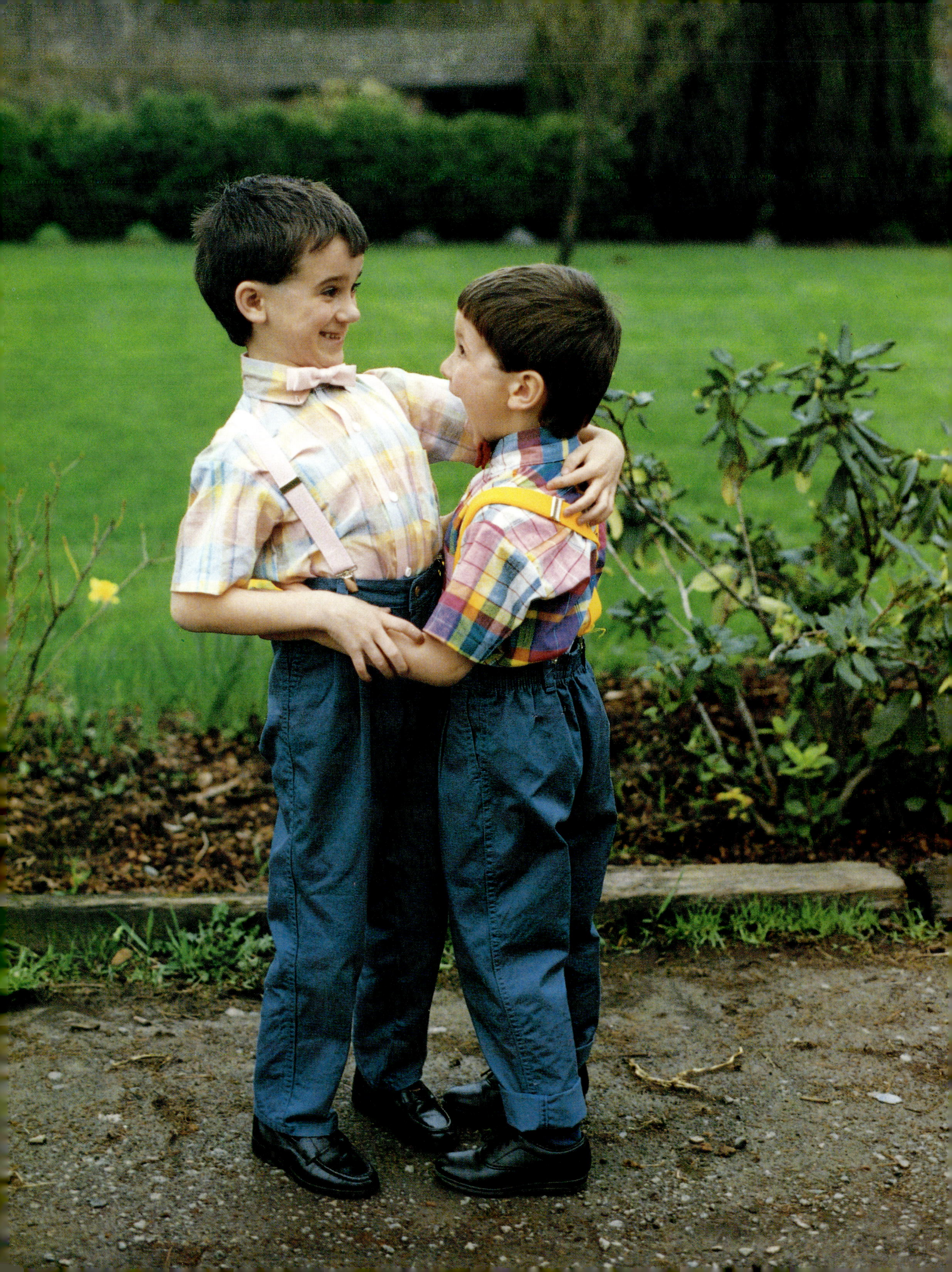

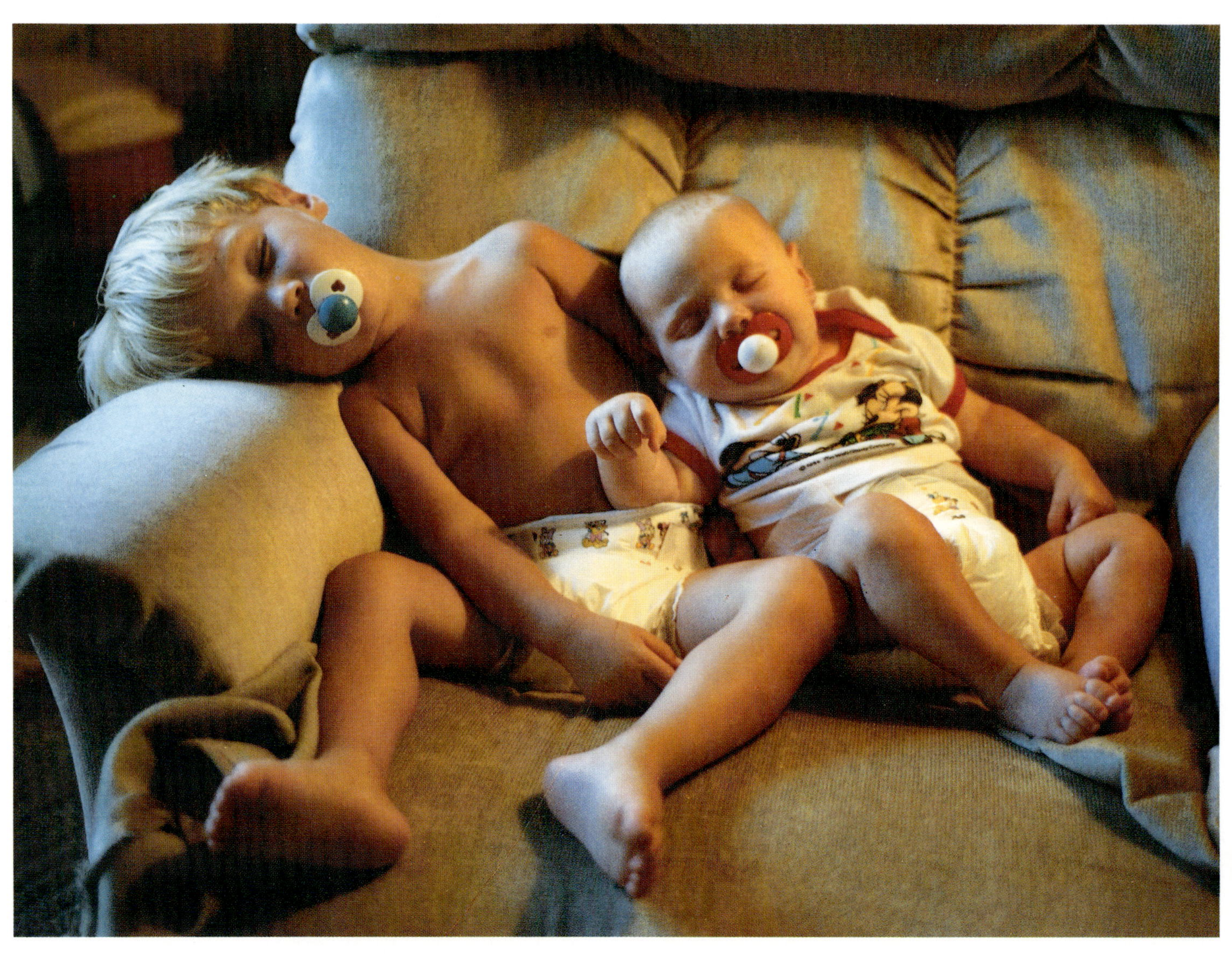

Snoozers: Kenny Norkiewicz, 2, and his brother, Danny, 3 months, nap in Dad's chair. Photo by their mother, Nancy Norkiewicz of Orland Hills, Ill.

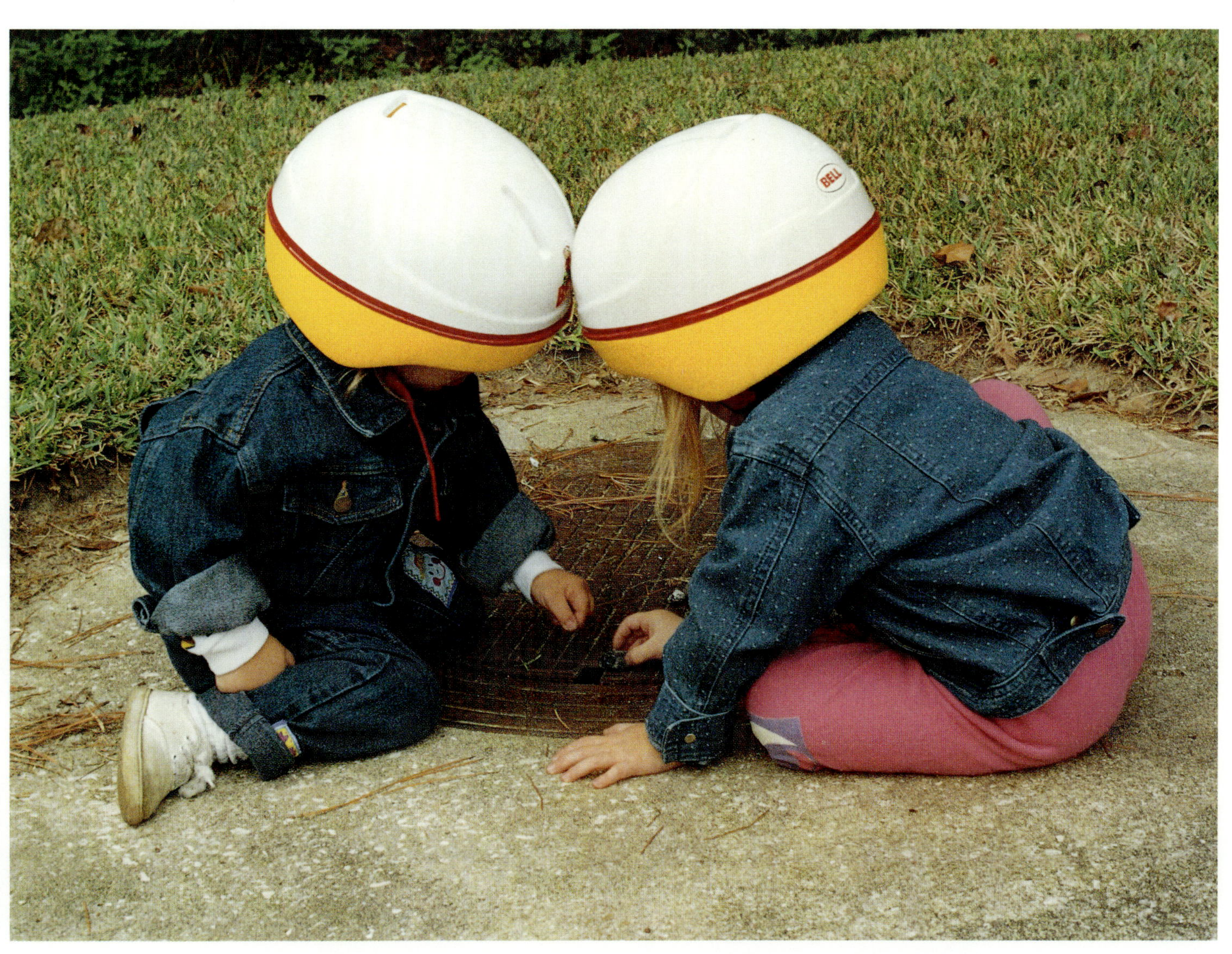

Lost in Play: Danielle Lee Keeter, 4, and Sydnie Ann Keeter, 3, are totally absorbed in…well, only they know for sure. Photo by their mother, Peggy Keller Keeter of Gainesville, Fla.

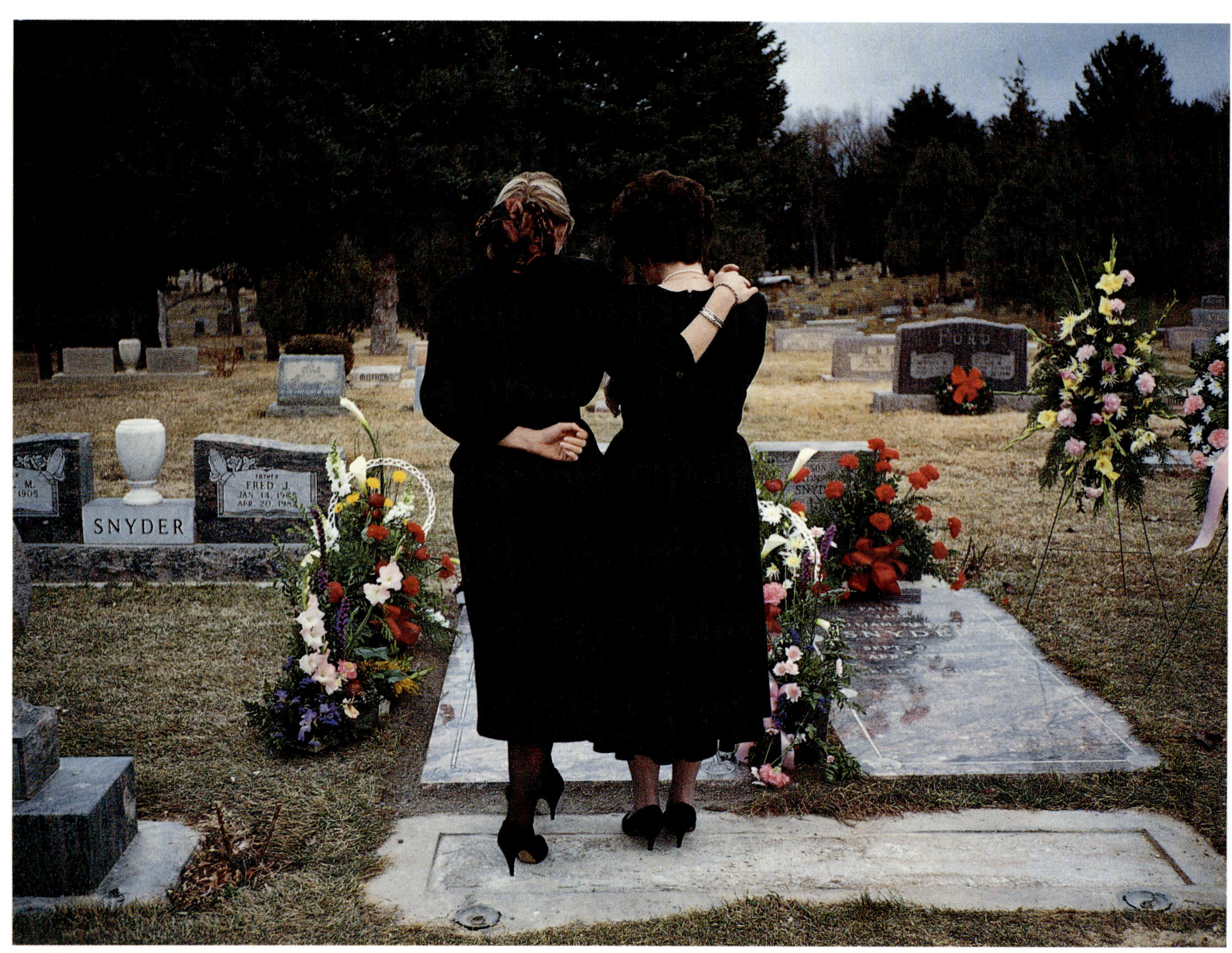

Sisters and Friends: Cynthia Snyder Baiardi of Durango, Colo., and Susan Snyder Ricks of Grand Junction, Colo., mourn the loss of a grandmother. Susan's husband, Galen, took the photo.

Hello to a Friend: Joey Orbe, 7, of Portage, Ind., took a flower to the grave of Ryan Bogart, with whom he used to play. Photo by Linda McPeek of Portage.

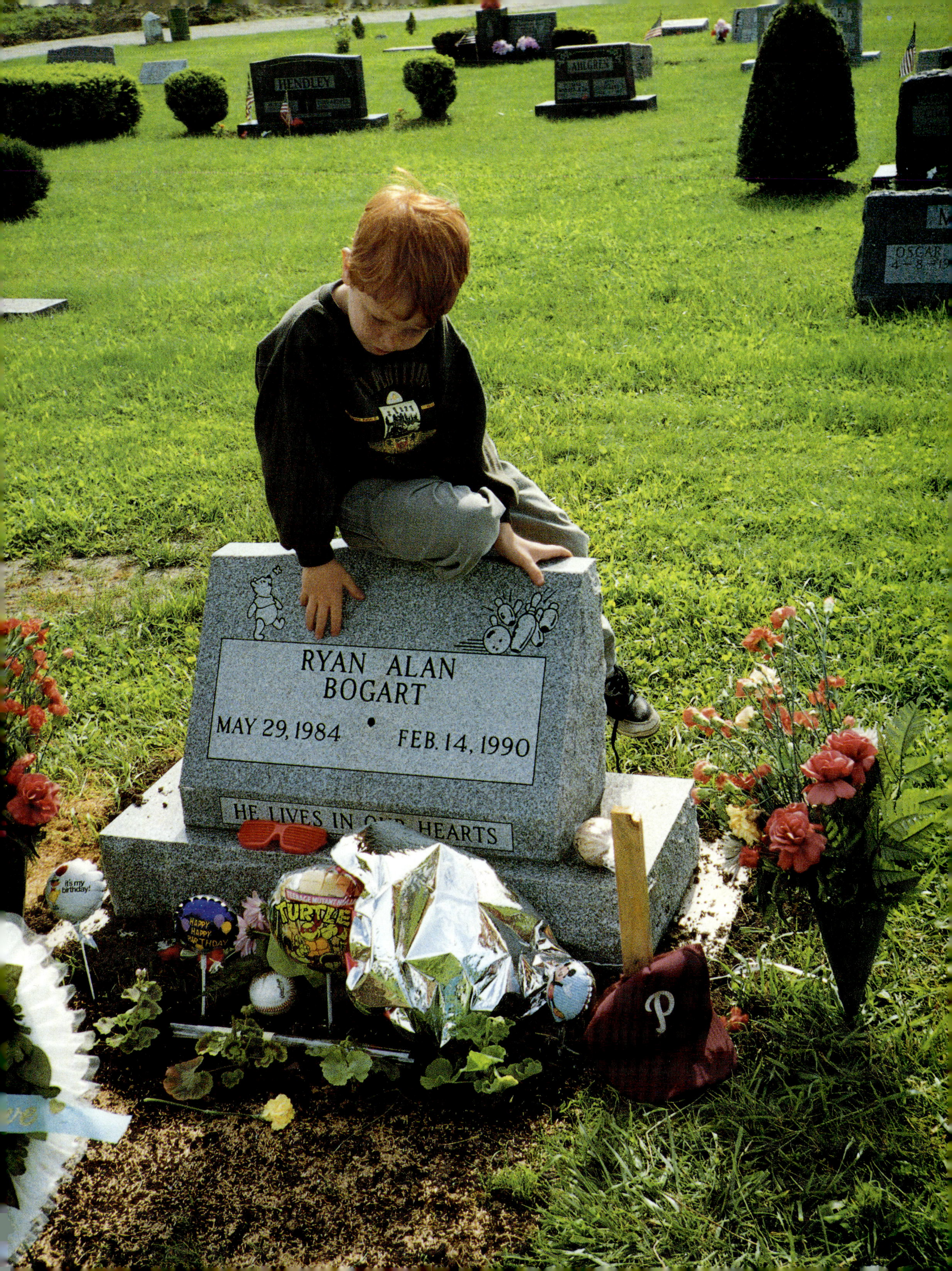

RYAN ALAN
BOGART
MAY 29, 1984 • FEB. 14, 1990
HE LIVES IN OUR HEARTS

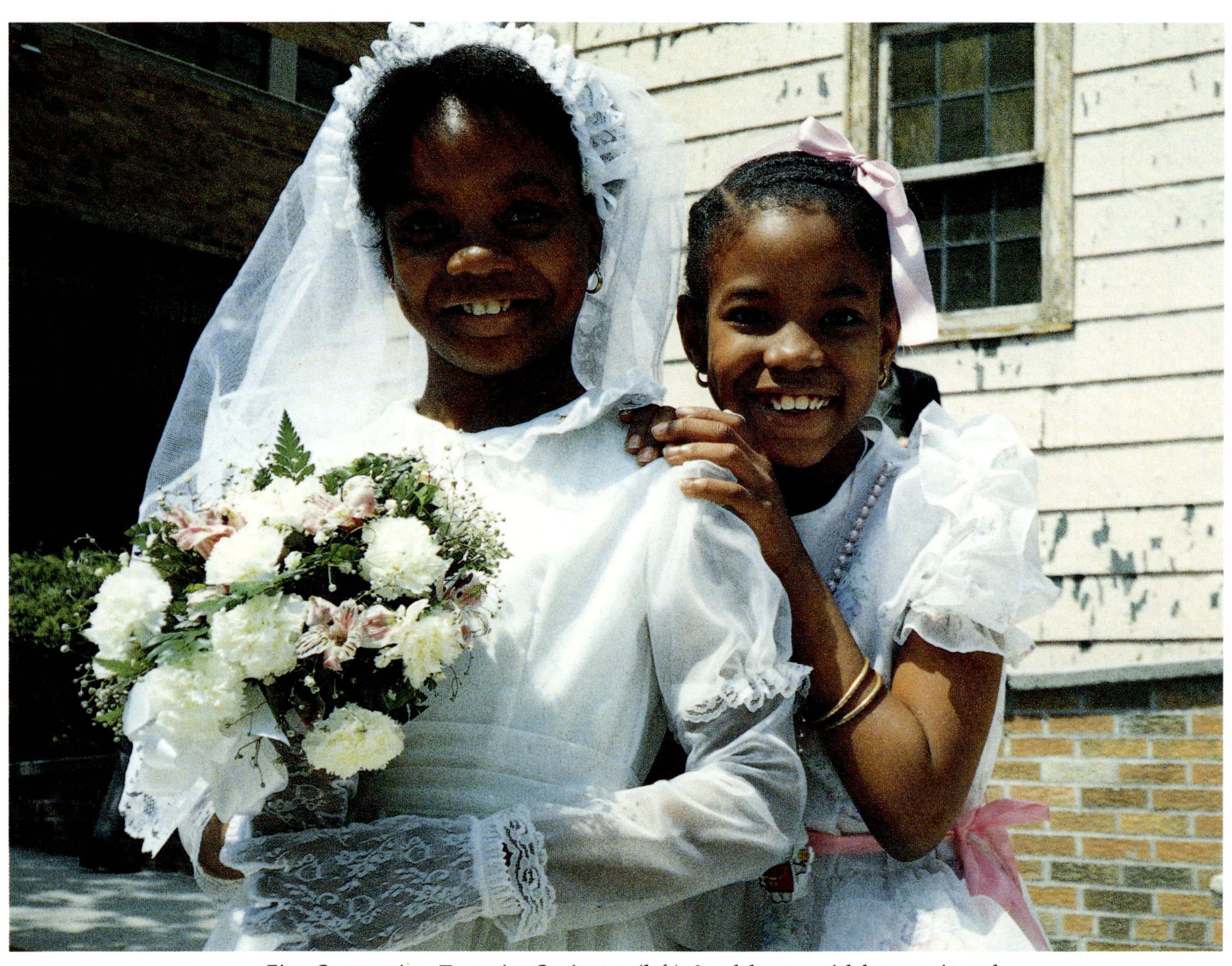

First Communion: Tramaine Covington (left), 9, celebrates with her cousin and best friend, Rahsheeda Covington, also 9. Photo by their aunt, Leslie Phillips-Covington of Albany, N.Y.

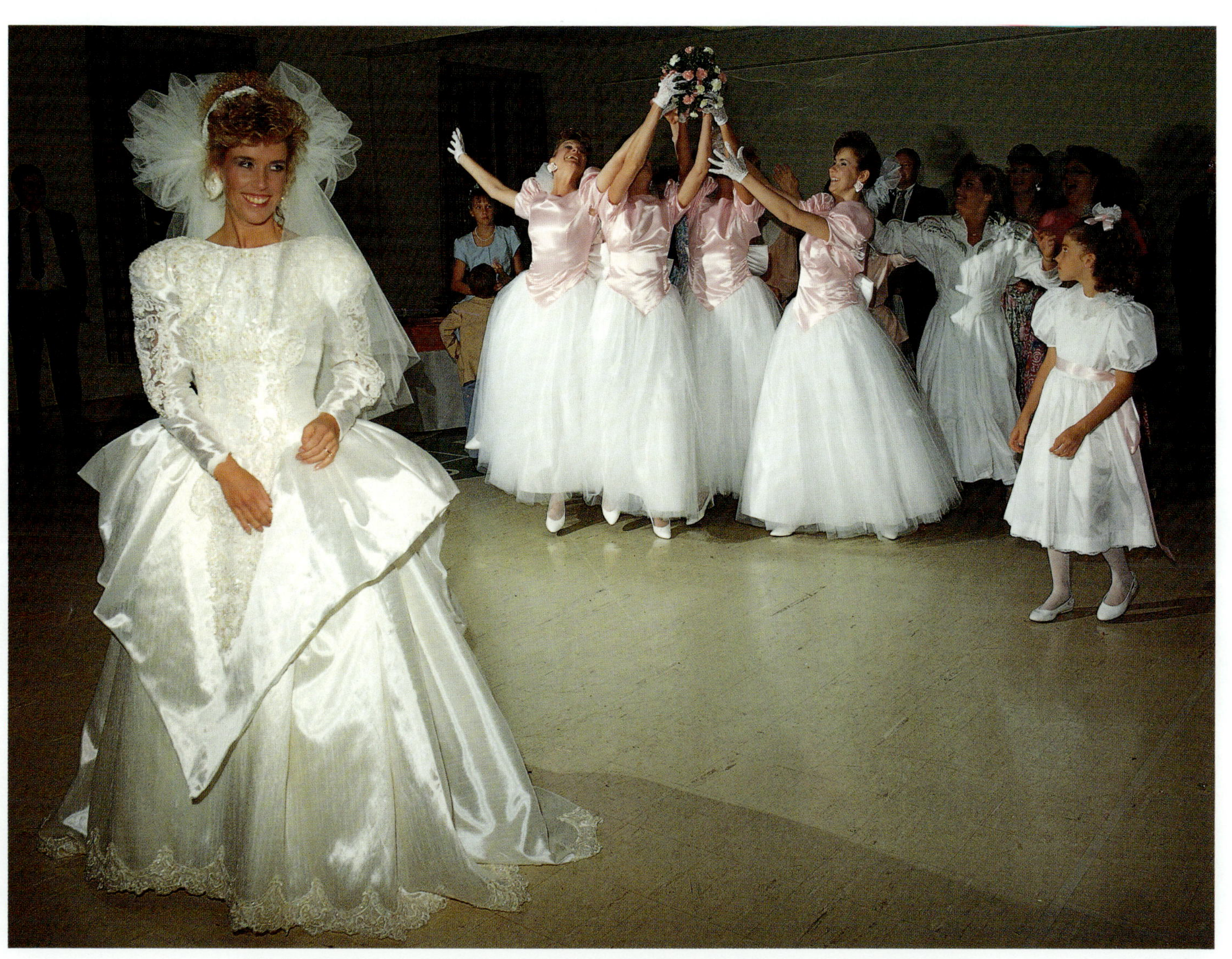

Sharing the Joy: Lada E. Horn, 24, just wed in Morristown, Tenn., celebrates with (from right) Kendra Shastid, 8, Melissa D. Livesay, 24, and lots of other friends. Photo by George Keener of Morristown.

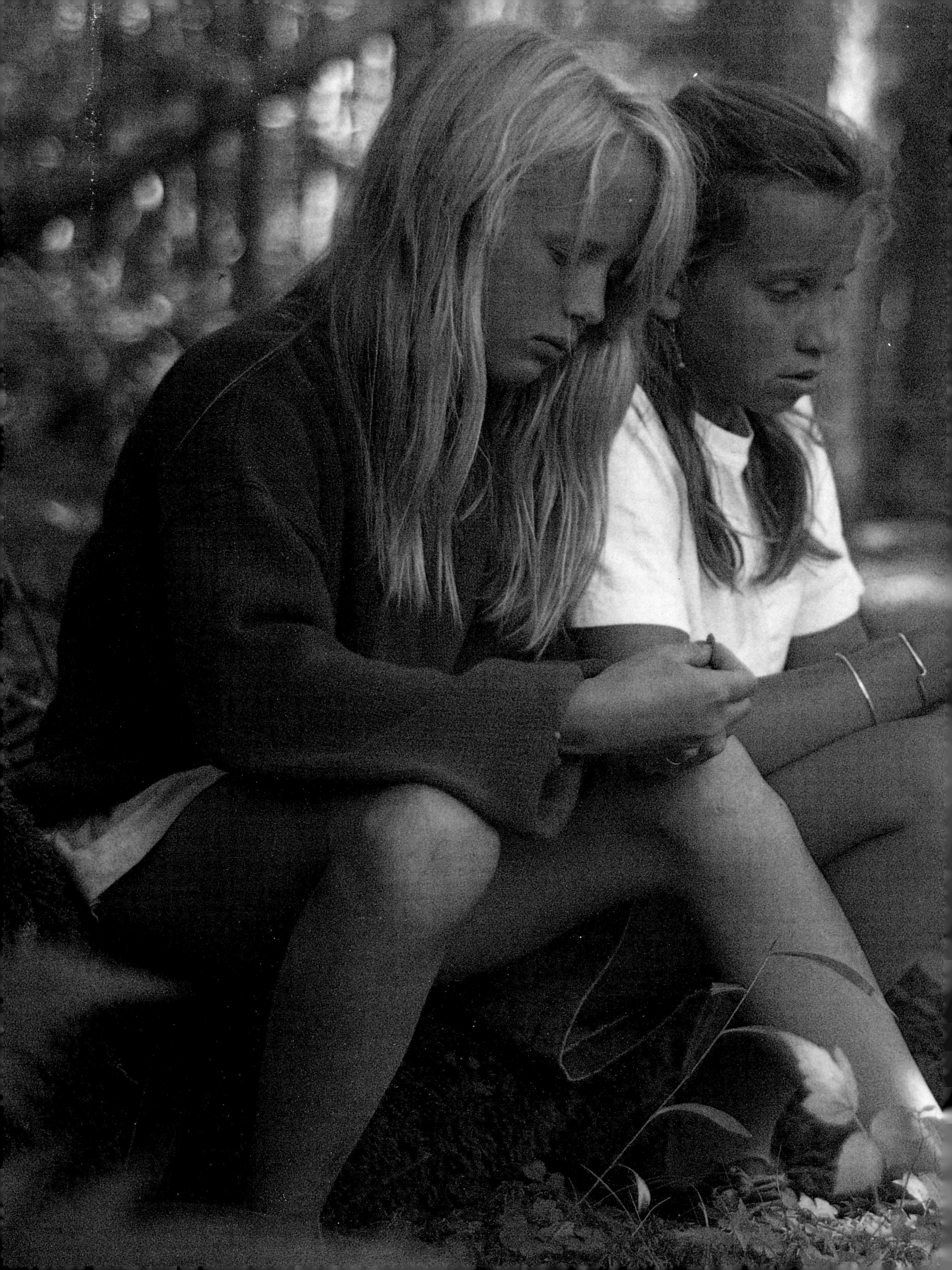

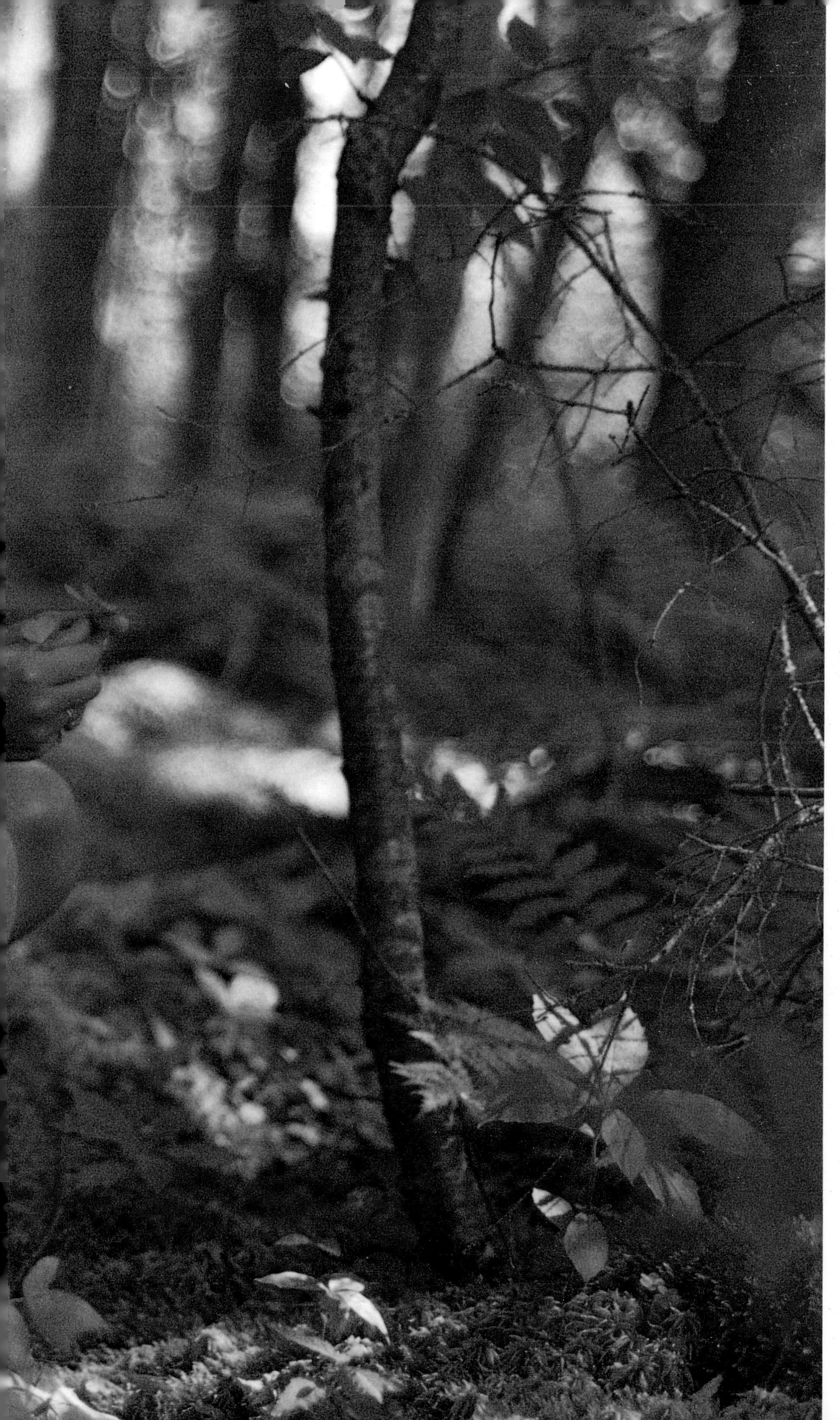

A Place To Be Alone…Together: Leah Bicknell, 15, with her friend Jesse Robinson, 14, in the woods of Metinic Island, Maine. Photo by Leah's cousin, Elizabeth Tarr Carey of Dedham, Mass.

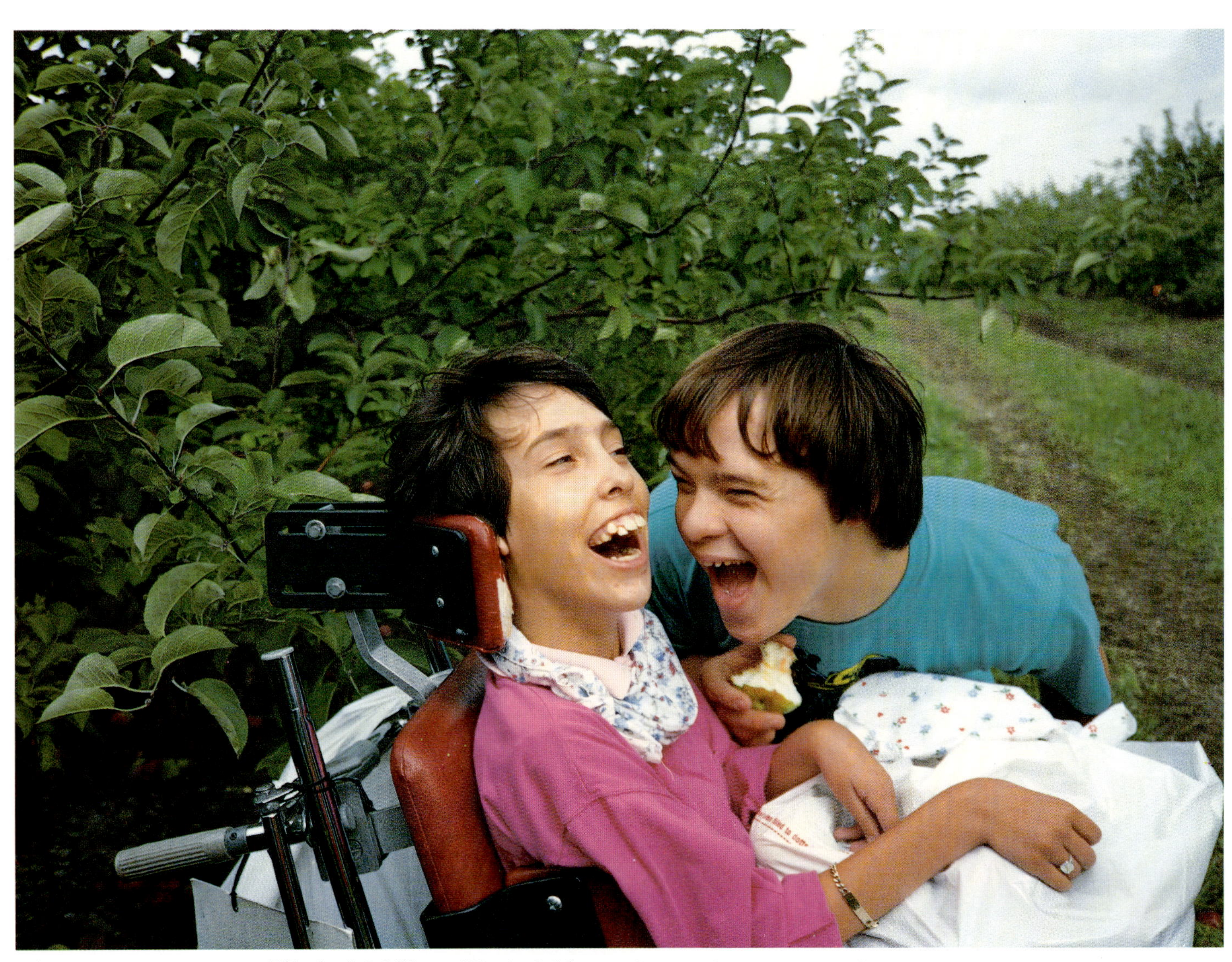

Elizabeth Schilly and Kevin Cobb—students and part-time employees—enjoy an outing to an apple orchard. Photo by Tom Parker of Fayettesville, N.Y., a teacher in the Jamesville-Dewitt special education program.

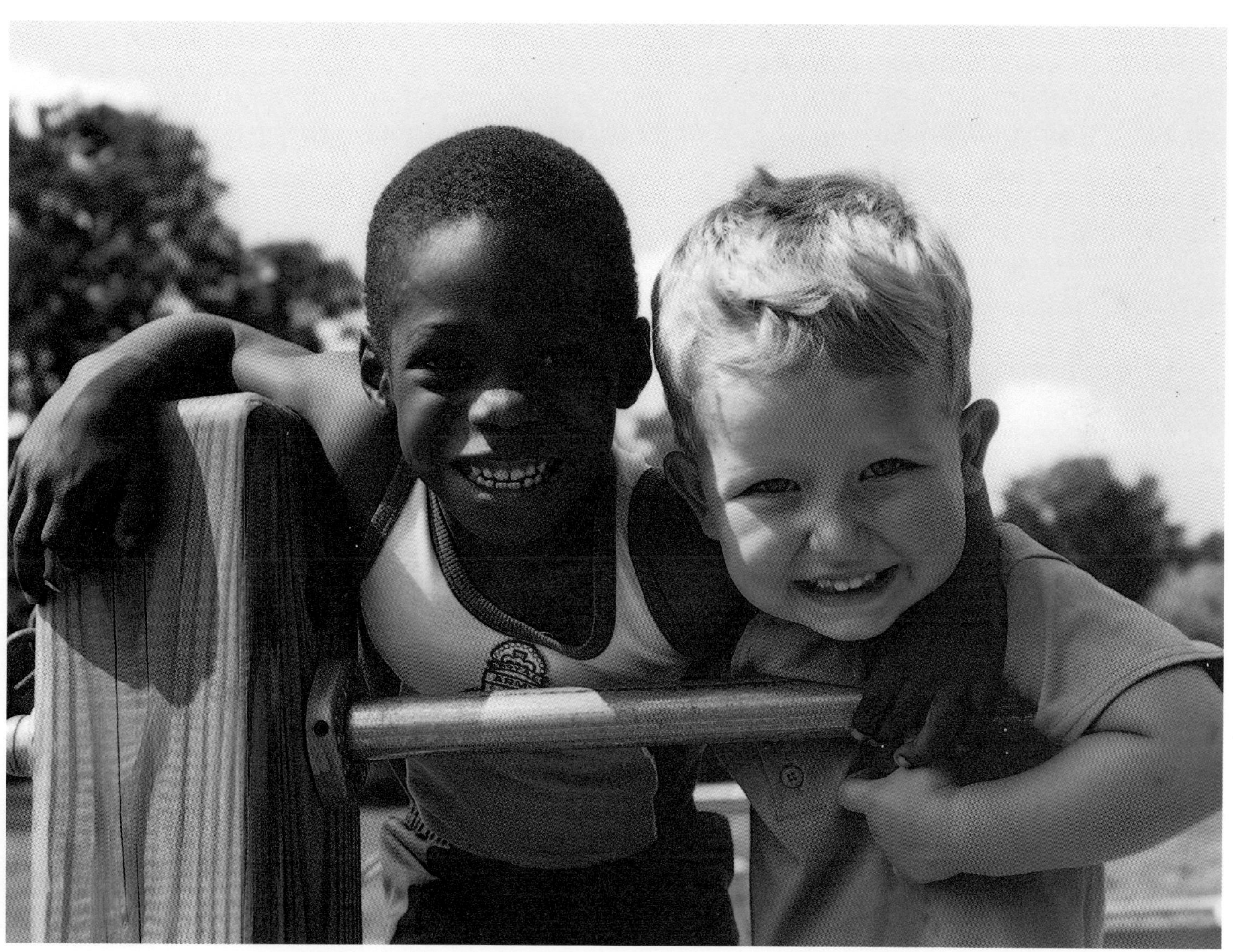

*At the Playground: Timmy Cooper Paris (left), 7, and Seth David Klinger, 3,
pause in their play to muster a grin for Seth's mother, Kiki. Both boys live in
Lima, Ohio.*

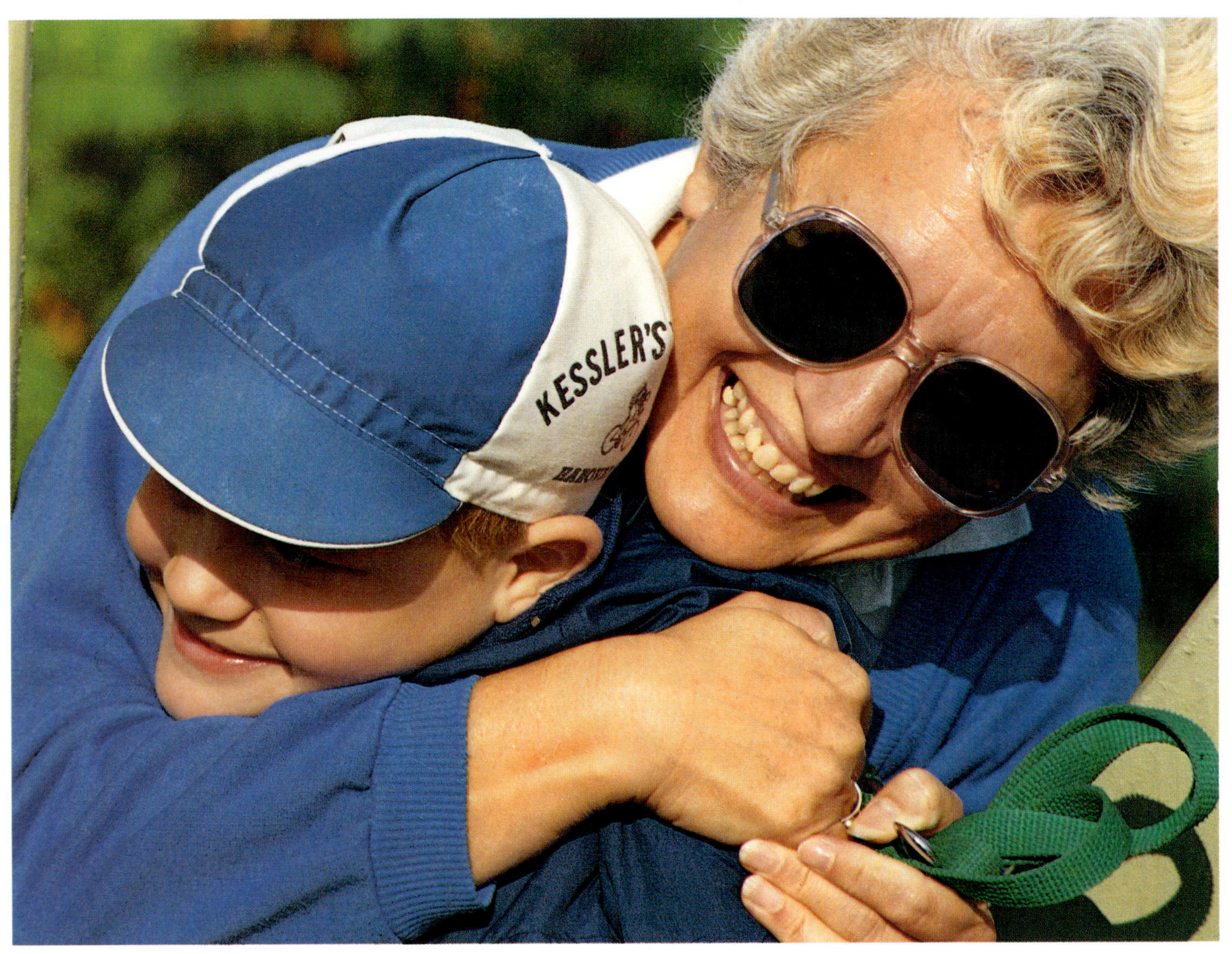

The Simple Pleasures. Nancy Jenkins, 52, and grandson, Tommy, 8, spend a brisk autumn day together. Photo by Russell's mother, Pamela M. Jenkins of Norfolk, Va.

For George F. Grant III of Denver, the best catch of a fishing trip is a happy moment with his son, Alexander, 19 months. Vienna M. Grant took this photo near Wright's Reservoir in Florissant, Colo.

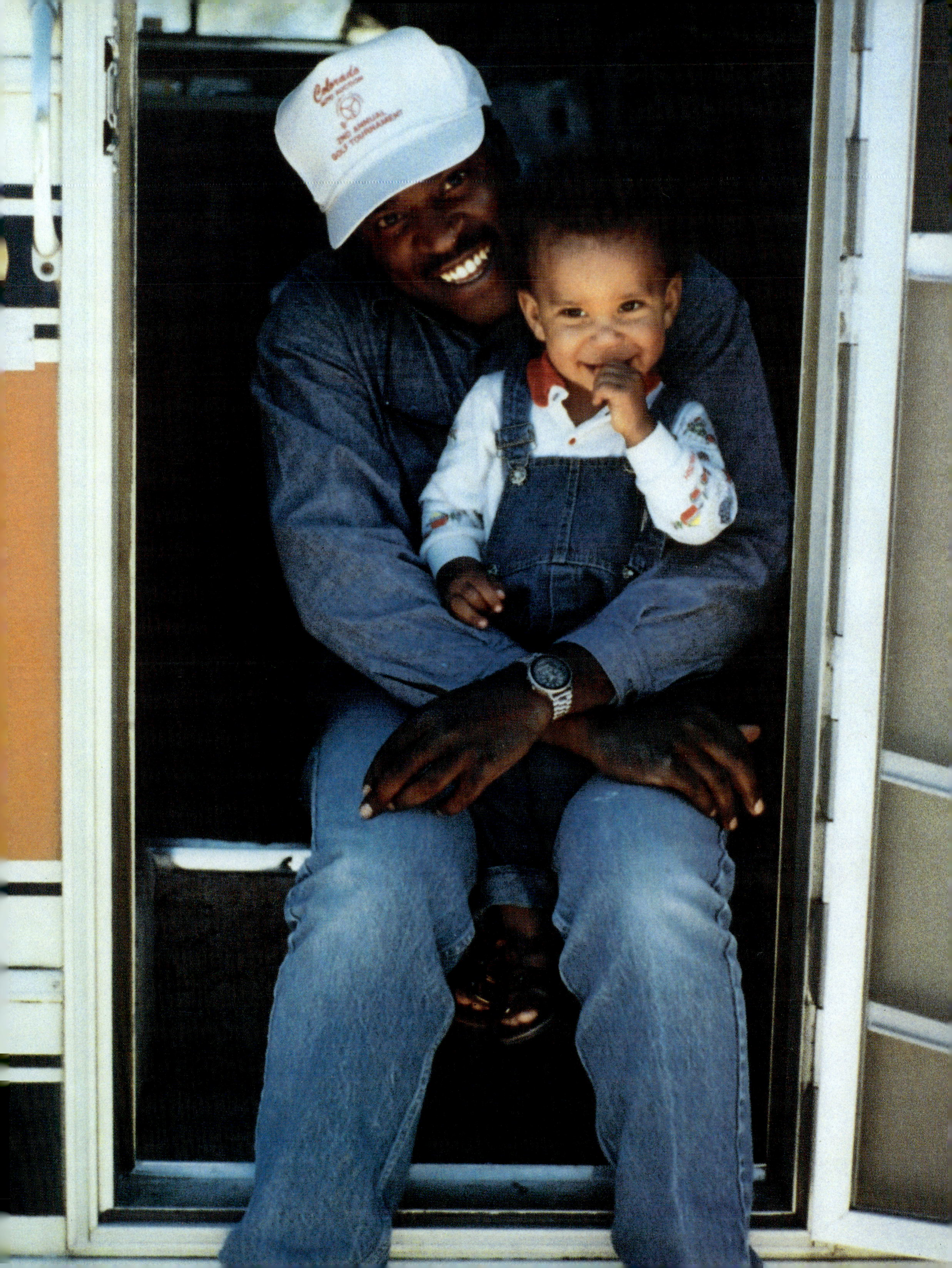

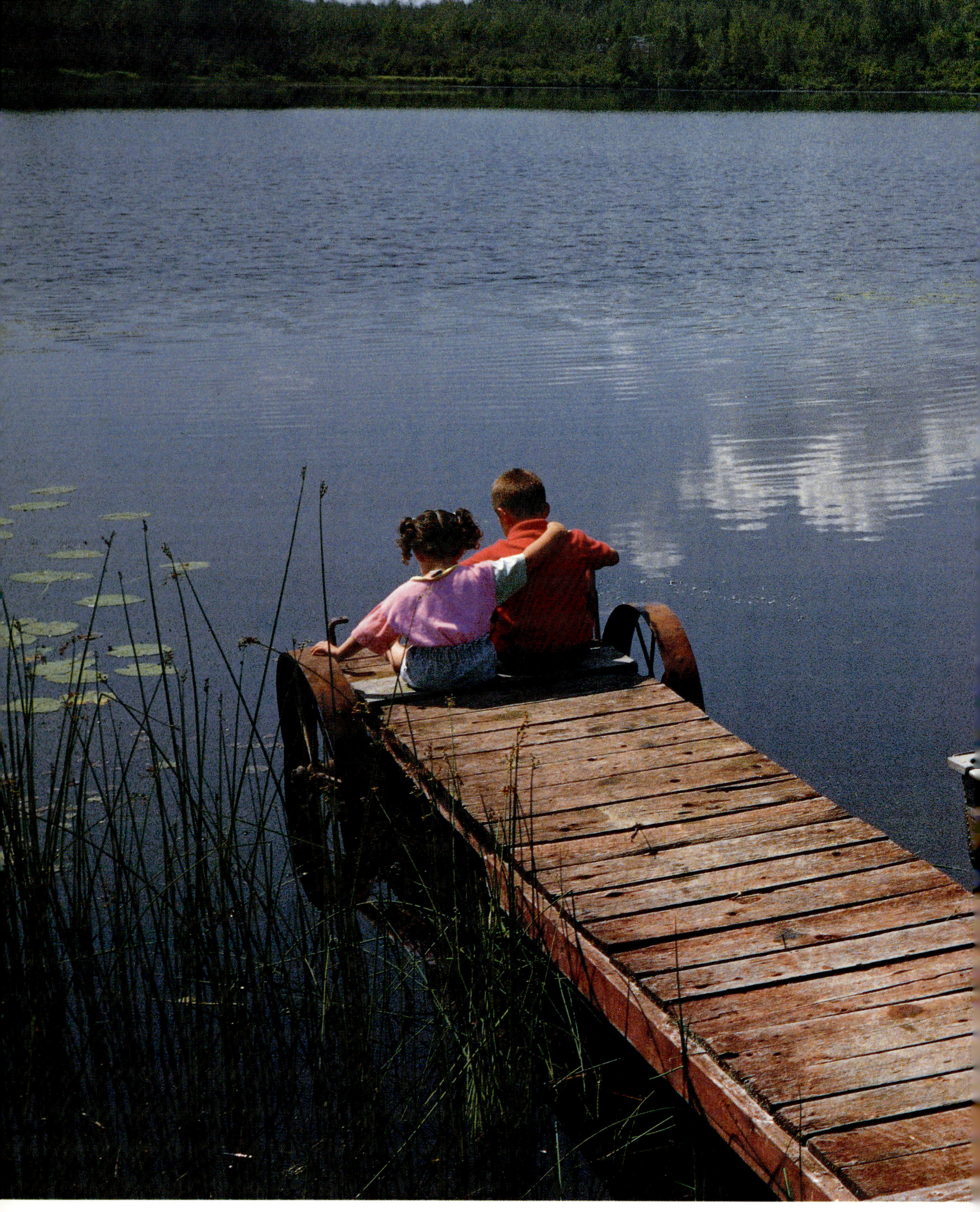

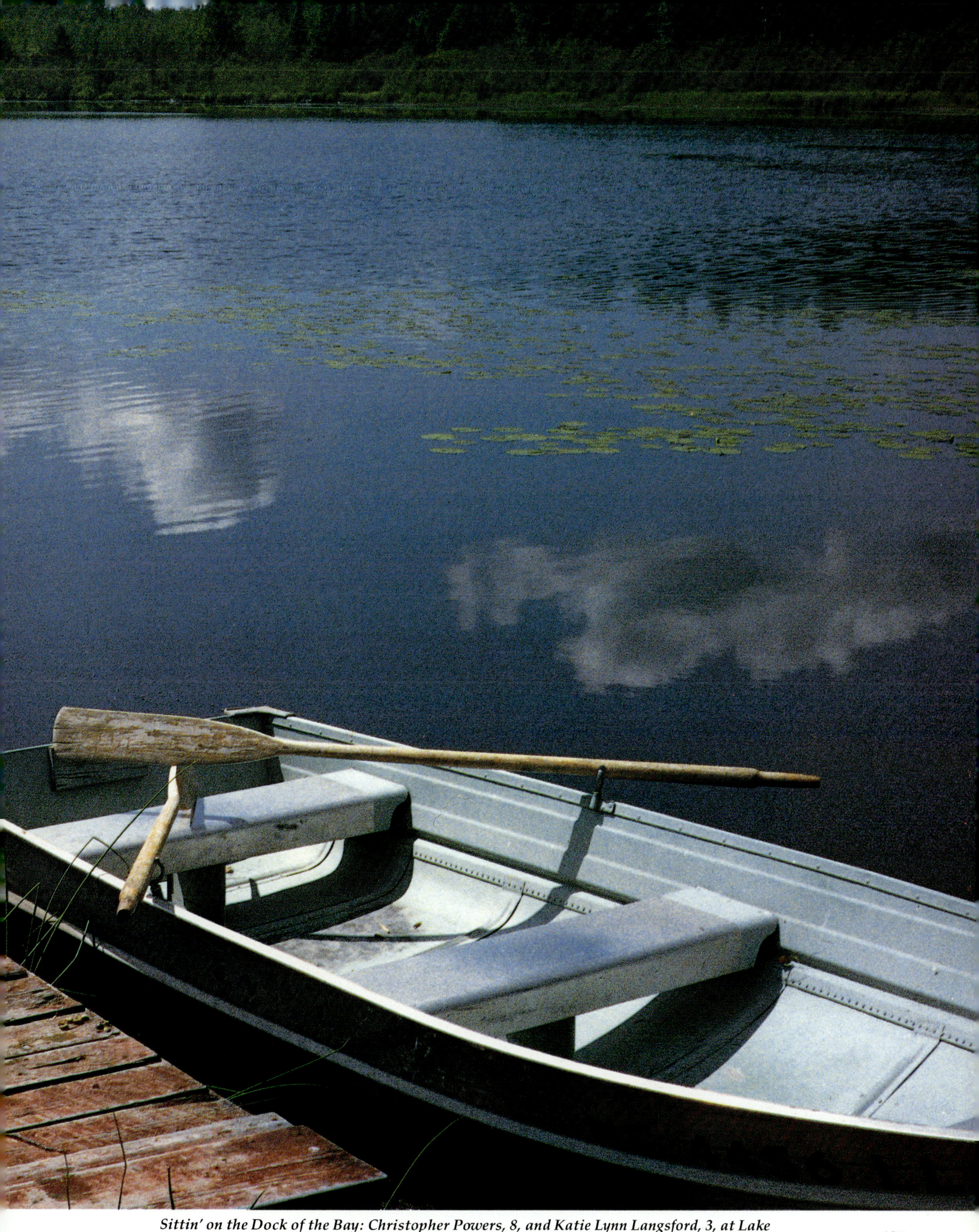

Sittin' on the Dock of the Bay: Christopher Powers, 8, and Katie Lynn Langsford, 3, at Lake Benton in Dickinson County, Mich. Photo by their great-uncle, Mark Bollone of Boston.

"What is a friend? A single soul dwelling in two bodies."
—Aristotle

"A friend is a poem."
—Persian Proverb

"When a friend speaks to me, whatever he says is interesting."
—Jean Renoir

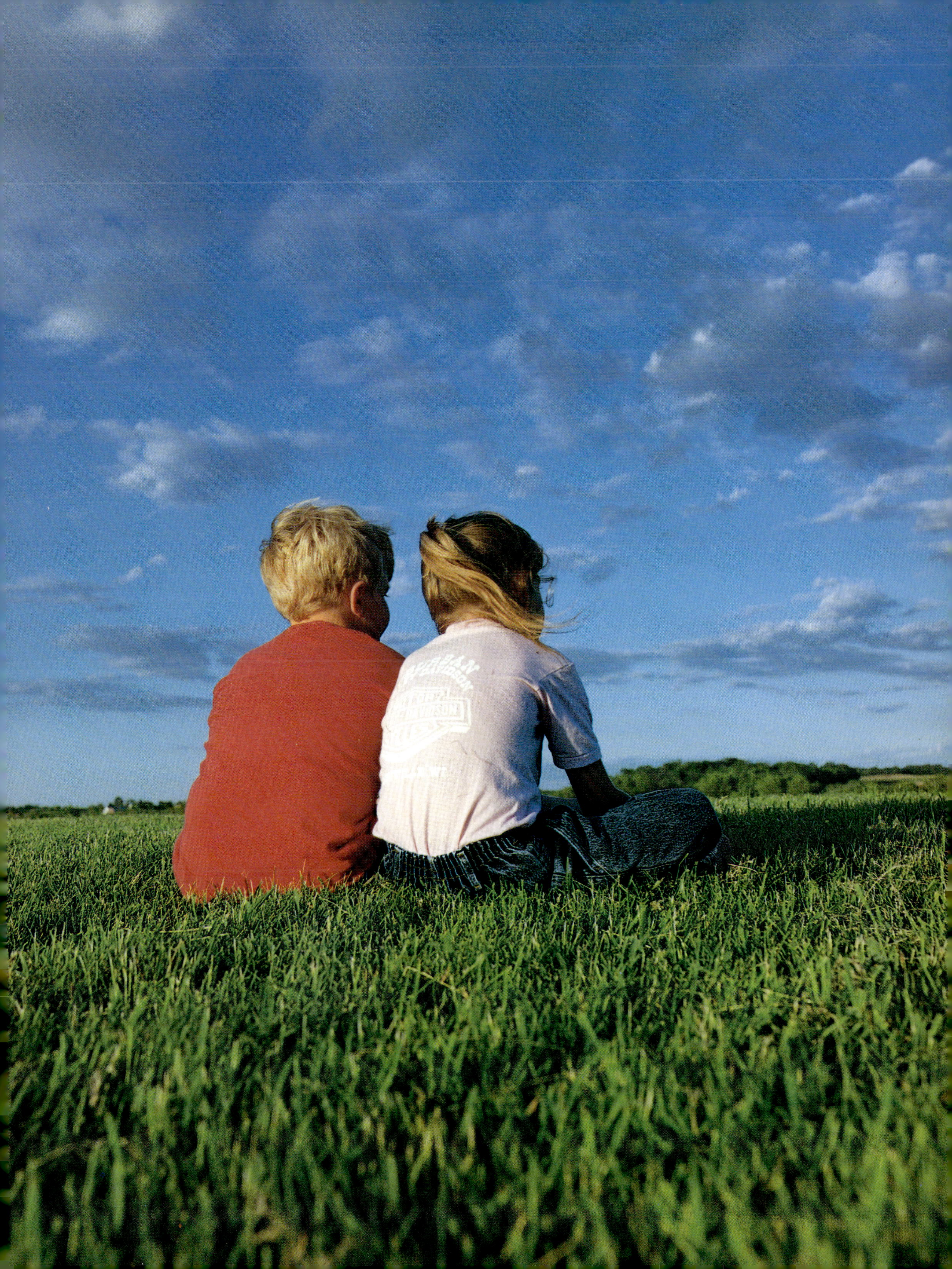

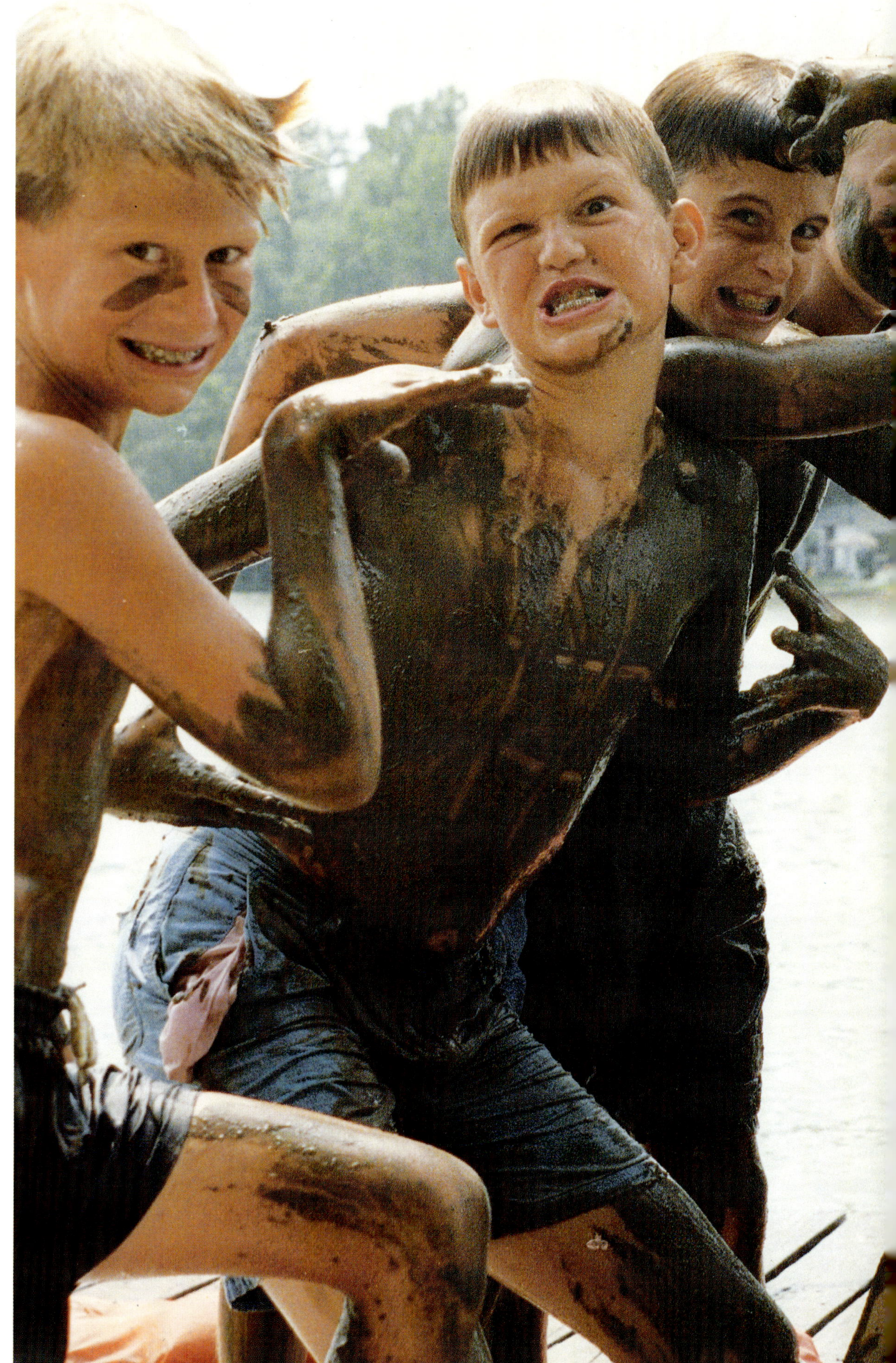

Good, Clean Fun: At a spend-the-night birthday party for Rob Bouton, the boys decide to cover themselves with mud from the bottom of Saluda Lake in Greenville, S.C. Front: Stewart Caldwell. Back (from left): Worth Beacham, Will Dellinger, Bill Bouton, Paul Holder, Will Dennis, Rob and Clay Mardre. Photo by Ralph R. Bouton, Rob's father.

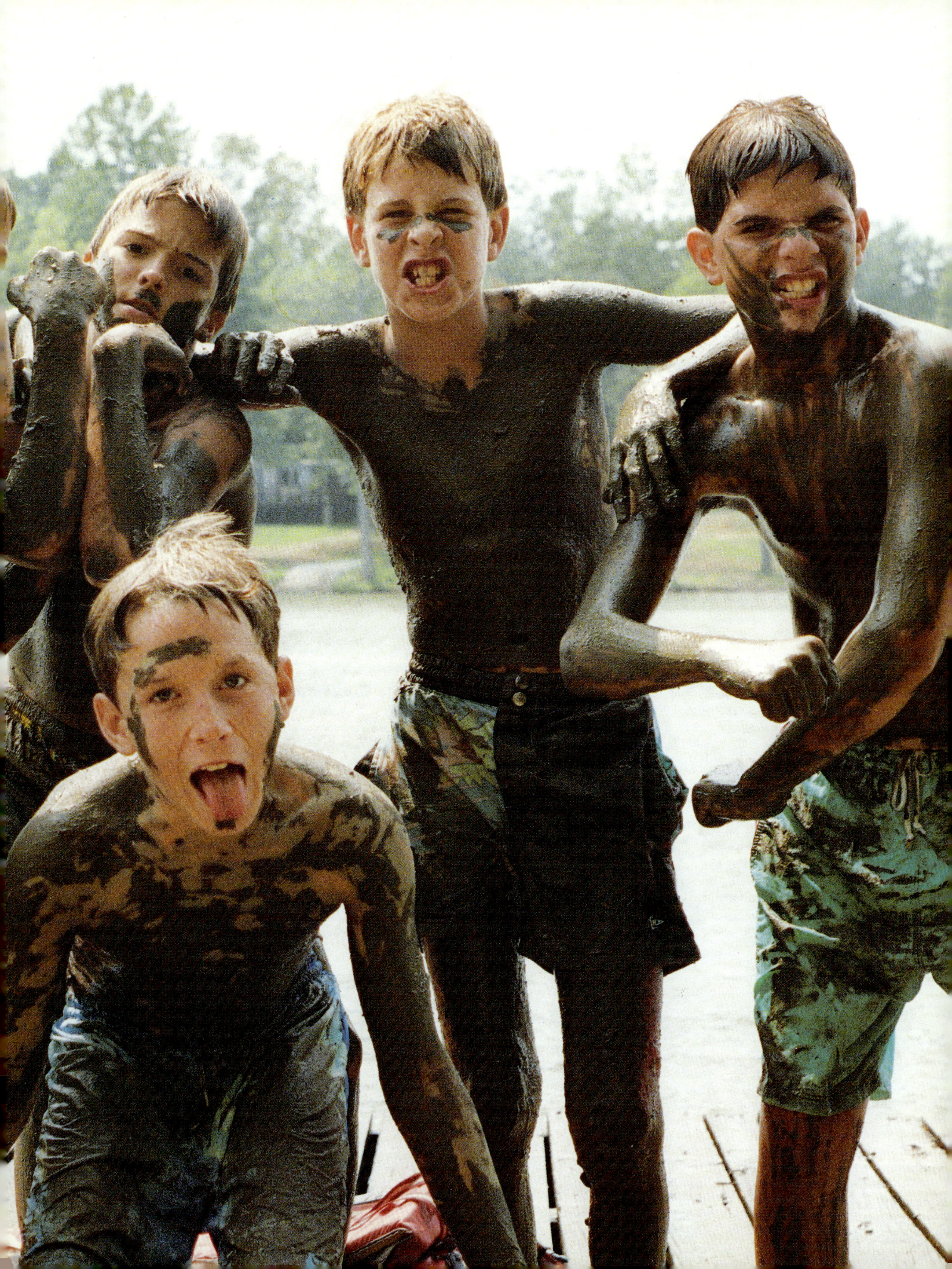

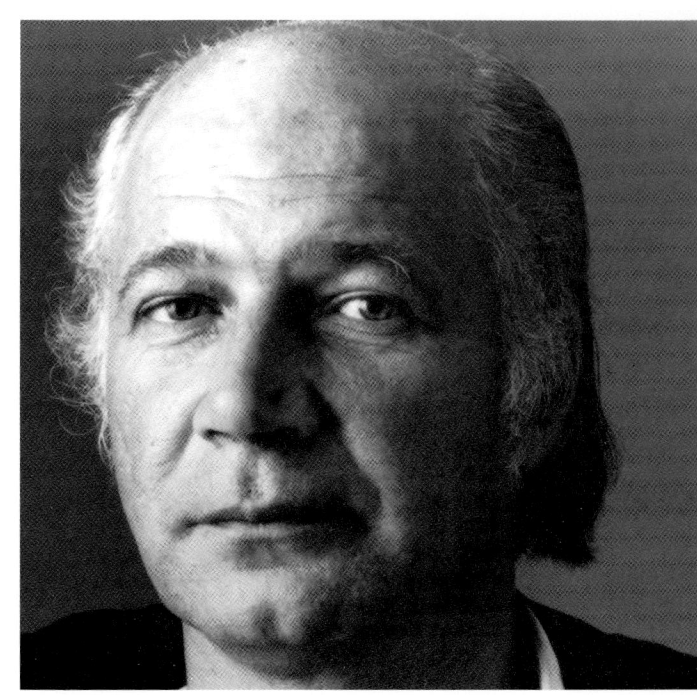

Eddie Adams

The subject for this photo book was a hit with *Parade* readers. And why not—"Best Friends" is a topic that allows for all the trappings of great photography. There are people in almost every picture—something that I feel is most important for a successful photograph—and because they are best friends, there is love, warmth, humor and honesty.

Spontaneities is another important element in these pictures. These photographs are not formal portraits, nor were they intended to be, but rather they are nice, wonderful moments between best friends. With the technically advanced but easy-to-use cameras available, capturing a spontaneous moment has become much simpler. There really is no longer a need to concentrate on distance or light because the new cameras adjust to conditions automatically. The result: Everyone, no matter how amateur they think themselves to be, is capable of taking fine photographs, both in the technical and emotional senses.

I have been a judge for many, many picture competitions. No matter what the subject matter, no matter what the contest rules, there are always entries that have that certain something wonderful, that tug at the heart or grab for any of the emotions. This contest was no different. All the winning photographs in this book meet this criterion. I am happy to have been part of this contest, and I am happy to say that this is a book filled with truly great moments.

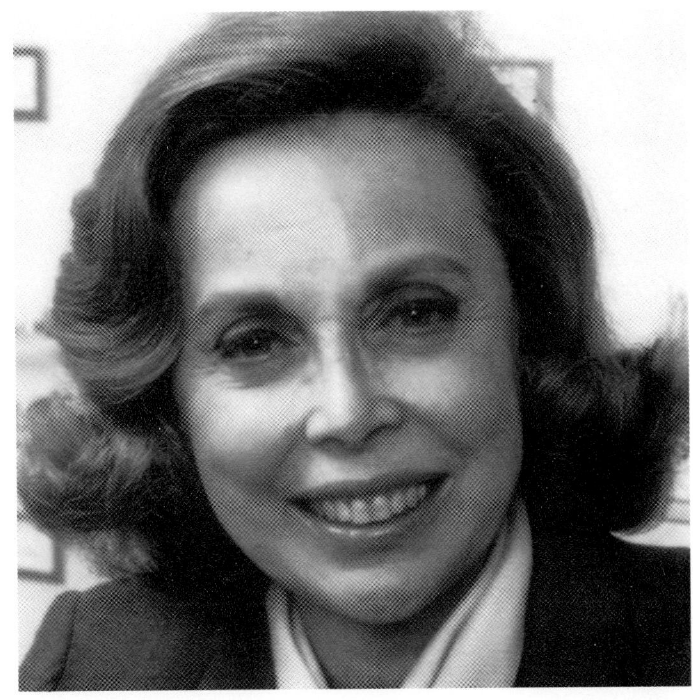

Joyce Brothers

Friendship is a pledge that covers varying degrees of strength and intensity and is as universal as the smile. We need all kinds of friends—neighbors, high school buddies, work mates and spouses alike. Whether we swap theories on child rearing over a cup of coffee, or just good mystery novels, all friends offer us the invitation to be ourselves.

Best friends, however, are considered a delicacy, an elite breed. Not everyone has the capacity to become your best friend, even though you share with them a special part of you. Best friends reach a higher level, nirvana if you will. It is a meeting of the minds, bound loyalty, and the person you want to go to first with good news or bad. As soul mates, best friends can speak with their eyes—just a knowing glance tells a thousand words. The common ground is endless. In short, they are irreplaceable.

Each winning photograph in this charming book tells its own story of friendship and affinity. In every shot, action or still life, everyone is sharing—whether it be a mud pie, a walk on the beach, a braid, a ripe carrot or a kiss. It illuminates a moment in time between the friends, like the shot of young Joey Orbe, 7, resting atop his best friend's gravestone (p. 125), maybe reflecting on the fun they shared?

These photos pinpoint a three dimensional view of friendship—intimacy, trust, and just plain 'ol fun! When I look at these pictures my heart strings are tugged.

Some of the photos, because of the diverse age range, remind me of similar instances in my life. When I judged the pictures, what stood out the most was that everyone, young and old alike, is enjoying the pleasures of comradeship. See the knowing look and caring touch between the friends! It tells a thousand words.

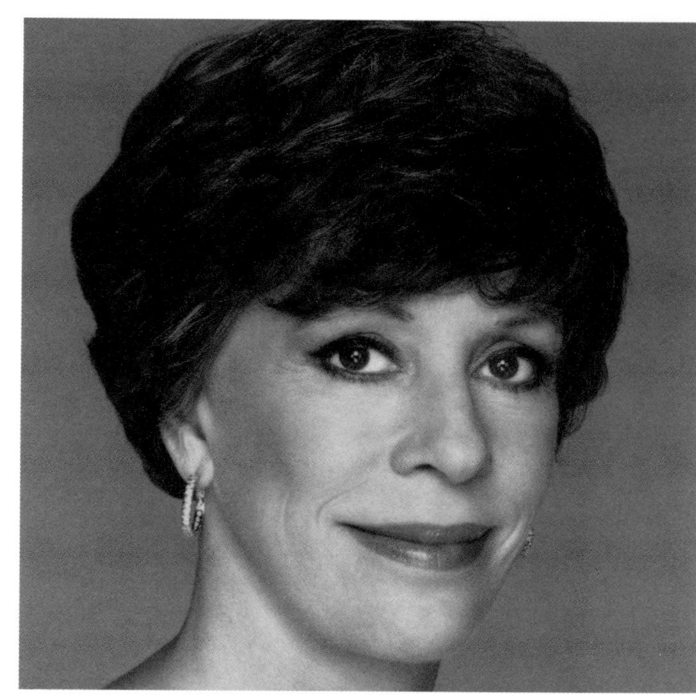

Carol Burnett

What a challenge! When I undertook my role as a judge of the *Parade/Kodak* Best Friends Photography Contest, I never expected to see *so many* wonderful examples of friendship.

In a time so clouded by war, it's refreshing to see such unabashed expressions of love—of people sharing, and learning and having fun together. In times like these, I think you realize how very important friendship is, how it must be nurtured and cherished and held dear, and that is what comes through in these photographs.

When I was asked to be a judge for the contest, I thought, "What fun!" And it was. It was also touching and funny, and even sad. But that is what makes a *best* friend—someone to share with, laugh with, and cry with.

I was impressed by the diversity of these friendships—it is truly inspiring. They transcend age, race and even species! You, too, will be moved by the faces you see here—the young, the old and the furry.

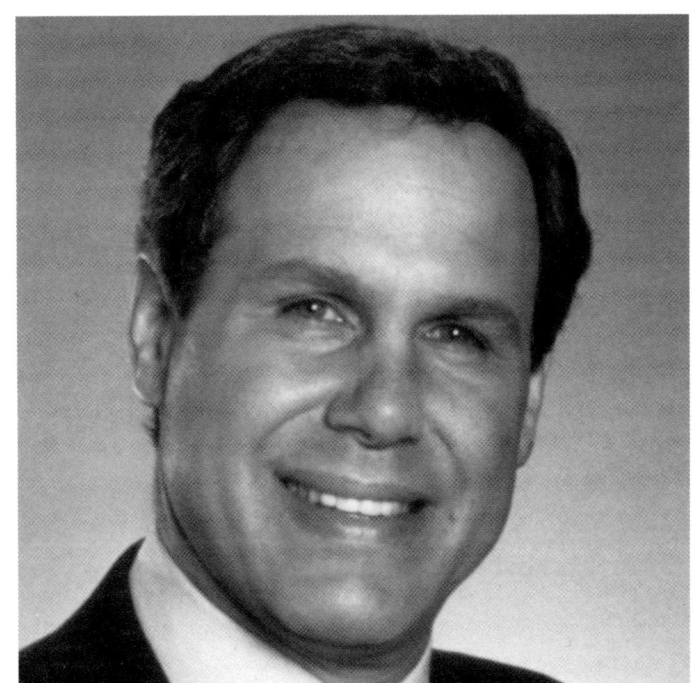

Michael Eisner

As chief executive officer of the Walt Disney Company, I keenly recognize the importance of friendship and togetherness. After all, that's what my business is all about—helping people enjoy a special moment together.

In judging the *Parade-Eastman Kodak* Photography Contest, I enjoyed the privilege of sharing personal moments with people I've never met. Each photograph is simple yet complicated, different yet alike. Each tells a unique tale.

As I write this, I am reminded of the adage that a picture is worth a thousand words. Surely that is a profound understatement.

No matter how many words I might write, I could not even begin to do justice to these photographs, which communicate so much emotion and wonder in a single frozen frame of time. Each is an essay on the warmth of human relationships. Each reflects what is best in all of us.

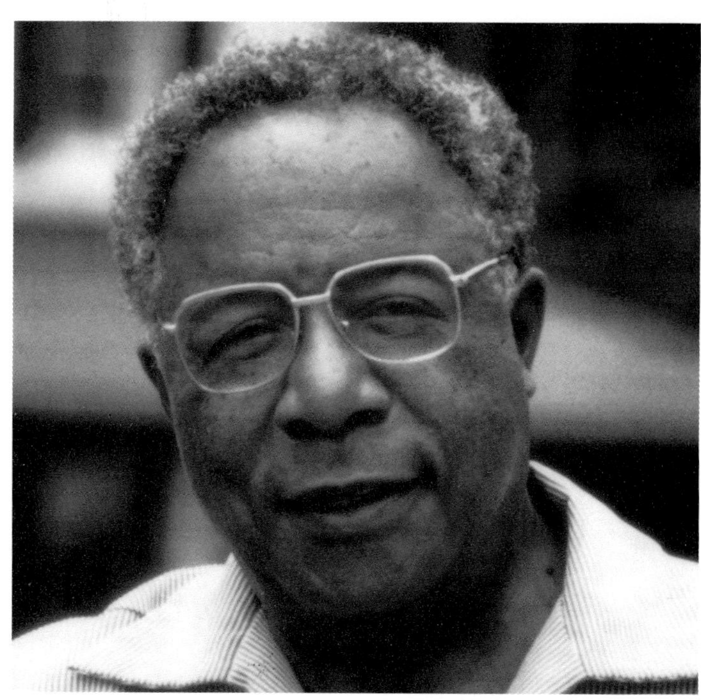

This year's photo contest exemplifies perhaps the most intimate, yet underrated side of personal relationships—Best Friends. Most of us know someone who we feel close enough to tell anything. It is reassuring to know you can share a thought or experience with someone else without fear of being criticized, misunderstood or ridiculed.

You will see a wide variety of images, emotions and ideas that reflect the idea of best friends when you look at these award-winning pictures. For instance, there are photographs of a grandmother hugging her grandson, two brothers enjoying a mudbath, a father kissing his three-month-old son, children of different races playing together, three elderly gentlemen enjoying a rest at day's end, sisters comforting each other at their grandmother's gravesite, a bride sharing her day of joy with her bridesmaids, and a kitten curled up beside a sleeping baby to share a nap.

All of the situations listed above were chosen as winners because the photographers were able to capture a special moment in time being shared by more than one person. I found that each of these pictures contains the same underlying theme—the comfort of companionship.